MW00962029

Red Skies At Night

The True Diaries of
Irving J. Schaffer

Written by
Irving J. Schaffer

Editor
Stafford "Doc" Williamson

This is a copyrighted book. All rights

reserved by the author.

© 2004 Irving J. Schaffer

Any reproduction in any media
whatsoever, including, without limitation
on the foregoing, derivative works,
dramatizations, animations, audio or video
recordings or the words or images in
whole or in part, is strictly prohibited
without written permission from the
copyright holder. Violations will be
vigorously pursued by Dao Chi Media and
any other license holders to protect rights
licensed to them and the rights of the
author.

Cover Design copyright:

Dao Chi Media © 2005

ISBN   1-4116-4277-5
Library of Congress Control Number: 2005930425
Published by Dao Chi Media
div. of Williamson Information Technologies
Corp.
19128 N 84 Dr., Peoria, AZ 85382

Printed in USA

DEDICATION

To my children and my children's children, and to their children from generation to all generations, may we all study history that we all may study war no more.

To Shyrle, without whom I doubt I would have survived, she is my wife and my life, my love and my heaven on earth.

To the brave men and women who serve our country, may you never face the lonely night without the support of your family, your mates. May both you and they receive the necessary guidance, training and support, material and spiritual, mental and medical needed by those whose lives have born the burden and the torment of the aftermath of past wars.

Be sure to look for other Dao Chi Media books online or in a bookstore near you. Other titles include:

Children's books

PUPPYFISH
By Stafford "Doc" Williamson

Puppy Goes to Lambergarten
By Stafford "Doc" Williamson

General Audience books

Science

The Day I Changed the Shape of the Universe
By Stafford "Doc" Williamson

Dao Chi Media is a division of
Williamson Information Technologies Corp.

PUBLISHER'S NOTE and Introduction

Irving J. Schaffer's life has been remarkably ordinary, except that everything about him seems to have touches of the extraordinary. He is of slight build, about 5 feet 6 inches tall (about 165 cm.) yet he beat a Mr. Universe in a boxing match. That remarkable feat happened when Irving was still in high school, before Mr. Universe had grown to 6 foot 3 inches (190 cm.) and 245 pounds (112 kilos) and taken up professional wrestling under a pseudonym. And speaking of pseudonyms, Izzy Demsky was Irving's Alpha Beta Gamma fraternity brother at Wilbur H. Lynch High School in Amsterdam, New York. Izzy's high school yearbook photos of himself (there are plenty of them, Izzy was on the yearbook staff) look almost indistinguishable from Irving's photos of himself during World War II. (I showed my wife 6 photos, 4 of Irving, 2 of Izzy and she could not tell which were of whom.) Izzy changed his name when he became an actor. He is better known as the Lifetime Achievement Academy Award winner, Kirk Douglas, or these days, to a younger generation, as the famous-actor father of famous-actor and multiple Academy Award winner, son Michael Douglas. Both Izzy and Irving are still handsome, though well into their eighties.

But even more remarkable in our opinion is the love story between Irving and Shyrle (pronounced like, "Shirl"). Sixty years of marriage and they are still devoted lovebirds, cooing over each other at dinner, full of admiration and appreciation in their eyes on both sides as they take the time for prolonged gazes at each other. That alone could justify the publication of Irving's diary. It is, in effect, one very long love letter to his lovely bride-to-be, written, at least in part, in the hope that it would never be read, yet preserving the possibility that she would be allowed to know the depth of his love if the worst should happen to him. We are pleased to report that she eventually did read all those thoughts and musings, even though it was many years later. They are still happily married at this time.

Irv Schaffer, lived a life that is familiar to many millions of readers, a life not all that different from hundreds of others from his generation, though the version that readers know is a fictional one. Irv Schaffer's experiences in the 12th Air Force during World War II are incredibly similar to those experiences of Joseph Heller, the stuff that inspired Heller's masterpiece of anti-war literature, *Catch-22*. If Heller himself had not lived through the same experiences, all he would have had to do was read Irv's diary for sufficient inspiration to form the basis for his famous novel. In that sense, this book is not a work of literature, it is a book of fact. Irv tells his daily life in the simplest of terms, with a soldier's typical attention to the daily details of every meal, sleepless nights of torment and fear, wounds to himself and his fellow flyers, death and destruction, lust and bureaucracy. Above all, we see his longing for home, safety, and a safe return to the love of his life, and a hope for the future.

We have attempted to preserve as closely as possible the accuracy of Irv's diary. We have tried to correct typographical and transcription errors from the hand-written diary, but have, in many cases, included spelling errors as they occurred, including a few inconsistencies in place names. We note that the term "negro" was considered socially correct and polite in the context as was "colored" at that time. We believe too that although Irv makes note of the fact that local military called some indigenous people "wogs", that he was unaware that this was a deprecatory term, since it was completely unfamiliar to him, and indeed he remained unaware of the origins and connotations even into the 21st century. Being a nice, Jewish boy from Amsterdam, New York, Irv is probably not eligible for sainthood, but his gentle nature and purity of heart are a strong hallmark of our friendship of many years.

It is also our knowledge of Irv's gentle nature that makes poignantly clear the anguish Irv was suffering during his tour of duty in the Mediterranean. Not unlike the revealing perspective on the American *Civil War* provided by the personal glimpses into diaries and letters of the participants shown in Ken Burns' epic 10 hour PBS Television production, we hope that Irv's diaries will give you a new insight into both the literal 10,000 foot view as well as the daily dirt and drudgery of at least one narrow slice of the end of World War II, and of one man's literally heroic struggle to survive it.

We are privileged to be allowed to publish this book. Irv doesn't like to talk about his wartime experiences. You will notice that in his diary, in the few times that he mentions earning the Distinguished Flying Cross, one of the highest medals of military honor, it never rates more than a couple of brief phrases. At rough count, we make it about 7 sentences in 3 instances referring to the announcement, the presentation and writing to his father about the award. Even though he received 4 medals in a single ceremony from the general of the 12th Air Force, it passes in his diary with less detail that the three meals he ate that day. Irving J. Schaffer is a proud man, and deservedly so, but he is no boaster. He deserves his story told, and he has told it well himself. We sincerely hope you enjoy reading it.

AUTHOR'S FOREWORD

Why did I keep a day-to-day diary of my war service, when I was clearly told not to do so? When I knew I could have charges brought against me, if it was discovered. And here is my answer.

To have someone you love literally drop off the face of the earth under mysterious circumstances, and no matter what efforts you make to find out what, why, or when, no one will tell you anything. I watched my parents change right before my eyes. Their pain was palpable. If they had been told that my brother Jerome had been killed, even if his body didn't come home, they could have grieved through it and moved on with their lives as best they could. But with quiet desperation they spent each day, each night waiting, praying for some word, trying to get through one more day. The unknown was almost more than any of us could take. And my brother's twin sister Merriam was especially affected. So was our other sister Geraldine and my brother Elliott. And then after the Pearl Harbor surprise attack stunned the nation, Elliott joined the Navy, doing dangerous anti-submarine warfare in the North Atlantic.

And that is why I made the difficult decision to keep a diary. If I didn't come back, there was an even chance that my loose-leaf notebook would make its way to my parents. They wouldn't have one more unbearable unknown. They could hold my writings in their hands and take some comfort from reading my day-to-day entries, including what I ate, if I slept, who I bunked with, who my comrades were, and the missions I flew.

What surprised me after the war was that not only could I not show the diary to the very people I had written it for, my parents, I could not even read the entries I had made. I could not attend war movies or read books about war. And I could not fly in an airplane for many years. I kept making entries for a few months after I was discharged, then I put it away. And then the first year I was married, my wife gave premature birth to twin boys, and both died. She was very ill, so I alone took care of the burials. Fighting an internal whirlwind that nothing seemed to make better, I tried to forget anything and everything connected with the war. My wife seemed intrinsically to understand what I was going through, did not probe, and stood by my side. Years passed, then decades. There was the Korean War, then Vietnam, and others. Still I couldn't talk about war.

The tragedy of 9/11 plunged me back in time and brought it all back. I knew down deep that it was time for me to open the diary and read it, face it, remember it. And maybe, just maybe, share it with my wife and two daughters. So I began reading.

In late 2003, as the war in Iraq raged on, deep feelings of empathy welled up in me for our troops, both in combat and what they faced when they returned home. I wanted their families to know the important role they needed to play when their soldier returned home. Maybe my story would be helpful to them. So I began looking for a publisher and found one whose father had served with the ground forces in Italy at the very same time and in the very places where I few combat missions.

Many of the physical evidences of World War ll are long gone, but my combat missions and all the tragedy I saw and experienced are burned into my very being. In combat, the luxury of acknowledging your feelings is not available. Instead of mentally and emotionally handling and processing a traumatic event right after it occurs, the combat soldier must store and store and store, one on top of another, stuffing them deeper and deeper into a dark and inaccessible place. Until it feels as if it will all explode. Even today, if I go deep enough, I find the humbling, terrifying, deep grief of sixty years ago.

I remember well the young man in my squadron who committed suicide. He just couldn't take it any more. And coming back from a bombing mission, there was the gunner who suddenly let loose on a bunch of civilians down below. He was angry, and out of control in his rage.

During and after World War II, little was known about the

ongoing effects of combat on a returning soldier. No one talked about it. Returning soldiers had to get back to earning a living right away, for themselves or for a family. The country was in the midst of a major transition. Ceiling prices were still in effect, war effort jobs were no longer needed, and thousands of men were returning and they all needed a job.

When I returned to the U.S., I was a wreck and knew it. But I needed to maintain and present to others that I was okay, that I was ready to get back to work and create a life. And I had Shyrle waiting for me, I hoped.

In the *Arizona Republic* on March 27, 2004, Robert Burns of the Associated Press, did an article entitled "Soldiers in Iraq short mental health support." Excerpts of the article follow:

Washington – The Army's first-ever survey of mental health in a combat zone showed that soldiers in Iraq last year suffered from low morale, high stress and holes in the Army's support system. . . .

Seventeen percent of soldiers were assessed as suffering traumatic stress, depression or anxiety and were deemed to be "functionally impaired." Of that group, about three-quarters said they had received no help at any time in Iraq from a mental health professional, a doctor or a chaplain. . . .

The point I wish to make is this. When fighting a war, the first goal is to win, and everyone knows to expect casualties. Dead or broken bodies are understood. But those soldiers who can walk and talk receive little or no help. Yes, it is a difficult thing to try and set up mental health assistance for hundreds or thousands of men and women, and each one having different problems. But the fallout that can occur when people return from war is real. In untold ways, it affects the individual, their family, their community, and their country. The ability to hold a job, to succeed in raising healthy children, and keeping families together all are affected. Not to mention the ongoing health care costs.

Where these returning soldiers can get help is from their families, if the family members understand what is needed: the emotional wounds of war, how the person is likely feeling whether he or she can express it or not, what to do to help and what not to do, and how long it may take.

Our country is now familiar with and accepts the positive results that can come from support groups, where a person can talk among others who have had similar experiences. To go to one is no longer considered a sign of weakness.

If we lived in a perfect world, we would have a required phasing out period after war of support type classes, before and after discharge, so that the soldier can be taught how to express what he or she is feeling and why it is important to do so. Basic training when inducted into the military is designed to give the soldier the training needed to fight and to survive. Back home, they need similar training on how to physically, mentally, and emotionally re-enter family life and society. They need to understand that it won't ever all go away and that inappropriate words or actions can slip out. All this takes time.

And family members need similar training. What to expect, when to recognize that the soldier needs reassurance and understanding, how to just let them talk when they need to, and to know when to use words and when to remain silent.

Having said all this, I realize we don't live in a perfect world and the government does not have an endless supply of money, and neither do taxpayers. So funding may never become available except in crisis situations. But this kind of re-entry training would likely save taxpayers a ton of money in the long run. And here is an incentive for local, state, or national government: Productive members of society pay taxes and keep the country economically strong. Non-productive members necessarily do not.

At the end of my diary I talk about some of what I experienced when I came home. And anyone who has returned from war will also read between the lines. I share what my wife did for me and how she did it. Without her, I'm not sure I could ever have gone forward in life and succeeded.

Now, my diary

AUGUST 3, 1944

As I commence this overseas diary, the thought foremost in my mind is that someday, my dear brother, Jerome, shall return to the United States to continue on with his journalistic ambitions that abruptly came to a halt on March 25, 1941. My secondary reason is the hope that perhaps an accurate account of one's travels in this modern global holocaust will be of literary benefit to his writings. Lastly I shall use it for remembrance.

In the event misfortune overtakes me, I trust the one responsible for return of my personal belongings shall include this compilation.

May the Lord guide Jerome home safely.

Irving J. Schaffer

AUGUST 3, 1944

Awoke 7AM. Ate breakfast. Bid the boys adieu. Twenty-five crews departed Columbia for Hunter Field, Georgia, by train. Played bridge with Lieut. Crisp, Sheffield, Steiner. Trip was very hot. Complete physical and record checking at Hunter. Made out Class E Allotment for $50.00 in Merriam's name. Contacted several Savannah girls whose addresses were given to me by Dorothy Miller and Mrs. Roskin. Made dates for the enlisted men. Ate supper at the service club and attended dance. Returned at midnight - a bit worn out.

AUGUST 4, 1944

CQ called at 6:00AM. Unkemptness of mess finds me missing breakfast. 7:30AM Crews were briefed. 8:30AM Radio Operators briefing. Took code check twice to pass 18-WPM check. Assigned our ship 1225-J (327793) Test run and calibration check OK. Right eng. went out at 4000 feet. Crisp made a beautiful single engine landing. Crash and fire trucks and ambulances were standing by. Oil seal on prop governor broke. Put about 2 1/2 hours on ship. Crew decided to name it "The Melting Pot", because of the religious mixture. Ate a swell chow at the service club. Bernard Bass (Bronx NY) sat in a few numbers at the dance. Waltzed around a few times. Canceled dates in Savannah, as all transient combat crews are restricted to the base. Retired at 11:30PM (Bunked in barracks 1214).

AUGUST 5, 1944

Awoke at 7AM. Managed to swallow a little of that undesirable food at the mess hall. Having thoroughly checked out, we received our orders for departure to Morrison Field at West Palm Beach, Florida. Twenty-five ships flying in formation of threes and fours. Each formation has an A.T.C. navigator on lead ship. Land Morrison Field at noon. Every type of ship about, especially C46's, C47's. Processed and sat in on a medical briefing. At this point, we commence taking Atebrine, malaria preventative. The anopheles mosquito is scarce in this area. Smitty is guarding the ship tonight. Taylor and I spent a sociable evening at the service club. Everyone is friendly. In fact our female warriors are too generous. La Bella made some WAC. Retired midnight.

AUGUST 6, 1944

Awoke at 8:00AM. Weather en route bad. Grounded today. Taylor is doing guard tonight. Kibitzing, letter writing and reading comprised the day. All the boys have dates for the evening. I still maintain discretion is a standard to be maintained. Eating all my meals at the service club. Food is desirable and a wide selection. We are quartered in what is known as the "Transient Area" for combat crews en route. The barracks are clean and spacious. We have a daily change of bed linen. Navy crash boat outfit stationed here. The crew "Step Lively" (that's us) was photographed professionally. Retired 10:30PM.

AUGUST 7, 1944

Area P.A. system called us at 4:30AM. Briefed at 5:30AM. Ditching procedure stressed. Pilot received our secret orders to destination. Not to be opened until one hour after departure from the United States. Checked out, loaded our side arms. (APO #16413BH10) Take off. 7:33AM Pilot informed crew of destination, Tunis. Passed over a continual session of islands. Landed Borinquen Field, Puerto Rico at noon. Processed through billeting. Our quarters are of modern cement and tile structure of three stories. Chrome and tiled lavatories are exceptionally clean. The temperature is most agreeable. There is always a breeze. Digested a steak supper at the NCO club. Drank a few bottles of 5. "India Beer". Briefed at 5:30PM for tomorrow's flight. Journeyed to the service club. It was pointed out by a friend that many of our U.S. soldiers have married Puerto Ricans. Their complexion and skin is beautiful. Being slight in stature and speak Spanish. Sugar cane is the chief product. Coconut trees pepper the island. Retired at 9:00PM.

AUGUST 8, 1944

CQ called at 3:30AM. Picked up our box lunches. 50 cents per man. Password "Florida" was necessary to pass guards to our ships. Puerto Rican guards speak with raised firearms. Tower clearance at 6:30AM. Climbed to 9000 feet. Flew over Antigua, Martinique and Barbados. Landed Waller Field, Trinidad 12:15PM. Lunch and refueled. Take off 1:30PM. Maintaining 1500-foot altitude. Search for two B25's that went down yesterday. Spotted flares that turned out to be smoke flares for wind direction. Arrived Atkinson, British Guinea 5:00PM. Airport was cut out of the jungles and is about 5 miles from our barracks. Lions, tigers, snakes, wild pigs, etc. prowl the vicinity. Malaria is again stressed. Taking Atebrine and using mosquito bars. Chow, as a rule is poor. Powdered milk, native bread, etc. Purchased a pair of silver wings for mother. "13-G" (British Guinea) The natives are black, very unkempt. Natives perform as K.P.'s latrine orderlies, barrack boys, etc. They are known as wogs. They speak Spanish and Portuguese. British money is used. Mud huts comprise their homes. Sleep on ground with thatched roofs for ceilings. Gasoline supply is underground. Picking up Spanish. Our barracks are 6 feet off ground to prevent prowling animals entrance. Natives carry supplies atop their head. Showered and retired at 9:30PM.

AUGUST 9, 1944

CQ called at 5:00AM. Take-off at 6:30AM. Still searching for lost B-25. Flew over Paramaribo, Cayenne (French Guinea). Landed Belem, Brazil 11:45AM. Since leaving Puerto Rico we have been receiving $7.00 per diem. While receiving such we pay for our lodging and food. Passed over equator and Amazon River. Jungles below very dense. Native villages dot the area. It will take some time to become accustomed to the food. Visited the Red Cross and was invited to complete a foursome for a bridge game. Yours truly was the hostess' partner. Transient censor played opposite me. Retired at midnight feeling OK.

AUGUST 10, 1944

Awoke 8:30AM. Remaining at Belem today. Purchased a handmade inlaid jewel chest for Shyrle's birthday. Purchased a box of cigars for Dad. Cigarettes are 5 cents per pack. Ship's radio equipment under repair. Met another Red Cross hostess from Rutland, Vermont. Wooden structures are replaced with cement and stone. Most all buildings are painted white and some pastel color. Roofs are of Spanish tile. Windows are of framework and screen. Uncle Sam is making much progress in Brazil. Certain things don't appeal to me. Prostitution is almost public. The rate of venereal disease is exceptionally high. Attended a movie, "Cowboy Canteen" which was shown in the old hangar and is now a theater and gym. Walked out in middle of show. Retired 10:00PM.

AUGUST 11, 1944

CQ called at 5:45AM. Checked off and take-off was at
7:00AM. Flew over Fortaleza. Dense jungle below.
Much has never been penetrated by white men.
Arrived Natal at about noon. Interphone out. Three
B-29's under inspection. Sand storm in action.
Brazilians are very fond of Americans. Especially so
for their money. Water is still a scarcity. Certain
hours are allotted for showering. Toilets are hand
flushed with buckets. Architecture as well as the
language is strictly Spanish. B-29 blew up on take-off.
Bombardier only survivor. Beer is sold in quart
bottles. Transients must obtain ration cards to
purchase necessities at the PX. All the boys are
buying the "Natal Mosquito Boot" and $5.00 watches.
Looked for my bridge partner at the Red Cross. Night
off. Retired 9:30PM.

AUGUST 12, 1944

CQ called at 5:00AM. Take off at 7:15AM. Entire trip
over Atlantic. Weather clear. Flying at 9000 feet.
Landed Ascension Island 2:30PM Radio transmitter
out. Side-tone intermittent. This airfield is known as
Wideawake Field. This volcanic island which is
completely covered with lava belongs to the British.
British authorities claimed it could not be converted
into an airfield. 1200 engineers from Ft Belvoir,
Virginia did the job in three months under naval
protection. Georgetown is the only city on the 'rock'
with a population of 50 civilians. Ascension is 6 by 9
miles. Chow is fair. One palm tree on the island and
no other vegetation including grass. Supported by the
navy band, a USO camp show. Gave us a real laugh.
Everything is open air. A continual breeze cools the

island. Attended the evening movie "Toughy Gang".
Retired at 11:00PM.

AUGUST 13, 1944

CQ called at 5:00AM. Trip canceled, weather closing
in. Operations gave us clearance at 9:00AM. Runway
is cut between peaks ranging about 2000 feet on either
side. Entire trip over water. Land Roberts Field,
Liberia, Africa. Liberian natives are used for labor.
Slight drizzle. Processed through billeting and
assigned barracks. IFF left in ship. Field has
permanent compliment of 150 GI's. Radio briefing
5:30PM. Medical briefing 6:00PM. Barracks very
comfortable. Native youth ranging from 15 to 18 years
attending American missionary schools service us from
head to foot. Being a previous Pan American airbase,
many facilities are still intact. Individual chrome,
leather-covered chairs, tablecloths plus waiters
service. Steak topped our first meal. Against
regulations, we tipped the boys. No matter what their
task, they never wear shoes cause they haven't any.
The officers eat at the same mess. Purchased a few
Liberian coins. Rations cards are effective. Theater
and PX are one and the same building. Retired at
10:00PM. Unable to sleep.

AUGUST 14, 1944

Awoke 9:30AM. Grounded due to weather at
destination. Missed breakfast but made up for it with
chicken for dinner. We hitched at ride on a Firestone
1/2 ton truck to the "Trading Post." Firestone has a
rubber plantation in excess of 1/2 million acres. One
half-pint glass bowls are fastened to the trees. Rubber
liquid drips for almost a day to fill the cup. On rainy

days the natives don't tap. Their wages are 18 cents per week. Many are paid off with rice or other necessities. At the "Trading Post" natives purchase and exchange articles. Firestone also controls it. Fruit juice drunk from the can is like the American Coca-Cola. Half clothed, barefooted and naked Liberians crowd the area. Filth is outstanding. Saw a case of Elephantitus. All the natives have malaria, many seriously. Mothers nurse their young in public. Commenced raining at 3:00PM. Never seen it rain so hard. American and English missionaries have done a wonderful job in progressing the education of the younger generation. Many speak fair English. Struck up an acquaintance with several traders from Morovia. One reminded me of a New York sharpie, dressed in American style. Purchased an ivory letter opener for $1.00. Swapped a jack knife for a brass snake made by the natives. Purchased a silver ring from a native chief for $1.50.   Liberians are very curious about we Americans. La Bella, Lieut. Bane, Lieut. Ivory, Lt. Kimball, Taylor and I hitched a ride to a native village. Incidentally, all native huts and villages are off limits to US forces. We were curious about a place called "Mama Luiz." She is about fifty and sells liquor in her hut made of mud and straw. Five girls, who are Liberian prostitutes, provide her a financial income. No one patronized her. Taylor bought a quart of Gordons Gin. Raining steadily. Retired 9:30PM. Very restless.

AUGUST 15, 1944

Awoke 8:30AM. Weather still bad. Visited the officers of our crew. Returned radio equipment. Hitched a ride to the "Trading Post". Very dull day. Returned to camp. Through conversation with Richard, our houseboy, Mama Luiz reared this lad of twenty, who is about to be a father. La Bella visited Mama Luiz - mm mm. Most of the cargo and supplies are brought in by DC 47's. At operations, I met Bishop Kroll, head missionary for the country of Liberia. His home is in Brooklyn. Tall and stalwart reminds me of movie actor. C Aubrey Smith. Kibitzed and retired about 10:30PM. Unable to sleep.

AUGUST 16, 1944

Awoke 8:30AM. Weather keeping us on the ground. There is much mud. Natives are cutting grass with an odd shaped cutter. At the end of a 30" round stick a small 4" knife blade is attached. They swing it to and fro. Very tedious and slow. Discussed navigation with Rudy. Prowled about, did a bit of reading. Retired 9:00PM.

AUGUST 17, 1944

CQ called at 6:30AM. Take-off at 8:00AM. Low ceiling, very hazy. Lieut. Crisp (pilot) very eager, but seems quite sure of himself. About 1 hour out encountered a violent storm. We encountered several more enroute. Flying over Atlas Mountains. Very treacherous and uninhabited. Ascended to 13000 feet to clear "Pass." 16000 foot mountains on either side. Passed over Waterloo, Bathhurst, Conkary, Portuguese Guinea. Landed Dakar about 2:30PM. The field is huge. In fact it is one of the few plateaus. Very hot. No humidity. Malaria very serious. Dakar off limits as there is an epidemic of Bubonic plague or commonly known as the "Black Death." Our forces were OK. Old French prison about 10 miles from field at base of mountains. No more per diem. Usual set up.

Remnants of sea battle between British and French still about. Not a very clean place. As in all these spots, prostitution prevails. American money to be changed into francs. Retired 10:30PM.

AUGUST 18, 1944

CQ called 4:30AM. Take off 6:22AM. Passed over Sahara Desert. Thermo waves jogged the ship about quite a bit. Two hours after take-off interphone system went out. Sometime later ship was beginning to draw heavy amps. Drawing over 250 amps, resets did not pop. Engineer cut investers and battery disconnects. Gunner called me to prepare to bail out. 15 minutes of gas left. Rather a queer feeling. Field sighted. Trap door sprung for jump. Pilot said we could make the airdrome. Pilot pushed Channel "A" VHF to call tower. VHF on fire. All power cut. Playing fire extinguisher. Fire out. Came in downwind. Didn't notify tower. Good landing at 12:30. Never felt so good to be on the ground. The boys feel the ship is cursed. Ship under repair. Marrakech is about the same as Dakar. Good is poor. Retired at 10:30PM (Prisoner of war camp - glass studded walls - young boys)

AUGUST 19, 1944

Take off Marrakech at 6:30 Z. Beautiful day. Ascended to flight altitude of 9000 feet. One half hour in, flight voltage regulator for engine beginning to burn. Engineer repaired trouble. Flying over desert and mountains. Passed over Casablanca, Alanya, Algeria, Phillipeulle. Land Tunis 11:30Z. Time changes to 1330Z (2nd) meridian. Airfield still battlefield scarred. Spitfire, Thunderbolts, P40's,

C47's, C46's, Wellingtons Handley Page and various German planes parked on field. Transportation picked us up and we are quartered in a former French hotel. Pilot sold our ship. Chow is pretty good. Still taking Atebrine and sleeping under mosquito netting. Land mines are still about. The city is still war torn. Freed Italian prisoners are the main source of labor. Very friendly and like Americans. Was pleasantly surprised by the crew with a gift of 500 francs. The boys went to town. Feeling a bit woozy. Retired at 7:30PM.

AUGUST 20, 1944

Awoke 8:30AM feeling gay and happy. Today is Shyrle's birthday. Hope she received her gift in time. Being Sunday, we cached away a good chicken dinner. Fruits and vegetables are plentiful. Departed by truck at motor pool for Tunis at 1:00PM. Ride was about 25 minutes, witnessed mass wreckage of Axis equipment. Arabs, Jews, French make up the main populace. Not very clean. Streetcars (electric). Boarded train (electric) for La Goulet to swim (5 francs). Enroute we stopped at seven stations. Each car is divided into two compartments. Seats for about 10 people. Very crowded. Red hats, known as "Fez" are commonly worn. Arabs still dress in age-old regalia. Struck up an acquaintance with a mademoiselle who is a native of Tunis. Being handicapped by lack of French or Italian our friendship came to a happy ending. Arrived La Goulet 2:00PM. Upstairs in the casino, drinks and food are being served. We are not allowed to participate due to various illnesses caused from public cafes. Changed to our trunks in an unkempt bathing house below the casino. It was quite a thrill to swim in the blue Mediterranean. French gals are plentiful but undesirable. Venturing up the beach we were permitted entrance to the French Armed Forces rest camp. Barbed wire entanglements are still about the beach and shipping wreckage in the harbor.

AUGUST 21, 1944

Lozowski was pulling my toe at 9:00AM. Sun is bright and the sky is cloudless. Going to La Marsa for a day of swimming. Enjoyed 11:30AM chow. Arrived La Marsa Beach 1:30PM. Met Rosette Jenimia and Jenimia's Aunt. Played volleyball, rowed. Popular American recordings continually play. Can be heard over the beach. Italian prisoners are better treated than in their own army. Tunis is same longitude as Virginia. Sun very hot, but little humidity. Dinner served in the patio at 6:00PM. Chicken was the main course. USA financed the US troops. Relations with pick-ups are extremely serious. Returned El Alovina at 7:00PM. Attended "Gas Light" open air theater. The screen is a white square painted on the side of a partly demolished building used by snipers. Retired 10:00PM. Boys came in at 11:00PM. Couldn't sleep. We went to midnight chow. Retired at 1:00AM.

AUGUST 22, 1944

CQ called us at 4:30AM in room 302. Loaded baggage aboard C47 transport. Take off 7:30AM. Delay was due to bombers returning from a raid on southern France. Flew over Sardinia and Pantelleria. Landed Corsica 10:00AM. B25's were gathering for formation. Bombers were returning from a mission. A bomber fired red flare, declaring serious injury on board. We are to be split up. I am assigned to 321st bomb group 448th bomb squadron. Sgt. Joe Ryan (detail Sgt.) bunked me in a tent with a swell bunch of "Joe's". I made the fifth fellow in tent "Nelson". Still using mosquito bars and taking Atebrine. Chow is OK. Trucks transport us to showers about 8 kilometers down the road. Went over to see Taylor and Smitty in the 445th. Taylor was quite ill since leaving Tunis. Wrote a few letters. Went over to the club for a few drinks. Evenings are quite chilly. Retired 10:30PM.

AUGUST 23, 1944

Nelson awoke me 7:45AM for breakfast. Oatmeal, fried potatoes, coffee and bacon. Organized my equipment. Steve (Shockey) Wallanoski 446th ordnance brought over Leonard Resnicki of Amsterdam. Remembered me from Mortans. Leonard and I are going down to the 340th group AUGUST 25th. Attended "Always a Bridesmaid". Punk movie. Retired 10:45PM.

AUGUST 24, 1944

Awoke 7:45AM. Charles Schoffner, Jim Blackard left for mission briefing. Hot cereal, pancakes, coffee. Slept until chow. Corned beef hash and trimmings. No fresh milk since leaving USA. Bass and I went swimming. GI swimming hole about 10 kilometers from camp. An ancient dam. The wall is composed of square cut stones about 30 feet high, 150 feet long. Hand operated 36" drop locks release water. Spillway is in center top of wall. Naked swimming is allowed. Water is clear and cold. Read "Time" magazine and the Mediterranean issue of "Stars and Stripes". Romania surrendered. Stomach nervously upset due to irregular living caused by our trip across. LaBella, Hulse, Molesky and Baird arrived 5:30PM. "Nick" Martinelli and Bellan were killed in a crash (calibration check) at Hunter Field. George Huka and I had a few drinks at the club. Retired 11:00PM.

AUGUST 25, 1944

Awoke 7:30AM. Scratching both arms at elbow. Right arm swelling. Coffee, bacon, pancakes. Leonard Rosnicki called at 8:30AM. Hitched a ride to the 340th. Met Frank Nasuto, an old friend from Amsterdam. Worked for Rappels Junk Co. Photography is his financial sideline. Ate at squadron mess and left to meet Ted Bryce also of Amsterdam. Toured the area and some of the wreckage was still about from "Jerries" raid in May. Pro-Germans in the mountain towns of Corsica. Guided them in. Ack-ack guns were knocked out first. Then 80 B25's. Then the fuel dump. 18 of the 340th were killed. Many injured. Returned to camp at 5:30AM. Hash topped the evening meal. Sad-sad-sad. So far our only beverage has been coffee. George and I killed a couple of rum cokes. Attended "A Guy Named Joe". About 10:30AM searchlight batteries went in action spotting our planes in tactical maneuvers. Schoffner pulled his 60th mission along the Swiss border above Italy. Rumors are circulating that shortly our outfit will be moving into France. Bomb lines are too long. Retired at midnight.

AUGUST 26, 1944

Nelson awoke me at 7:30AM. Bread, jam, coffee, cereal. Bernard Bass and I were detailed to commence digging a latrine. Dinner was an all time treat with chicken. John Carruthers, Gene Fley went swimming. Our aquatic rendezvous is about 10 miles from camp. 1 mile is trudged up the mountains. At the base of the mountain there is a solid rock abyss at which point a creek empties itself. The water is crystal clear plus a natural sand beach. The mountainous setting reminds me of the Adirondacks and the water of Lake George. On way back we looked over century old mill and dilapidated forts. The "Maque" is almost impassable in spots (under growth). Blackberries are plentiful. Climate is ideal. Schaffner completed 61st mission over Marseilles. Lately the "partisans" have been knocking out our targets before our bombers get there. Supper was topped with stew. George and I killed a few "Tom Collins" at the club. LaBella, Hulse, Radcliffe, Abecuneas and I played poker. Finished 15 francs ahead. Commencing a collection of paper money. Steve Wallanowski gave me a cigarette lighter. George sprays the inside of the tent with "Flit" every night. Night is very clear and cool. Read from "Time" magazine. Retired at 11:15PM.

AUGUST 27, 1944

Awoke at 7:50AM. Feeling tired. Stewed apricots, cereal, coffee. Cleaned pistol for small arms inspection. Nelson and I picked up suntans at a native's abode. Wash and press them for 10 francs. Consistently being about finds me picking up French and Italian. Met Julio and Guiseppee, two KP's from Sicily. Eating from mess kits. Washing our utensils outside in four waters (disinfectant tub). 50-gallon drums cut in half. Heated by an oil line running underneath. A basketball court is directly in front of the barbershop. Earthen floor, no markings. Horseshoe court alongside. We are situated about two miles inland. Towering mountains are directly behind us. Any desirable uniform is passable at camp. Neckties are not required. We wash from metal helmets. Flying combat personnel are entitled to sleeping bags. Ground men have medium canvas bed rolls. Bordering the entrance to our squadron is about a half dozen homes. The homes are usually two stories. Being made of natural stone and cemented in. Wooden doorlike windows. Very few have glass. No porches. No lawns or flowers. Burros, donkeys roam the area. Black is the general color. The natives don't wash their clothes very often. Beauty, even among the younger females is a rarity. There are only army vehicles traveling the highways. The peasants bring containers to hold our leftovers from chow to feed their livestock.

AUGUST 28, 1944

John Nelson (Saratoga Springs, NY) called me at 7; 30AM for breakfast. Pancakes, hot cereal, bread, jelly and coffee. Operations called to learn of my decision in becoming an airborne photographer. Will give answer tomorrow. Visited Lt. DiFulvio at the 445th squadron. Completed two missions. Hash, mashed potatoes, diced carrots, fruit salad, sliced cabbage and coffee for dinner. Started Stephen Crane's "The Red Badge of Courage". Took pictures of "Ike" (1st Sgt), "Mike" (Mess Sgt), Joe Ryan (Work Sgt), John Nelson, Fred Jacobson and James Blockard. Operations asked if I might like to be an airborne photographer. Operations told me I am to be a photographer. In fact I believe I'll like the job. Spoke with Capt Moss and T Sgt Hours. Played a bit of blackjack. Won 20 francs. Cold corned beef, hash, unseasoned mashed potatoes, boiled onions, fruit salad. Attended "Fired Wife". Evening very clear. Searchlights in tactical maneuvers with our ships. Milton Slafkes was over discussing sex. Retired 11:00PM (Merriam's and Jerome's birthday)

AUGUST 29, 1944

Awakened to the "merrimacs" coming from Radio Rome of the American Expeditionary to the tune of "My Darling Clementine." Marines mission still standing by. French toast, syrup, hot cereal and pineapple juice. The squadron sgts gathered for a morning bull session. John Ryan of Boston, Mass. Still popping off. 310th on 24 hour alert. Meatloaf, mashed potatoes, peas, chocolate pudding, bread and peanut butter. Today's mission canceled. Feeling a bit restless. Want to get going. Hitched down to the dam to go swimming. Roads are very rough. Communication lines are just laid through the foliage of trees. Aviation pipe line runs complete length of island. 4" pipe. Ack-ack outfits are scattered throughout. Some heavy-duty trucks are armed with fifty-caliber hand held turret machine guns. Mountains ranging up to 13,000 feet along the east and north coasts. Since arriving the sun has continually shone. Met George Huka at dam. George pointed out "prune Face" a woman who runs a house of ill repute that is "off limits" to all US Forces. No mail as yet. Ate early chow doing 1st shift guard duty on line from 6 to 10. Struck up acquaintance with a free French anti-aircraft battery. Jack and Harry from Algiers, Algeria are in charge. They speak good English. Harry was formerly a French aviator. Both have families in Algeria. The ack-ack gun is a 40mm remotely and hand controlled. Accurate range about 5000 feet. Two German ships to their credit. A Focke Wolfe 190 in Sept 1943 and a Junkers 88 November   1943. Slanksy (sgt of the guard) picked me up at 10:10PM. Had a quick once over at the club. Retired 11:00PM.

AUGUST 30, 1944

Natural awakening at 7:05AM. Pancake with raisins, hot cereal, fruit juice, coffee. Attended aerial photography class. Lectured on K20 (hand held) K8AB (electrically operated stationary). Permanent aerial photographer in conjunction with radio operating and gunnery. Corned beef hash paddies, canned corn, kidney beans, bread and butter. Read Stephen Vincent Benet's "Johnny Pye and the Fool Keller." Flight officers Robert Lesser (448th) and I hitched down to the 15th field hospital to visit Lt Da Fuvlio who was stricken with malaria the night before last. Schaffner and I picked up our suntans at the native's abode. They charge 20 francs. Showered at the 445th squadron. P38 belly tank on raised platform holds 125 gallons and is piped to enclosed shack. Chicken fricassee, beef dumpling, diced beets, string beans, bread and jelly, coffee. Unloaded bottled beer from Tunis. Transported by plane. Killed a few on the way to the squadron. Shot the breeze awhile. 3/4 moonlit night. Retired 9:45PM.

AUGUST 31, 1944

Nelson awoke me at 7:55AM. Powdered eggs, hot cereal, bread and jelly, coffee. Dreamed I was home from the European jaunt. Getting ready to push off for the Pacific. Water for the tent is kept in six canteens. Several water trailers are about the squadron. The latrine is a six passenger, open-air mosquito covered affair. Due to a rough and rocky terrain, there is no sequence to the layout of the tents. Being of the more fortunate our tent has a wooden floor with spacious cracks between the boards to catch the dirt. A gasoline energizer provides electricity for the squadron lights and our radios. Yesterday's mission, which was a stand down, is to go out today. Picked almost a helmet full of thimbleberries. Turkey a-la-king, canned tomatoes, string beans, diced beets, bread and jam. 12:45PM ships returning from mission 7 miles north of Venice. 1st formation missing 2 ships. Hulse, Moleski, Ratcliffe OK. Ten flak holes in ship. 2 ships hit over target with flak. Engine one knocked out. Made emergency landing in Italy. Jim Blackard OK. All squadrons policed runway, picking up large stones. Roast beef, creamed mashed potatoes, creamed peas, butterscotch pudding, bread and jam. George and I ate thimbleberries I picked this AM. Squadron hardball team playing 334th service group (colored). Attended "Hi Good Lookin" (corny show). Went swimming after supper at the dam. Retired 10:30PM. Low ceiling, no stars.

SEPTEMBER 1, 1944

Awoke 7:53AM. It's Friday, the first day of September. . Corn pancakes, oatmeal, coffee, grapefruit juice. Washed sun tans. Played blackjack for a spell. Sauce and spaghetti, peas, diced carrots, cocoa, bread and butter. Steve Waltanowski 152 Front St. Schenectady was over for chow. Clarence Donovan Schnaffer 51 Olean St, Bolivar, New York and I hiked through a narrow rocky winding trail to the village of Ventessere. About 12 kilometers from camp. Village is situated on side of mountain about 7,000 feet high. Stopped at the caf, for water. Una mademoiselle and deux French soldats were there. Colored troops. Intermingled sexually with the Corsican whites.

Malaga and blue grape vineyards dot the hillside. Fig
trees, sassafras, thimbleberries and cork trees
dominate the heavier wooded sections. Peasant
women still laboring although 80 years of age. From
this village of Venetessere, one can plainly see the
321st airdrome in the valley. Native villages are up in
the mountains to keep out of the mosquitoes reach
and malaria. Viewed an ancient graveyard and
monastery. The church bell is atop a high stone tower
ranging about 75 feet in height. 15-foot ladder
sections are the path, which the bell ringer uses to
reach his objective. Small American school in village.
At the village water spring we met the priest.
Commenced our return journey at 4:20PM. Arrived at
Travo at 6:10PM. Jeep picked us up for remainder of
1 miles to camp. Pork chops, mashed potatoes, peas,
bread and marmalade, coffee. Our motor at the
shower was stolen. Showering at Steve's of the 445th.
Fragmentation bombs being loaded for tomorrow's
mission. Celebrating Schaffner's being grounded on
his 62nd mission. 4 other radiomen were grounded.
Sure will miss Charles. Retired at 11:45PM. Feeling
somewhat inebriated.

SEPTEMBER 2, 1944

Awoke at 7:35AM. Boys informed me I am on the
morning's mission. Pancakes, oatmeal, prunes and
apricots, bread and jelly, coffee. Mission canceled,
standing by. Operations called. Seward, La Bella and
myself to go up for practice camera mission using k20
aloft for 1 3/4 hours. Pilot Lt Ovard will see results
tomorrow. Canned corn beef, many beans, fruit salad,
bread and butter, water. Slept for 1-1/2 hours.
Haircut and shave at the barber shop. Dirt floor, four-
foot wooden side, mosquito netting, canvas roof. Box

with back support for chair. Read "Young Man Axelbrod" by Sinclair Lewis. Day is very clear. George Huka, Hutchinson, Mine, Hermansi, Pennsylvania informed me that Master Sgt. George Parsous has appointed me chief radio operator. Fried hot dogs, kidney beans, canned corn, fruit salad, bread, iced tea. Visited Taylor and Smitty at 445th. They have three missions. One quart of beer per man at club. Charge - 20 francs. On tomorrow's mission as cameraman, carrying 1000-lb demolition bombs. Retired 10:00PM. Thunderstorm awoke us at 2:00AM. We let down and secured flaps. Unable to fall asleep for some time.

SEPTEMBER 3, 1944

PA system called us at 6:30AM for a 7:25AM briefing for today's mission. 6:35AM mission canceled. Pancakes, coffee, tomato juice. Smitty, Taylor and I attended Protestant services. Chaplain (Captain) Johnson presided. Went over to photo lab. Results of practice mission were fair. Received our rations for two weeks consisting of 5 cans of beer, 1 coke, 15 pkgs cigarettes, 8 candy bars, 1 box gum drops, 1 tooth brush, 1 tube toothpaste, 1 jackknife, $3.30. Hot mashed potatoes, sliced beets, spinach, bread and butter, coffee. Called in for briefing at 3:55PM. Target 30 miles north of Genoa, Italy. 23 span railway bridge and highway. Acting as photographer using K20. Take off 4:10PM. Encountered flak about 5:31PM. 5 minutes before target. First element hit target, snapped 3 photos. Didn't salvo our 1000-lb GP. Landed 7:05PM. Several ships hit, but returned safely. I had no fear on my first mission, but my stomach felt very strange. Fred Bixler of Indianapolis, radio operator was most helpful. Using Schaffner's flack helmet. Flack suit and sitting on frequency meter. Altitude 12000 feet, about 45 degrees F. Clear weather. Interrogated by S-2. Stew, stewed tomatoes, lima beans, vanilla pudding, bread and coffee. Schaffner, Huka and I ate cheese sandwiches and drank a can of beer each. On tomorrow's mission. Flew on "Cheery Fizz" today. 29 missions. Retired 11:30PM.

SEPTEMBER 4, 1944

Awoke 6:10AM. It <u>may</u> be Labor Day, but you would never know it on this island. French toast, orange marmalade, coffee. Pre-brief and briefing. 3 bridges at Pavia, 1000 lb. GP. 6 nine ship formation. Altitude 9, 10, 11,000 feet. Take-off 9:13AM. Over target 11:02. 100% hit. No flak - P47 escort. Landed 12:20PM. Did not get any photographs (my fault). Lieut (1st) Rogers pilot. Flew on "Silver Belle" which has 39 missions. Felt much better on my second mission. Red Cross served doughnuts, coffee, lemonade at interrogation. Salmon (canned) spaghetti, diced carrots, peas, bread and marmalade, iced tea. First shift of guard 6 to 10PM. Full moon. Chilly evening. On tomorrow's mission. Schaffner brought me a roast pork sandwich. Retired 11:00PM.

SEPTEMBER 5, 1944

PA system awoke us at 6:00AM. Cold Tuesday morning. Canned grapefruit, powdered scrambled eggs, bread, apple jelly, coffee. Attended 7:50AM briefing. 1 hour standby. Same target as yesterday. Jerries making repairs. Take off 8:50AM. Over target 10:33AM. Reconstruction in progress. Dropped 1000 GP bombs. Direct hit. Milk run. Saw snow covered Alps. Everything looks very peaceful below. Flew at

10,000 feet. Pilot Lt. Kruse 28 missions on ship 327791. Using K20, took some good photos. Interrogated. Red Cross serving. Every day of a mission, combat crews are entitled to a shot of whiskey. Navy beans, spaghetti, carrots and peas, chocolate cake, tea, bread and apple butter. Feeling very tired. 445th encountered fighters in Po Valley. Shot down over FW190. Attended lecture on "escape and evasion" by a Captain from the underground. (Llenard). The group theater is open air. Individual 12" square metal stools are placed together. The hill is inclined about 30 degrees. The screen on a 25 x 15 wooden stage is in the pit. Enlisted men have one side reserved, officers the other. Due to the inconsistency of the power supply (energizer) the show is usually interrupted. Commenced "The Seventh Cross", Anna Seghers. Vienna sausage, tarter sauce, mashed potatoes, string beans, canned pears, coffee, bread and apple jelly. Nelson gave us some fresh tomatoes he bought in Solenzara. Meeting of all enlisted men at 7:15AM at enlisted men's club. Major Bell broke down as soon as "Ike" called upon him. A new CO has been appointed. They say Major Bell was the best CO we ever had. Read a bit. Retired at 9:30PM.

SEPTEMBER 6, 1944

Awoke 7:30AM. Cloudy Wednesday. Pancakes, stewed apricots, wheaties, coffee. Standdown on this morning's mission. The showers are about five miles down the road along a stream about 50 feet wide. A gasoline pump draws the water to a 500-gallon tank. From here it passes through large coils that are heated, then to the shower. There are 20 overhead sprinklers in two rows. The ceiling is the sky with six-foot burlap walls surrounding the spot. Out drinking

water is drawn from the same water supply to a large
water bag atop a 30 foot wooden tower. The bag is
open on top and canvas side. Holds 500 gallons.
Chlorine is mixed in and water trucks are refilled to
bring aqua to the various squadrons. Hash paddies,
lima beans, canned tomatoes, bread, coffee. New CO
Captain Damon McClain took charge today. Tent and
area inspection tomorrow. Schaffner and I went hiking
up in the mountains. Tried to reach an ancient
structure about 3 miles up the mountain. After
several hours we were unable to reach objective. On
return we picked grapes, berries and peaches. Figs
are still green, as are the olives. Snitched 7 ears of
corn from a farm. Mike Koscis (mess Sgt) brought a
huge cake over for Schaffner's birthday. Smitty and
Taylor bought a motorcycle. Listened to a few musical
programs and read. Retired 10:45PM.

SEPTEMBER 7, 1944

Awoke 7:30AM. Fried powdered eggs, tomato juice,
bread, apple jelly. Schaffner's 29th birthday. Stand
by on today's mission. Corned beef hash, navy beans,
fruit salad, bread, apple butter, tea. "Ike" got weapons
carrier, 10 of us started for Bonafacia. Narrow
winding mountain roads. Bridges were blown by
Germans. Railway line on Corsica put completely out
of commission. Passed through Port Vaccio where
321st landed. Viewed castle with drawbridge. 500
years old at Bonafacio. Bombed freighter still in
harbor. Took photographs. Very hilly. Drank cap-
corse and muscatel wine. Joe Ryan really played the
women - no luck. Ate at cafe in Bonafico. Vegetable
soup, French rye bread, tomatoes, pepper eggplant
and ground meat. French-fries, fresh peaches and figs
for dinner. Kibitzed with several prostitutes.

Inhabitants are not very clean. Streets are of cobble stones and about 15 feet wide. Typical of book reading. Fork as souvenir from Bonafacio. Returned by Port Vaccio, very similar to Bonafacio. Joe Creighter drove back. Arrived camp 8:30PM. 22 new men came in today. Lemonade, coffee, doughnuts brought over to the tent by Mike Koscis, 150 Lenox Avenue, Bridgeport, Conn. Starry sky, beautiful evening. Stand down on today's mission. Retired 11:30PM.

SEPTEMBER 8, 1944

Awoke 7:30AM. Dismal and dreary morning. Oatmeal, pancakes, grapefruit juice, coffee. Stand down on today's mission. (Nickeling mission) Picked up 5-A from Crisp at 446th. Visited Rudy, Taylor. Stew, diced carrots, navy beans, beets, chocolate pudding, bread and marmalade. (Low ceiling) John Nelson, 14 Greenridge Place, Saratoga Springs, NY. Oldest tent member? Smitty and I took a trip down to Salizara on his motorcycle. Beef and gravy, green beans, mashed potatoes, canned applesauce, bread and butter, coffee. Evening shower. Weather turning. Sgt Kern brought back watermelon, cantaloupe and tomatoes from Salizara. Very enjoyable. Chilly evening. On tomorrow's nickeling mission. Retired 9:45PM.

SEPTEMBER 9, 1944

Awoke 6:50AM. Damp Saturday morning. Pancakes, syrup, coffee, oatmeal. Standby on "Nickel Mission". This is a mission on which pamphlets are enclosed in a bomb, timed to explode 10 seconds after release. Information regarding war news and to continue fighting is useless. Secured "Citizen Tom Paine" by Howard Fast. Very clear and warm. Open buns chicken a la king, peas, potatoes, bread and marmalade, canned pears, coffee. Tracy reported prisoner of war. Take off 5:30. Flew at 15,000 feet. Very cold. Flew tail position as gunner became sick. Dropped "nickels" at 6:35PM. No fighters, no flak. Landed 7:50PM. Vienna sausage, navy beans, sauerkraut, canned tomatoes, bread, orange marmalade, coffee. Jim Blackard returned from Rome. 1st mission returned OK. Retired 10PM. Nelson staggered in at midnight. Quite sick. Schaffner and I put him to bed. Awake until 3AM.

SEPTEMBER 10, 1944

Awoke 6:25AM to check mission. Not on today. 100 lb demos up in Adriatic sector. Soft boiled eggs, wheatena, bread, marmalade, coffee. Clear morning. There are five cots in our tent. Wooden floor and table in center. "frag" boxes act as locker trunks. Wash from a helmet. Drinking water in canteens. 60 watt bulb from energizer. Most of the time it remains very dim. Radio inoperative due to lack of power. Nelson is really under the weather this morning. Just scheduled for today's mission. Flying 791 Lt Lonsdorf pilot. Target is ammunition dump and command post about 25 miles north of La Spezia. Take off 12:32PM. 13:55PM encountering heavy moderate inaccurate flak. Over target 1400. Hit target squarely. Could see explosion. Threw window out "Escape hatch" to allude radar detection. (stencil) Had quite a mess with "window". Using K20 #11. Took some good photos. One of formation. Interrogated. (Landed 1505) Stuffed peppers, boiled onions, beans, bread, marmalade, coffee. 1st shift guard 6 to 10. Quite chilly. Very

starry night. On tomorrow's mission. Met the new
CO, Captain McClain at the club. Bought him a drink.
Retired 10:00PM.

SEPTEMBER 11, 1944

CQ blowing whistle awoke me at 5:30AM. Standby for
6:30AM. Fresh fried eggs, oatmeal, bread, marmalade,
coffee. Briefing at 6:50AM. Target is supplies. North
of Bargo San Lorenza. Take off 7:35AM. Carry light
500lb GP bombs. At 9:00AM encountered flak.
(moderate) Fighters were in vicinity but did not make
a pass. Did not drop bombs. Over target at 9:20AM
on second run over target. Hits looked good (75%).
6th mission. Landed 10:30AM. Red Cross served
doughnuts. Interrogated. Photos should be OK.
James R Blackard, 4081 Boulevard, Indianapolis,
Indiana (tent mate) also flew as cameraman. Flew on
791. Stew, fresh cucumbers, onion, beets, canned
tomatoes, pineapple, bread and marmalade, water.
Over at photo lab, Sgt Sheldon said one of my photos
would be used for public relations (ammunition
dump). Collecting additional per diem (Marrakech).
Rode with Smitty on motorcycle to showers. Roast
beef, mashed potatoes, vegetable salad, chocolate milk,
chocolate ice cream, bread and marmalade. Attended
"Presenting Lily Mars." Very clear, starry sky. Retired
11:00PM.

SEPTEMBER 12, 1944

Awoke 7:00AM. Stand down on today's mission.
Fresh fried eggs, oatmeal, bread, marmalade, coffee.
Clear and warm. Bonafacio pictures came out badly.
Replacements came in today. Pork and beans,
spinach, sliced cheese, cake, iced tea. Truck ride down

to a small French estate about one mile past "Travo". Bought one and one half kilo of tomatoes at twenty francs a kilo. Capt McClain asked Nelson to open bar at club at 3:00PM. Meat paddies, beans, canned tomatoes, chocolate pudding, bread, marmalade, eggnog. Received a letter from Shyrle (quite a bracer). Attended "GI Pie" show presented by a British troupe. Brawl over at club. Retired at 11:30PM.

SEPTEMBER 13, 1944

CQ blowing whistle at 6:30AM for 8:55AM briefing. On a "frag" mission. Scrambled eggs, oatmeal, ground sausage, tomato juice, bread, marmalade, coffee. Take off 9:40AM. Target is troops and supplies fifteen miles northwest of Borgo S Lorenzo. Fighters - did not make a pass. No flak. Over target 11:00AM. Made three runs. Hit target. Landed 12:40. 1st Lt Bard, pilot. Flew as radio-photographer. Good photos. Seventh mission. Canned corn beef, kidney beans, canned corn, peach pie, lemonade, bread, marmalade. Nelson went to Catonia, Sicily. Gray, a radio gunner of 445th, cut my hair. Graduated from U of Kentucky. (Bachelor of Science) Read all evening. Received mail today. Clear and starry evening. On tomorrow's mission. Retired 10:00PM.

SEPTEMBER 14, 1944

Awoke 6:35AM. Briefing at 7:40AM. Very clear. Pancakes, hot cereal, coffee. Troop concentration and gun emplacement on the "Gothic Line" just above Runini at the Adriatic Sea. Fighters at 3 and 6 o'clock - did not make a pass (friendly). First element dropped bombs. We didn't drop. Pictures of fighters and heavy flak to our rear. One ship in our formation hit.

Making emergency landing in Italy. Several bombardiers were slightly cut. Holes in several ships. Weather slightly cloudy 3/10th. Seen the island of Monte Cristo. Landed 11:50 with bomb load (500). Hamburgers, beans, diced beets, canned tomatoes, fruit salad, bread, marmalade. Ship in distress at 12:45 over field. Hydraulic system shot up, crew bailed out. Pilot crash landing ship. On another mission this afternoon. Troops and ammunition dump at the "Gothic" line. 48 ship formation. Briefed at 2:00PM. All set to take off. Mission stand down. Public relations to publish my photo of target (bridge) and B-25 showing destruction of target at La Spezia. Back aching quite a bit. General Cannon, General Knapp inspected the squadron. Rode to showers with Jeffery Lynn (Hollywood actor). Colonel Smith from Washington spoke on personal affairs. (National Life Insurance) On tomorrow's mission. Frank Julio, Italian interpreter for Catherine Cornell and Brian Aherne, Ethiopian Governor joined our outfit. Very clear night. Had a Tom Collins at club. Retired 9:30PM.

SEPTEMBER 15, 1944

CQ blowing whistle at 5:45. Still dark. 9/10th coverage. French toast, oatmeal, grapefruit juice, coffee. Stand by until 2:00PM. Schaffner leaving for Rome at 8:30AM. After briefing, which is held in an all-metal portable bomb shelter, trucks transport us to the line. Gunners, radioman, pilot, etc., make a last minute preflight. Bombs are loaded the evening before by ordnance. About five minutes before engine time, we first put on whatever clothing necessary. Next comes our "MaeWest" or life preservers. Over this is our parachute harness. The takeoff is somewhat rough due to an earthen runway. We sweat out many takeoffs with a bomb load. After the formation has assembled and reached flight altitude, we set course. As we approach the Italian coast, flak suits are donned, plus a flak helmet. A flak suit is composed of small individual squares of metal linked together. The back, front and lower front are individual sections snapped together. In emergency, the pulling of the front cord will dismantle the three units. The flak helmet is of medium metal. Hinged earflaps are held in place with a strap under the chin, holding the helmet in place. At this point, one is quite weighted down. As we approach our IP (initial point) where we begin our bomb run, the human tension becomes quite alive. Eyes pierce the sky, expecting fighters, flak, ships in trouble, etc. Once we leave our target, the crew finds relaxation. However until we departed Italian soil, maximum effort is required. Each man is entrusted with an escape kit consisting of money, maps, compass. Escape kits are to be used should you land in enemy territory. Meat loaf, canned tomatoes, mashed potatoes, (dehydrated) peas, fruit salad, iced tea, bread, marmalade. Slight drizzle. Taylor and I purchased tomatoes, Spanish melon, cantaloupes at a small French market. Nelson returned from Catonia. Boiled beef, beans, canned tomatoes, fruit salad, coffee, bread, marmalade. Listened to British heavyweight fight for title Jack London (champion) Fred Mills (contender). Ate a piece of Spanish melon. Rum coke at club. Retired 9:30PM.

SEPTEMBER 16, 1944

SQ blowing whistle over PA system at 5:50AM. Briefing 6:45AM. Very clear morning. A bit of diarrhea. Pancakes, oatmeal, coffee. Carry 500-lb amiable incendiaries. Target fuel dump 3 miles SW of Bologna. Over target 9:31AM. Good hit. Good photos. Flak was moderate and inaccurate. Pictures of Florence and ship "Cherry Fizz". Landed at 11:10AM. Very cold upstairs (12000) right wing lead element. Mission (9) a bit nervous. Hash, eggplant, canned beans, fresh tomatoes, cake, coke, coffee, marmalade. Received rations - 9 bottles beer, 4 packages gum, 2 cokes, 3 cigars, 14 pkgs cigarettes, 9 bars candy, 3 bars soap, 1 face powder, 1 pipe, 2 cartons tobacco, 1 towel. Washed coveralls in gasoline. Captain McClean inspecting area. Slophes, Davey left for the states. Stew, fresh tomatoes, onion, cucumbers, bread, butter, coffee. Stomach feeling punk. Not on tomorrow's mission. Retired 9:15PM.

SEPTEMBER 17, 1944

Awoke 6:45. This Sunday morning, clocks were set back one hour. Was disturbed about 10:15PM last evening from a lot of jabbering in the tent. New combat man sleeping in Charles bunk for night. Commenced Alexander Woolcott's "As You Were". Retired 12:30. Bright and clear morning. Corn fritters, grapefruit juice, coffee. Assisted the "Chief" in reassembling club after a night of fury. Major Bell was over. On detail to pick up cement below Bastia at Casanova. Left 10:45. IR - 600 lb cans of cement (10 1/2 tons) Arrived at camp 4:30PM. Traveled about 70 kilometers. Light rain on return. Stopped to pick grapes along way. Farmer came out with shotgun. Took a couple of eggplant sandwiches. Some of the boys left for the mountains to observe the holidays starting at sundown. Made S/Sgt today (Sept 15, 1944) Roast beef, mashed potatoes, canned corn, onions and beets, coffee, bread and marmalade. Over

at the club awhile. Killed a bottle of beer. Mike
stopped in, has infected hands. Clear evening.
Retired 9:00PM.

SEPTEMBER 18, 1944

Awoke 5:15AM. Briefing at 6:35AM. Sky 4/10
coverage. Scrambled powdered eggs, oatmeal,
grapefruit juice, bread, marmalade, coffee. Target,
troops and supplies northwest of Rimini. Pilot Lt
Moyer (541) Takeoff 8:10. Over target 9:29. 100%
hit. Flak - moderate inaccurate. P47 dive-bombers.
5/10 clouds. Very cold. Flew at 12,000 feet. One
ship 445th went down - bombardier, DiFulvio. Hit over
target. Three parachuted but were being fired upon by
German ground forces. Eating early chow for another
mission this PM. Stuffed peppers, onions and beets,
kidney beans, butterscotch pudding, iced tea,
marmalade, bread. Briefing at 12:35PM. Same as this
morning's target. Lt Swanson (563). Takeoff 1:45PM.
Lead ship 2nd element. Turned back at coast of Italy.
10/10 at 10,000. Landed 3:10PM. Capt Neprash gave
me another photo which is to be published. Feeling
knocked out after knowing of Rudy's ultimate fate.
Dreary day. Received 10 letters. Used K-8A for both
missions. On 1st shift of guard. Comfortable evening.
Prayed for Rudy. Schaffner returned from Rome.
Stuffed pepper, canned tomatoes, canned peaches,
bread, butter, coffee. Feeling blue. Retired 10:30PM.

SEPTEMBER 19, 1944

CQ blowing whistle over PA at 5:50AM. Raining but
clear in the east. Briefing 7:05AM. Pancakes,
grapefruit juice, coffee, hot cereal. Stand by on
mission. Rain is continuing. Laying in sack, reading

from "As You Were" (Edgar Allan Poe) (Ring Lardner). Cement and tarpaper coming in for winterizing tents. Sides to be built up with lumber from frog boxes. Meatloaf, string beans, sliced cabbage, mashed potatoes, fruit salad, hot tea, bread, butter. Working on roof of club. Still raining. Continual gab session in progress. Standdown on mission. Roast beef, beans, canned corn, rice pudding, coffee, bread, marmalade. Learned to play cribbage and gin rummy. Very windy, rainy, cold. Secured tent. Retired 9:00PM. Awoke 10:15PM. Heart burn, feeling punk. Drank two canteens water. Up several times urinating. Retired 11:30PM.

SEPTEMBER 20, 1944

CQ blowing whistle 5:15AM. Briefing 6:00AM. Slight rain. Carrying 1000 lb GP's. Railroad bridge 50 miles northwest of Valerno at Citta Della, Italy. Powdered eggs in pancake form, stewed prunes, coffee, bread. Played cribbage, read, kibitzed. Standdown on mission. Steel runway mats coming in. Boys are repairing club. Spamburgers, carrots and onion, canned tomatoes, applesauce, bread, butter, coffee. Very heavy rain. Rain ceased 3:30PM. New roof being put on club. Roast beef, mashed potatoes, cabbage, beans, fruit salad, coffee, bread, marmalade. Went to see Smitty and Taylor. Frag exploded causing Rudy's ship to go down. B26 outfit claims they saw 6 chutes open. Flak missed Taylor's head and his radio-gunner was put out of commission with a slug in his right side. (7 on lead ship). Rudy's wife to have baby next week. Read Ring Lardner's "Some Like Them Cold" and Edgar Allan Poe's "Murders in the Rue Morgue." Retired 8:50PM.

SEPTEMBER 21, 1944

CQ blowing whistle at 6:00AM. First day of autumn. Feeling like a million. Briefing at 7:20AM. Fried powdered eggs, wheatena, bread, marmalade, coffee, grapefruit juice. Standdown. Hitched to the 340th with Smith, Stanley. Found Lozowski in 486Sq (Usher, Stevenson, McLarin, Carter, Thomas, Lt Bain, Horton also in 340th group.) Ate chow at 340th. Headquarter tent, metal stools and board covered boxes to form table. Dirt floor. Area very scattered. Visited Lt Bain and Lt Horton. Lt Ivory from 448th was also at 340th. Spoke about Rudy. Complete crews fly on transition flight. Very clear day (Hash, canned tomatoes, rice pudding, bread and peanut butter, grapefruit juice - 340th meal) Lozowski came back with me to 448th. Joe Creighter's friend, Lt Ned Reiley came down from 340th (489th). Leonard and Ned stayed for supper. Roast beef, mashed potatoes, shredded cabbage, fried eggplants, bread, marmalade, coffee. We went through the chow line twice. Killed a bottle of Jamaique Rum. None for yours truly. Used squadron jeep to drive the boys back. Removed our caps and zipped our jackets up and drank with Ned at the 340th officer's club. Edith (Red Cross) acting bartendress. Sampled every drink. Creighter drank consistently (American whiskey and gin). Met Captain Taylor. Ned removed three cases of Rupperts beer for Joe and me. Tried to leave at 9:00PM. Finally departed at 11:00PM. Joe very stinko. Yours truly drove back. Arrived camp 12:15AM. Very tired. Clear night. Stumbled on way in tent. Chief (John Nelson) kidding me about being inebriated. Retired 12:30AM.

SEPTEMBER 22, 1944

CQ blowing whistle at 6:00AM. Briefing 7:20AM.
Pancakes, stewed prunes, bread, marmalade, coffee.
Very clear morning. Weather reconnaissance ship
sent out over target area to check weather. Target at
Cetta Della, northern Italy. Carrying 10000 lb GP.
Target is 1000 x43 foot railroad bridge. Flying #805 Lt
Poard pilot. Using K-8A camera. Takeoff 8:45AM.
Flying 12000 feet. Very cold. Over target 11:03AM.
Lead ship second element. First run on target, wing
ships dropped bombs. Bombs went all over
countryside. Second run was a 100% hit. Viewed
snow covered Alps. Milk run. Met a character Ben
Hospod. Landed 12:40. Feeling very tired. Schnaffer
left for the states via Naples. Moved to corner of tent.
310th men badly poisoned from lye in wheat cakes.
Played cribbage with James Blackard. Vienna
sausages with sauce, kidney beans, creamed peas,
coffee, bread and butter. Sleeping bag very
comfortable and warm. Retired 8:00PM.

SEPTEMBER 23, 1944

Light in tent awoke me at 5:10AM. Did not hear CQ
blow whistle. Briefing at 6:00AM. Fresh toast, syrup,
coffee. Carrying 1000 lb GP's. Lead ship last element.
Target is at Podwa, Northern Italy. Railroad bridge.
3/10 coverage at field. Lt Grady, pilot (067). Takeoff
8:53AM. One minute before reaching IP, beaucoup
flak. Evasive action. Over target 9:29AM. 100% hit.
Returned same route and caught more flak. Right
wing ship dropped out. Landed 11:45AM. Five flak
holes in our ship. Flew as radio-photographer. Using
K-8A. Reported beaucoup ground activity over enemy
territory (Convoys, barges, industry). Hash paddies,
tomato sauce, mashed potatoes, canned corn, bread,

butter, water. Winterizing tents. 2 x 4's form framework. Wooden floors. Tar paper and chicken wire form walls. Floor 12" off ground. Making company streets. Sides are 6' high. Still taking showers outside. Read "Outcasts of Poker Flat", Bret Harte. Issued air mattress. No mail. Fair weather. American whiskey at club. Steve came over. Joe Creightor, Wesley Kheen, Mike Green, Louey Dunbar and I drank beer at their tent. Retired at 9:30 PM

SEPTEMBER 24, 1944

James called me at 6:30AM. Not on today's mission. Partly cloudy. Pancakes, stewed apricots, wheatena, marmalade, coffee. Washed sun-tans. Read "The Last Will", Williston Fish, "The Duke and Dauphin Come Aboard," Mark Twain. Worked with detail assembling duplex building to house S-2, operations and orderly room. Spoke with Major Knieval. Fred Jacobson, returned from Rome. Boiled chicken, creamed peas, canned tomatoes, coffee, bread and butter. Filled out PR form at S-2. Picked up air mattress at tech supply. Mission was at SW of Venice. 10/10 sky prevented bombing. Hot dogs, tomato sauce, navy beans, diced beets, bread, butter, coffee. Ned Heilich came down. Had a beer, liquor and food party at Mike Kosses' tent. (Ned Creightor, Adams, Lynn, Jesse, George, Ned and yours truly (2 beers and 1 shot). Commenced Gene Fowler's "Good Night Sweet Prince". Retired 9:30PM.

SEPTEMBER 25, 1944

Hot sun beating against tent awoke me at 7:05AM. Stand by on mission. Pancakes, marmalade, coffee. Very windy morning. All the Italian KP's left the island September   23rd. This was a directive issued by

44

General Eaker. Too much friction between French and Italians. (I personally prefer the Italians). Standdown on mission. Jim Radcliffe and I went to the "villa" near Solenzara. Bought watermelons and tomatoes. Two watermelons the size of grapefruit and eleven tomatoes (80 francs). Attended USO show unit 265. "Hum and Drum" (Max Seides, Boston, Mass.) Ray Kretair, Amsterdam, NY. Remembered me from back home. Had quite a session. Still doing imitations. Max Seides knows Phil Saltman well. Capt Marshall (flight surgeon) drove the boys back to the 446th officer's area. Clear and cold night. Retired 11:00PM.

SEPTEMBER 26, 1944

Awoke 7:05AM. Not on today's mission. Hot and sunny AM. Powdered egg pancakes, wheatena, bread marmalade, coffee. Went to 446th. Met the USO troupe. Ned Purek, Leonard Roznicki, Mike and yours truly. Took picture with the troupe. Read. Meat loaf, creamed peas, mashed potatoes, chocolate cake, bread, butter, water. Nickeling mission for this PM canceled. George Herkas' day off. Lack of something to do and a place to go makes a man irritable. George and I repaired voice control of PA system. Pork chops, peas, mashed potatoes, cocoa, bread, butter. Attended "Shine on Harvest Moon". Ideal for the movie as there was a full harvest moon. Nelson kept nine eggs from the Catania shipment. Brought us two oranges. Retired 10:00PM.

SEPTEMBER 27, 1944

CQ blowing whistle awoke me at 6:30AM. Not on mission. Cloudy morning. Pineapple pancakes, tomato juice, marmalade, coffee. Wilkinson (radio) somewhat shaky today. I am to replace him on today's mission. Briefing 7:50AM. Standby until 12:00PM. Showering outside is becoming quite chilly. Evenings are fine for sleeping. There are never any games of vice in our tent. One can sleep most any time as no one disturbs you. James Royce brought in a couple dozen oranges this morning. Blackard and I played cribbage. Stew, rice, fresh tomatoes and peppers, bread, butter, iced tea. Mike Kassis infected thumbs slowly healing. Captain Marshall (flight surgeon) is not too well thought of by the boys. Doesn't pay any attention. I pray to God that someday it shall be my good fortune to write what I see on men's faces and my own. Standdown of today's mission. Called on Lt Carl Fisher, but was out. Gene Stanley and I went for a 3-hour walk. Watched a group of mother pigs and their sucklings. Blackberries are no longer present. The grapes have been picked as well as the figs and peaches. Huge wine casks in the cellar are being filled. Hash, navy beans, canned tomatoes, onions, cucumbers, fruit salad, bread, apple jelly, coffee. Dark at 7:00PM. Very chilly. Ike, Khun, Leo returned from Rome. Met Angelo Surrino former football player at Temple University. Played with Dave Smukler. Angelo was in stockade for 6 months for breaking a soldier's nose, jaw and eliminating teeth. Was a PT instructor at Miami Beach, Fla. Retired 9:00PM.

SEPTEMBER 28, 1944

Awoke 7:25AM. Bright sun, slight wind. Awoke during the night to listen to a howling wind. Standby until 12:00PM on mission. Creamed corned beef hash on bread, oatmeal, orange juice, coffee, apple jelly. Washed clothes. Read "Fifty Grand" by Ernest Hemingway. Winter preparations are continuing but rumors are circulating of our departing. It's the longest the 321st has stayed in one spot. The boys are becoming restless. For the past several weeks I have been smoking a pipe. Cigarettes are slowly falling out of my life. Taylor, Stanley and myself rode on Taylor's motorcycle to the line to take pictures of the pin-up girls painted on the ship. Met Crisp coming back. Four rode back on motorcycle. Took my first try at driving the cycle. Sudden change in weather. Very cold. Pork chop, roast beef which I did not get any of, peas, mashed potatoes, fresh beets and onions, apple sauce, bread, marmalade, coffee. Bull session in tent. Played cribbage and casino with Blockard, Huka. Slight rain. Typical fall sky. Heavy dark billowing clouds. Damp, cold, penetrating wind.

SEPTEMBER 29, 1944

CQ blowing whistle at 6:50AM. Moderate rain. No briefing time for mission. Pancakes, stewed apricots, oatmeal, bread, apple jelly, coffee. Helped John clear up club. Vino, cognac, brandy, gin, anisette, vermouth comprise our liquor stock. Most of it comes from Catania, Sicily. The beer usually comes from Tripoli. Every so often a plane is dispatched to pick up supplies. Glasses are made from liquor and beer bottles cut down. This process is done by merely filling the bottle with hot oil until the desired depth of glass. Gently tap and you have your glass. As a rule it leaves a smooth edge. The oil cannot be used again. Standby on today's mission. Played cribbage, stud and draw poker. George Huka pulled last shift guard. Briefing at 12:50PM. Corned beef hash, navy beans, fried onions, sliced onion, fruit salad, bread, tea, peanut butter. Helped Nelson repair roof on club. Still taking outdoor showers. Getting colder.

Inconsistent showers. Meat loaf, gravy, navy beans, string beans (sour) chocolate pudding, bread, peanut butter, coffee. No movie this evening. Met Benchowsky, Aloyuseus, Royce at the club bar. Had three drinks of Marsala wine. Very cold night. Almost a full moon. Retired 9:00PM.

SEPTEMBER 30, 1944

Awoke 7:25AM. Brief for mission at 11:35AM. French toast, whole-wheat cereal, stewed prunes and apricots, coffee. As a rule I shave every morning. Cloudy, slightly warmer. Assisted Lewis Dunbar (telephone maintenance) in putting up a new line to Captain Marricks tent. Carry 500 lb GP. Target is a RR bridge at Voghera. Wear long johns and sheepskin boots. Lt Mitchell pilot (548). Take off 12:35PM. Over target 1400. 100% hit. Very rough upstairs. Feeling a bit nauseated. Carry K-8A camera. Should have good photos. Spotted traffic and beached barges on way home over enemy territory. Landed 1510. Just about to toss my cookies. Landing saved me. Paid 6000 francs, as this is the day. Windy, clear skies. Noon chow - Vienna sausage, tarter sauce, navy beans, fruit salad, bread, butter, coffee. On guard from 6 to 10PM. Cloudless, full moon, typical fall evening. Mike, George, Wesley, Lynn, Blackard and yours truly fried eggs and bacon on a double burner gas stove in the tent. Also made tea. Retired 12:00AM.

OCTOBER 1, 1944

CQ blowing whistle at 5:45. Briefing for first mission at 6:55AM. Second mission 7:35AM. On second mission. Powdered egg, omelet, oatmeal, stewed apricots, coffee. Carrying 1000 lb (GP) Last element of

18-ship formation from 445th. Target is ammo dump at Pracenza, Northern Italy. Over target at 10:45AM. Carry K-20. Good photos. Lt Carrington pilot. Commencing to feel tired at 13,500 feet. Lack of oxygen. Beaucoup flak. Evasive action. Take off 8:50AM. Landed 12:30PM. Circled field for one hour awaiting first formation to land. James Davis, engineer, flying tail was killed. Davis crash-landed and bailed out before, about 35th mission. Flak hit him just above the heart. Going completely through flak suit. Headache and I feel beat in general. Fried chicken, diced beets, canned pineapple, bread, butter, water. Moleski, Huka, Ratcliffe crash landed safely yesterday in Northern Italy at an allied field. Both engines on fire. Received rations today. 5 bottles beer, 2 cokes, 4 pkg gum, 1 box sour balls, 1 tropical Hershey, 1 towel (bath) 1 cookie, 4 O'Henry's, 1 Himac, 1 cigars, 14 pkg cigarettes. Clear and warm. Today was Davis' 57th mission. I flew my fourteenth. Roast beef, mashed potatoes, gravy, canned tomatoes, bread, peanut butter, hot tea. Clear, moonlit night. Retired 9:00PM.

OCTOBER 2, 1944

CQ calling at 6:45AM for chow. Not on today's mission. Pineapple pancakes, oatmeal, coffee. 3/10 coverage, warm. Met Ike's cousin, John Vink. To attend funeral of James Davis (killed in combat yesterday). Sent home 5000 francs ($100.00) Cpt McCall sealed envelope. Left area at 12:15PM for burial services. 2 1/2 hour ride over bumpy road. At 3:30PM about 25 attended. We awaited the ceremonies for a bombardier on a B-26 also killed in yesterday's raid. Captain Farwell was in charge. Being a US military cemetery there were many already laid to rest. In formation, we faced Jimmy's flag draped casket. Upon completion of Chaplain Johnson administering the last rites, the firing squad of six men shot three volleys. Against a clear mountainous background a bugler sounded taps. Indeed we shall miss James Davis. Against a W-D order, I took several pictures. Being but several miles outside Bastia we drove to the seaport town. In the harbor laid the wreckage of several freighters. An allied destroyer and freighter were also anchored. The outskirts was badly damaged; mainly a huge cemetery. It was here the Germans fought a sniper's war. Blue uniformed Gendarmes patrol the city. Boston streets are similar in construction. It'd been the first time in weeks since I've seen a well-dressed person. Stopped at the Red Cross for a sandwich and coffee (5 francs). A rather delightful and pretty mademoiselle was cashier. Bastia is several hundred feet above the harbor. Located on the side of a mountain. It is a large sized town, perhaps 100,000. Prostitution is prevalent. Returned to camp at 6:00PM. Roast beef, rice and gravy, vanilla pudding, bread, peanut butter, coffee. Washed thoroughly after that dusty trip. Full orange moon. Retired 9:00PM. Chest feels a bit congested.

OCTOBER 3, 1944

CQ blowing whistle at 6:55AM. Briefing at 9:50AM. Cool, clear, sunny morning. Pancakes, bacon, whole-wheat cereal, marmalade, coffee, tomato juice. Still shaving every morning. Briefing changed to 12:30PM. Eating early chow at 10:45. I have a premonition. Feel a bit nervous. Rather I didn't fly. Take off 1:50PM. Target is at Giota, Italy (fuel dump). Over target 3:35PM. Milk run. Lt Norris pilot. Rather cold, very clear day. Feeling rather punk. Hit target.

Landed 5:05PM. 445th lost two ships over target near Milan. A burst of flak blew up one ship. The concussion sent another ship into a spin. S-2 said a "May-day" was received. The first ship's crew is finito. Roast beef, gravy, navy beans, carrots, peas, fruit salad, bread, jelly. USO show this afternoon while we were on mission. Joe Ryan over and feeling a bit intoxicated. Being a rather boisterous individual causes one to get a rather bad impression. Visited Taylor at 445th. His bunkmate Hickey went down over target today. Came back with me to club. Had several Tom Collins. Feeling punk. Retired 9:30PM.

OCTOBER 4, 1944

CQ blowing whistle 6:50AM. Standby on today's mission until 10 o'clock. Egg, cheese omelet, oatmeal, bread, jam, tomato juice, coffee. Low ceiling, cold sun trying to penetrate ceiling. Looks clear out at sea. Feeling rather perky this AM. Commencing to rebuild tent. Briefing at 10:05AM. Carry 1000 lb GP's. Target at Pantipale, Italy (Railroad bridge). Heavy overcast. 10/10 coverage over target. Did not drop bombs. Captain Burks pilot. Landed 1:35PM. Tent with wooden floor and 2 x 4 supporting beams. Spaghetti and sauce, navy beans, bread, butter, fruit salad, cocoa. Helped build. Completed job just as rain commenced. Baked beans, peas, beets, celery, bread, marmalade, coffee. Smoking a lot lately. Received letter from #19 and Merriam. First meal in 12 days. Slight rain. "Hum Strum" and Ray Kretzer returned awaiting hop to Florence. To entertain 5th army. Staying at 448th officer's area. Standing in drizzle in coveralls. Ray came over for a few minutes. Retired 12:00AM.

OCTOBER 5, 1944

Awoke 7:10AM. No missions. 10/10 ceiling.
Oatmeal, pancakes, tomato juice, marmalade, bread,
coffee. Working on tent, making rear extension. Roy
came over about 10:15AM. We are constructing
extension to rear of tent. Yours truly has the GI's plus
a headache. Feeling punk in general. Mike invited the
troupe over for dinner. "Hum and Strum" entertained.
Hamburgers, tomato sauce, mashed potatoes, beets,
bread, butter, water. Feeling very weak. Went to
dispensary. Medic gave me 2 aspirins and a 3-ounce
shot of Paregoric. Laid down for a spell. Felt a bit
guilty in not helping on the tent. Helped toward the
end. The tent is 16 feet square, with wooden
fragmentation box tops providing the floor (72 pieces)
Six foot 2 x 4's are corner posts. 1 x 8's provide the
crosspieces. 2 x 4 pyramid from each corner to form a
center pole. Tarpaper covers the outside of lumber.
Chicken wire is placed atop this to prevent ripping.
The tent is next given a canvas roof and part canvas
side. George Huka supervised the job and did the
majority of the work. Roast beef, gravy, peas, mashed
potatoes, bread, butter, fruit salad, coffee. Roy and
the boys are in the kitchen, unknown to me. Body,
head etc. beginning to act up. After Dr Marshall
finished caring for a burned arm and hand of an
Italian KP, he looked after me. Took temperature.
Another dose of paregoric, 9 sulfa tablets to be taken
all at once. 12 sulfa tablets to be taken 4 every four
hours, quartered and ground. Went over to CM club
where the troupe was entertaining. Bid the boys
goodnight. Hit the sack about 9:00PM. Mike came in
and we discussed the CQ. Captain McClain has
outwardly accused Mike of selling coffee etc., from
mess supplies. He has cursed out Mike and all EM
men in general. He seems to be constantly drunk.

The boys in the 445th were mighty glad to see him go. Why was such a curse wished on us. He is also selling combat whiskey as well as bringing any surplus from the month's supply to the officer's club. Dozed off 9:45PM.

OCTOBER 6, 1944

Awoke 8:55AM. Feeling OK. Pancakes, bacon, wheatena, coffee. Did not go to breakfast. Still raining. Rained hard all during night. Heavy overcast. Standby on mission until 10:00. Standdown. Corn beef hash, navy beans, tomatoes, bread, marmalade, hot tea. Roy came over for negatives. Still taking sulfa tablets. Rested for several hours this PM. Awoke feeling better and to a bright sun beating against the canvas. Read and wrote several letters. No mail. Stew, peas, rice, fruit salad, bread, butter, coffee. Ike told me on the QT that our CO has been ousted. At present McClean is in France. Construction throughout the squadron is progressing. Moderate stomach cramps. A tent and area inspection by the colonel never came off. Writing by candlelight. Listened to a Limey musical program. World Series being rebroadcast from Radio Rome. Read from S-2. "Air Intelligence" branded as secret. Retired 9:00PM. Could not sleep. Stomach cramps. Dozed off about 10:30PM. Very windy.

OCTOBER 7, 1944

John called me at 7:30AM. Partly cloudy sky. Standby on mission. Fresh fried eggs, oatmeal, stewed apricots, bread, coffee. Standdown on mission. Feeling better today. Hawthorne and I discussed and reminisced over our connections with National and Martin-Rosebury. Still reading "Good Night Sweet

Prince." Pondering over an aircraft recognition magazine. Read the "Stars and Stripes" a daily publication printed in Italy. This Mediterranean issue is not printed on Sunday. Slight headache. Meat loaf, mashed potatoes, gravy, canned corn, bread, marmalade, water. Feeling mokey. Ham, beans, spinach, vanilla pudding, coffee, bread. Body racked with pain, headaches, sore chest. Medic at dispensary gave me three pills. Retired 6:30PM.

OCTOBER 8, 1944

Awoke 7:00AM. Very restless night. Inconsistent rain squalls throughout the night. Felling better this morning, but somewhat foggy. Must be the effects of the medicine. On today's mission. Standby. Mike Hersh (NYC) stopped in to discuss organization of a squadron band. Bernard Bass is playing piano with the "Mitchell-airs" who have just returned from Naples. Fresh fried eggs, stewed raisins, bread, coffee. Dreary day. Standdown. Steve was over this afternoon. Duplex orderly room and operations completed. Lynn gave me some more pills for fever. Severe pains are chest, neck stiffening. Doctor took a blood smear to test for malaria. Boiled chicken, gravy, beans, beets, peaches and apricots, coffee. Did some reading. Neck quite stiff, slight headache. Corn beef hash, rice, Worcestershire sauce, apricots, peaches, coffee. Lights very dim in mess hall. Captain Farwell new CO. Played cribbage with James by candlelight. Feeling punk. Doc says I still have fever. Gave me some capsules to take every three hours. Damp, cloudy evening. Wish I could be with Shyrle and those at #19. Quit smoking. Retired 8:30PM.

OCTOBER 9, 1944

Awoke 7:15AM. Feeling quite chipper. Fresh fried
eggs, oatmeal, bread, pineapple juice, coffee. Partly
cloudy, rather warm. Standdown on today's mission.
Weather over target bad. Rome trip been trying to take
off for four days. Read most of the morning. Fresh
roast beef, gravy, fresh tomatoes, peas, mashed
potatoes, applesauce. Meeting of combat men at
1:00PM. Captain Farwell (new CO) chewed us out for
tardiness in meeting time schedules. Moved a couple
of shacks. Worked on the tent a bit. Made another
burner for washing clothes. John Scallion,
Dorchester, Mass. moved in today. Seven fellows from
the 319th (B26 outfit) came to this squadron. Doing
away with the b26's and replacing them with b25's.
They are to have several weeks of schooling. Rather a
decent chap. Lt Ned Heilich from the 340th (Joe
Crider's buddy) came down. Played cribbage. Washed
beaucoup clothes. Fresh roast beef, peas, navy beans,
peaches, coffee, bread, peanut butter. Kibitzed with
Nelson about semi-notorious persons in Saratoga.
Wrote by candlelight. Feeling punk, neck very stiff,
slight headache, kidney pains. Medics gave me some
more dope. Retired 9:0PM.

OCTOBER 10, 1944

CQ blowing whistle at 6:45AM. Standby until
11:00AM. Huka just coming off guard. Bright sunny,
warm AM. Feeling great. Sweated a lot during the
night. Fresh fried eggs, bacon, oatmeal, tomato juice,
coffee, bread, marmalade. We always have powdered
milk for our cereal. James Herod let me borrow "God
is my Co-Pilot" by Colonel Scott. Fair day. Feeling
OK. Fried spam, fresh tomatoes, boiled cabbage,
beets, bread, jelly, water. Went over to the 445th.

One of the boys cut my hair (20 francs). Stanley took
me to showers in squadron jeep. Water is heated, but
atmosphere chilly. Semi-cloudy sky. Stew, fresh
vegetable salad, fruit salad, bread, butter, coffee.
Attended "Life is That Way" Donald O'Connor, Peggy
Ryan. Excellent movie. Still taking APC capsules.
Chilly evening. Lightning toward Italy. Reading in bed
by candlelight. Retired 10:45PM.

OCTOBER 11, 1944

Awoke 7:20AM. Stomach cramps. Diarrhea again.
Clear, bright AM. Standby on mission until 11:00AM.
Fresh fried eggs, whole-wheat cereal, bread, jam,
grapefruit juice, coffee. Washed mattress cover,
coveralls. Flight surgeon feeding me more sulfa.
Commenced "God is My Co-Pilot", Colonel Robert L
Scott. Hash, mashed potatoes, fresh mixed vegetables,
hot tea, bread, jam. Couldn't eat much. Mail from
Shyrle pepped me up quite some. First in a fortnight.
Intended to work on tent, but too weak. Stayed in bed.
Roast beef, mashed potatoes, onions and string beans,
canned sliced pineapple, bread, jam, coffee. Mess
lines are becoming very long. Confusion and noise in
mess hall isn't my idea of dining in quiet. Couldn't
eat. Felt guilty about throwing away good food. Mild,
clear and starry evening. Wrote a long letter to Shyrle.
Retired at 9:00PM. Chest and side pains. Restless.

OCTOBER 12, 1944

CQ blowing whistle at 6:30AM. Feeling pert. Cloudy
sky. Briefing at 7:45AM. Hard-boiled eggs, bacon,
oatmeal, tomato juice, coffee, bread, marmalade. Wear
OD's and sheepskin boots. Target is 3 miles SW of
Bologna ammunition and supply dump. Carry 500 lb

GP's. Flying as lead radio operator. 1st Lt Dossey, pilot. Smith navigator. Take off 8:51AM. Weather closed in, returned to field. Landed 10:15AM. No interrogation. Standing by for another mission. Cloudy sky. Jim Blackard receives a parcel. Haven't digested such delicious fruitcake in months. Baked beans, fresh uncooked peppers, onions, cabbage, bread, butter, coffee. Interrupted middle of meal for immediate briefing. Weather looks bad. Same as morning mission. Take off 1:30PM. Couldn't see to make landfall over enemy territory. When we finally did find an opening we were over La Spezia. We immediately went into evasive action and got away from there. It is a heavily defended harbor. We headed for Rome, called the field to tell them of our unsuccessful mission. Made good contact. Very picturesque, overcast. Looked like huge snow piles and billows of white smoke. Very cold. Capt McClean was co-pilot. Landed 4:00PM. No interrogation. Still showering outside. Ange, Frank and I went in Ange's truck. Feeling great. Wesley gave me heavy cellophane for tent windows. Roast beef, gravy, mashed potatoes, canned corn, fruit salad, bread, marmalade, coffee. Rewiring area and putting power lines on poles. Retired 10:20PM.

OCTOBER 13, 1944

Awoke 7:00AM. Feeling OK. Partly cloudy sky. Mission standby. Fresh fried eggs, wheatena, bread, marmalade, tomato juice, coffee. Put up chicken wire around tent. Ryan called me for detail to load gravel on truck. Didn't go as I was working on tent. Ike was over. Has bad cold. Lozowski and Usher came down. Usher has 9 missions. Lozowski 16. Stayed for chow. Corn beef paddies, tomato sauce, spinach, mashed

turnips, butterscotch pudding. Played blackjack at
Ratcliffe's tent. Won 50 francs. Danny Hury secured
Major Knievel's permission for jeep #4 Eleanor. This is
Captain Marrick's private jeep. Got jeep license.
Received special permission to go beyond officer's PX
resulting from shooting near Geshonnochi where
447th held a dance. Colored troops were denied entry
to the dance. They returned with arms killing a 310th
boy and injuring two from the 447th. Left area
5:15PM. Went over to 445th to see Taylor and Smitty.
Ratcliffe, Lozowski, Usher and I ate chow at 445th.
Hamburgers, tomato sauce, mashed potatoes,
butterscotch pudding, bread, coffee.   Lights in jeep
out. Returned to 448th. Motor pool obligingly put in
two new sealed beams. Back to 445th. Gene treated
us to several drinks. Cherry brandy and orange-
grapefruit juice. Beat Lozowski in ping-pong. Raining.
Sang all the way to 340th. Arrived 9:00PM. Had
coffee at Red Cross club. Met McClane at 340th, an
old buddy from Scott Field. Left at 9:45PM. Picked up
Walter Rogusky on way back. Gene Stanley drove
most of the way. Arrived 10:45PM. Kibitzed with
LaBella a spell. Mission went to Bologna, carry 500 lb
for fuel dump. Successful. Starry night. Retired
11:45PM.

OCTOBER 14, 1944

Awoke 7:30AM. Interrupted night. Partly cloudy sky.
Feeling OK. Standby on mission. Fresh fried eggs (4)
bacon, bread, marmalade, coffee. Gave Ike some
Vick's nose drops to help his cold. Sun came out.
Feeling exceptionally fine, greeting everyone with a
melodious "hello". Hamburgers, tomato sauce,
mashed potatoes, creamed peas, bread, butter, hot
tea. Picked up pictures at photo lab. Went to wing

post office with Rogusky - to 310th. Picked up mail at
group. Mild weather. Roast beef, gravy, mashed
potatoes, string beans, bread, peanut butter, coffee.
Pulled 1st shift of guard. Very starry evening. Guard
duty is really a big job. Chilly. Retired 10:45PM.

OCTOBER 15, 1944

What awoke me I do not know at 7:25. Hurrying and
scurrying to get myself organized as briefing was at
7:20AM. Ate a hurried breakfast. Fresh fried eggs,
oatmeal, bread, butter, coffee. Ran to catch trucks
leaving for the line. Hailed one on highway mission
south of Turin, Italy. Carrying 500 lb GP's for oil
dumps. Lt Kruse, pilot. Lead element. Have on all my
winter flying clothes. Flew over snow covered Italian
Alps. Target covered 10/10 stratus. Made two passes.
Milk run. Headed for secondary. Also covered.
Landed 11:30AM with bombs. This is the first time
the Red Cross has served doughnuts and coffee on
Sunday. Received rations today (2:20). 14 pkgs
cigarettes, 2 cokes, 1 box vanilla snaps, 2 tropical
Hershey's, 4 pkgs dentine gum, 1 box hard candy, 2
tubes peanuts, 2 pkgs gum drops, 1 peanut bar, 4
candy bars. Rations are rather snafued as is our
squadron supply. Underhanded activity is evident.
Much of our equipment designated for squadron
personnel use is being disposed of for financial gain.
Ham, canned tomatoes, chocolate pudding, bread,
butter, water, fresh apples. Warm and clear today.
John Scallion of Dorchester, Mass moved back to the
319th (formerly B26's). Played the squadron football
pool yesterday. Sorta hoping Wisconsin U would beat
Ohio - no luck. Been thinking about Shyrle a lot.
Flew my eighteenth mission today. Roast beef,
mashed potatoes, green beans, fruit salad, bread,

butter, coffee. Dozed off until 9:45PM. Capt Farwell called meeting of all radio operators at operations. Discussed messages and frequencies. Clear, cold evening. Retired 11:00PM.

OCTOBER 16, 1944

CQ blowing whistle 7:45AM. Briefing at 8:15AM. Sunny morning. Pancakes, wheatena, bacon, grapefruit juice, coffee. Fred Jacobson was grounded on 55 missions. Mission for today is standdown. Meeting at operations at 9:00AM. Meeting was for gunners to clean guns at line. Stomach cramps and diarrhea. Spam paddies, fresh tomatoes, mashed potatoes (dehydrated), spinach, bread, marmalade, water. No appetite. Swapped Joe Creighton 2 cokes for 6 pkgs cigarettes. Went out to see Capt Hayes at ordnance. Checked out on tail and top turret. Read and slept. Clear day. Showered. Commenced building portable bookstand for reading in bed. Roast pork, succotash, canned tomatoes, rice pudding, coffee, bread, butter. Met Lt Bechtle, a distant relation of Kirsten Flagstad. Commenced Hamlet, Prince of Denmark. Received mail from Geraldine and Shyrle. Retired 10:00PM.

OCTOBER 17, 1944

DQ blowing whistle at 6:55AM. Standby on mission until 9:00AM. Cloudy morning. Fried powdered eggs, wheatena, tomato juice, bread, marmalade, coffee. Nelson spent the day in the mountains yesterday. Stuffed peppers, fresh salad of tomatoes, onions and peppers, peas, canned sliced pineapple, water. Huka and I built door for tent. Slightly cloudy. Sanford Wellington Will, North Plains, Oregon, stopped in.

Sanford is about six-three, slightly stooped. A daily part of his dress is a beret obtained from a Frenchman. He likes to talk about his drunks. As an individual he is outstanding for his gold trimmed front teeth and odd way of expression with his lips. Stew, fresh onions, tomato and pepper salad, kidney beans, butterscotch pudding, coffee. One of the tents caught fire this evening. Attended "Background for Danger" with Ben Moleski of Gary, Indiana. Ben is about 5'9" - 150 lbs and of Polish extraction. Likes to dress ostentatiously. Talks about many things of which he knows little or nothing. Goes out of his way to associate with officers and the cream. Does a lot of brown-nosing. Does a lot of bull throwing. He is a clean liver. Good habits. Retired 10:00PM.

OCTOBER 18, 1944

CQ blowing whistle over PA system (just recently repaired at the Signal Corps). Briefing at 8:35AM. Clear, sunny AM. Raisin fritters, whole-wheat cereal, apple butter, coffee. Mission standby until 10:35AM. Million standdown. Meal loaf, gravy, shredded cabbage, applesauce, bread, peanut butter, hot tea. Immediate standby on mission. Briefing at 12:45. RR bridge west of Milan. Carry 1000 lb GP's. This is to be a hot target. Take off 1:50PM. Very heavy cumulous. Target area 10/10. Inaccurate flak. Did not drop. Instructed to stay with ship in distress at 4:58PM. Watched 7 chutes open between Cape Corsa and Bastia. Crash and PT boats out. Sea Gull (air sea rescue flying boat) over area. Continued circling area spotting chutists in water. Lt Kruse excellent pilot. Circled area until everyone was picked up. Do not know of ship or its crew. Seen smoke flares. We departed in the dark for our field. Salvoed bombs on

way. Sweating out gas consumption. Landed 6:30PM.
Greeted by CO and Captain Moss. Rumor about that
they were practice chutes. Ate a few sandwiches and
hot dogs. Having a party at club. 321st band is
playing. 1st Sgt Isledykes' father died on Flt 6.
Received telegram and letter today. Mitchell-Aires, led
by Capt (flight surgeon) Smith of 445th, Corsican girls,
about fifteen, were secured. Sandwiches, cake,
doughnuts and orange juice. Bar did not have any
American liquor. Yours truly left about 9:00PM. No
drinking. Boys feeling high. George Parsons, Master
Sgt in charge of communications told me I am to act in
capacity of Chief radio operator. Retired 10:00PM
(very windy).

OCTOBER 19, 1944

Awoke 6:10AM.   Very restless evening and night.
Standby on mission until 9:00AM. Very windy, but
clear. Still have diarrhea. Club and mess hall a mess
from party last night. French toast, oatmeal, coffee.
Briefing at 10:00AM. Same target as yesterday.
Strong cross winds on runway causing standby.
Canned corned beef, fried onions, fresh boiled
potatoes, canned tomatoes, applesauce, bread, butter,
hot cocoa. Meeting in mess hall at 12:45. Ike asked
for voluntary contributions of $2 per man to organize
squadron band. To purchase instruments. Spoke
about athletic committees for basketball and touch
football. 2 sand buckets in front of each tent a fire
precaution. Standdown on mission. Over to group
communications inquiring about air-sea rescue.
Showering outside. Steak, fresh mashed potatoes,
canned corn, fruit salad, peanut butter, water. Wind
has quieted down. Very cold. Getting a cold. Clear
and starry night. Retired 9:30PM.

OCTOBER 20, 1944

Nelson awoke me at 7:40AM. Tent rather cold inside.
Very sunny, cloudless AM. Briefing at 9:00. Same
mission as yesterday. Pancakes, whole wheat cereal,
apple butter, orange juice. Target is Gazette Road
Bridge. Carrying 1000 lb GP. To be a hot mission.
Might encounter fighters. Take off 10:10AM. Flying
lead radio operator. Lt Dossey, pilot. Lt McKinley,
navigator. Lt Comfort, bombardier, Anderson, co-pilot.
Bouman, top turret. Bergestrom tail turret. Throwing
window from ship out of camera hatch as we have not
special chute. Very clear. Flak on bomb run. Tail
gunner hit. Flak hit in bomb bay. Rudder shot up,
wings hit. Radio shot out. Hydraulic system shot out.
Hole in Bergestrom's jacket. Called pilot informing
him of a possible injury and removing his chute etc.
Blood showed as I peeled off his clothes. Hole about
the size of a nickel in his back just below kidney.
Bleeding not very heavy. Ran into more flak. Yours
truly was missed by inches. Applied sulfa - nullified
powder and compress. Removed my clothing to made
a comfortable bed for Bergestrom and keep him warm.
Didn't let him know seriousness of injury. He is a real
scout, no complaining or fear. Injected complete
morphine surety in arm. Broke formation and tailed
for home. Preparing to land at Gisonhacci for 15th
field hospital. Could only lower 1 wheel 45 degrees.
Prepared Bergestrom for crash landing. Bouman
slightly injured. Engineer managed to pump to
hydraulic system and get landing gear down and
locked. Pilot unable to lower flaps. Called on
interphone inquiring as to whether he intended to
lower flaps. Said he couldn't. Yours truly ranked
down flaps mechanically from radio operator's room.
Got full flap. Beautiful landing. Doctors, ambulances

greeted us. The medics took over. Bergestrom walked out. What a brave guy. Ship completely shot up. While waiting two hours for ride, flight surgeon came out and told us the flak lodged between his heart and lung missing both. Condition is good. Doctor complimented me on first-aid measures. 100% hit on target. Douman grounded on 62nd. Took my first shot of liquor since being in combat. Interrogated by Capt Liquart. Had a snack at kitchen. Feeling OK aside from chest cold. Steak, beans, string beans, fruit salad, peanut butter, bread, coffee. Attended "Beautiful But Dumb" at theater with Jerry Kures. Very cold night. Heavy chest cold. Taking aspirin. Retired 10:30PM.

OCTOBER 21, 1944

CQ blowing whistle 6:10AM. Briefing at 7:25. Cold and clear. Fresh fried eggs, whole wheat cereal, grapefruit juice, bread, marmalade, coffee. Standby on mission as weather is closing in. Raining. Lt Tilton stopped over. Gave complete report to intelligence on yesterday's mission. Standdown on today's mission. Canned turkey, string beans, potatoes, fruit salad, bread, apple jelly, coffee. Harold Phares who just arrived on Corsica from the states is in 447. Knew him from gunnery school. Flying as a private, he was busted at Greenville for letting a buddy use his pass. Salmon salad, fresh vegetable salad, string beans, potatoes, bread, apple butter, coffee. Major Knieval gave me jeep to visit Bergestrom at 15th field hospital. Pateet, Reeves, Kraus and I met some other boys at hospital. He is doing OK. Very nervous. Cannot eat and must remain in one position. Returned to squadron 8:15PM. Fair evening. Stove assembled

today. Throwing good heat. Cold about the same.
Retired 9:30PM.

OCTOBER 22, 1944

CQ (Danny Hurley - Dorchester, Mass) blowing whistle
at 6:45. Cloudy AM. Standby on mission for
10:00AM. Fresh fried eggs, bacon, oatmeal, bread,
butter, coffee. Fill out PRO form at S-2. Blackard and
I put up radio antenna. Boys came back from Cairo
and Rome. Meatloaf, gravy, canned peas, fresh
mashed potatoes, fresh tomatoes, fruit salad, bread,
hot tea. Checked out on tail and top turret at line.
Using energizer. Raining. Visited Harold Phares at
447th. Fresh frankfurters, tomato sauce, fresh boiled
potatoes, fresh tomatoes, fruit salad, coffee. Bad cold.
Medics gave me more pills and spoke of possibly
grounding me. Played casino with George. Retired
9:45PM.

OCTOBER 23, 1944

John awoke me at 7:40AM. Very uncomfortable night.
Clear and warm this AM. Mission standby 10:00AM.
Scrambled egg cheese omelet, oatmeal, tomato juice,
coffee. Standdown on mission. Stuffed peppers,
kidney beans, canned corn, bread, peanut butter,
coffee. Cold. Visited boys at 445th. Schall taught me
to play chess. Stayed for supper. Roast beef, canned
corn, tomato sauce, string beans, bread, canned
peaches, coffee. On 1st shift of guard. Lt Wyman of S-
2 called me in for additional information on Saturday's
raid. Raining. Relieved at 10:00PM. Retired
10:30PM.

OCTOBER 24, 1944

Awoke 7:30AM. Feeling OK. Standby on mission until 9:00AM. Cloudy. Pancakes and syrup, whole wheat cereal, orange juice, coffee. Finished filling in foxhole. John and George left for the mountains. Took majority of contents from Sullivan's package from home. (Sullivan went down over Verona on July 26th) to sell in mountains. Also took mattress cover. Standdown on mission. Turnips, fresh vegetable salad, macaroni and tomato sauce, peas, bread, marmalade, fruit salad, coffee. Camile Goethals and I visited Donald Bergestrom at hospital. Doing OK. Hospital moving near Bastia. Going to transfer Don to a general hospital on the mainland. On Rome schedule for rest camp. Beaucoup mail. Roast beef, lima beans, fried onions, gravy, peas, bread, butter, coffee. Fair evening. Issued OD's, overcasts, heavy underwear today. Cold better. John and George brought back walnuts. Ate my first fresh apple since leaving states. Packed. Retired 10:45PM.

OCTOBER 25, 1944

Awoke 8:10AM. Continual downpour. Rome trip canceled today. Missed breakfast. Started stoop. Very damp. Felling OK. Baked beans, peas, string beans, chocolate pudding, hot tea, bread, apple butter. Still raining. Put on weather strips around door. Erected half shelter over door to keep rain out. Finished bookstand for reading in bed. Supply was robbed last night. (4 pairs new shoes and beaucoup OD's were stolen) No clues. Cold much better. Spaghetti and tomato sauce, string beans, fresh boiled potatoes in jackets, apple sauce, bread, marmalade, coffee. Yours truly has quit drinking java as it gives me diarrhea. Borrowed fifty dollars from Nelson for the Rome trip (2000 francs, 1000 lire). Read in bed awhile. Retired 11:00PM.

OCTOBER 26, 1944

Awoke 7:30AM. Raining. Feeling OK. Fried powdered eggs, bacon, wheatena, grapefruit juice, coffee. Rome trip canceled due to weather. Sgt Charles Wemberly, Baird, Moleski and I going to Adjaccia to pick up released GI prisoner at stockade. Left in reconnaissance car at 8:50. Stopped in mountains at officer's rest camp where Charles used to work. Met Madame, owner of hotel. Treated us to a drink of real rum. Ascended to about 10,000 feet. In and above clouds. Mountains snow capped. Roads very rough. Mountain streams swollen from recent rains. Drove part way. Arrived Adjaccio 12:43PM. Stockade moved to Bastia. Ate at MP's transient mess. Purchased deux kilos of apples at cinq francs a kilo ($1.60). Took pictures including Napoleon's monument. Charles stopped at friend's home on return trip. Ben, Jim and I helped some mademoiselles gather fall chestnuts. Ate at a caf, in Ghisonia. Soup, rye bread, steak, french fries. (Cinquante francs - 50) Very enjoyable. Had a shot of cap-corse at Romano Bar. My Italian and French is steadily improving. My opinion of these people has greatly changed since seeing how well some live. The scenery through the mountains is beautiful. The chasms and dangerous precipices made travel hazardous. Returned to camp at 8:30PM. Clear evening. Very tired and sore from such a long jogging trip. Retired 10:00PM.

OCTOBER 27, 1944

CQ blowing whistle at 7:00AM. Cold, clear AM.
Pineapple pancakes, oatmeal, grapefruit juice, coffee.
Standing by on Rome trip. Capt McClean made major.
Lt Dossey made captain. Vienna Sausage, beans,
onions, peas, fruit salad, bread, butter, hot tea.
Standdown on Rome trip. George and I loaded
weapons carrier with roots to be used for firewood in
stove. Attended lecture on propaganda leaflets. Capt
Hargrove was in charge. Raining. Noticing change in
men about area. Rest camp at Rome to be canceled if
VD rate continues to increase in returning men.
Boiled beef, fresh mashed potatoes, gravy, fruit salad,
bread, apple butter, coffee. Danny Kinley (CQ) and I
played checkers and chess. Beat me in both games.
Read in bed. Retired midnight.

OCTOBER 28, 1944

Awoke 6:30AM. Stomach cramps. Cold, clear AM.
French toast, bacon, wheatena, orange juice,
grapefruit juice, apple butter, coffee. Rome trip
canceled. 3 bottles beer, 2 cokes, 4 pkgs gum, 2 large
Hershey's 2 small Hershey's, 1 pkg gum drops, 1 bar
soap, 3 cigars, 2 Clark Bar, 2 Zagnuts, 1 box cheese,
tidbits. Moleski picked up my rations. Nelson used to
pick up tent rations. As time goes on he appears to be
a very stubborn individual. His actions are very
obvious. Some of his activities are subversive. Clear,
warm day. Hash, diced carrots, fresh potatoes,
butterscotch pudding, bread, butter, water. Spoke
with Blackard about his civilian life. Was married at
18. Didn't graduate high school. Looks about 25 and
acts it. Intelligent, good clean looking chap. 445th
and 448th played touch football. Yours truly acted as
lineman for a while. We were defeated 6-0. Met Lt

Cremmion of 446th at theater. 446th lost ship on rest camp trip to Rome yesterday. After being refused a landing, the ship returned to Corsica with its eleven occupants. On way over a cylinder broke loose from the right engine hitting the rudder. Ditched the ship. Two enlisted men went under with ship. There were not enough Mae Wests to go around. One GI was keeping a bombardier afloat with just his own effort. This GI had no life vest. Bombardier was released. He afterwards floated by the life raft face down. Catalan landed, picked up crew but could not take off due to rough water. PT boats picked up crew members from Catalan. Attended "The Unwired". Dealt with the supernatural. Picked up a heavy parka at tech supply. Very clear, cold evening. Lost eight out of the eleven men. Canned salmon, boiled onions, kidney beans, string beans, bread, peanut butter, coffee. Herman DeGeorge, 212 Shrewsbury Ave, Redbank, NJ, recently grounded armory gunner on 64 missions. Small fellow about 5'3", age 25. Quite cocky. Doesn't smoke. Has an Atebrine appearance. Read in bed awhile. Retired 10:00PM.

OCTOBER 29, 1944

Awoke 7:30AM. Very clear and warm AM. Pancakes, oatmeal, grapefruit juice, marmalade. Ike, Ryan, White Benchowsky were soused last night. Roaming about the area around 1:00AM singing. Stopped in our tent to do a bit of serenading. Rome trip canceled again. Boys came down from island bakery to purchase liquor. John left for mountains again. Meatloaf, peas, fresh potatoes, stewed cut apples, bread, butter, hot tea. Fair day. Group having assimilated bombing of bridge. Putting up fifty ships. Watched touch football game between ordnance and group officers. Boiled beef, canned corn, canned peaches, bread, peanut butter, coffee. On first shift of guard. Raining. Blockard and I played cribbage, casino, gin rummy in shack at 805th. Very cold. Nelson did not open club tonight. No heat. Been wondering about Shyrle. Her correspondence is not very consistent. I do miss her. Retired 11:00PM.

OCTOBER 30, 1944

Awoke 7:30AM. Cold, cloudy AM. Fried powdered eggs, bacon, oatmeal, orange-grapefruit juice, coffee. Standdown of Rome trip. Worked on detail changing latrine. Used lime to kill odor. Corn beef hash, navy beans, canned tomatoes, bread, soup. Played chess with Schall at 445th. John Gray cut my hair (20 francs). Ate at 445th. Taylor, Smitty and I attended "You Can't Ration Love". Clear, cold evening. Mail coming in fine. Read Shyrle's letters over and over. Mike Kassis stopped in. Mike worked for the Decca Record Corp in Bridgeport, Conn three years previous to being drafted. He tested master records and made duplicates for sales release. Retired 11:30PM.

OCTOBER 31, 1944

Awoke 7:30AM. Cloudy AM. Pancakes, whole-wheat cereal, apple butter, tomato juice, coffee. Worked on detail constructing new mail tent. Rome trip standdown. Completed my adjustable bed lamp. Two stoves made of fifty-gallon drums installed in club. Canned chicken and spaghetti, canned tomatoes, fresh boiled potatoes, diced carrots and onions, bread, butter, water. George Huka attended high school at the Sewickley High Township about two and one half miles from Hutchinson. He graduated. Worked on the railroad previous to coming in army. Couldn't get a defense job due to being in the first draft. Received 7240 francs in pay line ($144.80). Paid back John $50.0. Spaghetti and tomato sauce, spinach, boiled onions, chocolate pudding, bread, jelly, coffee. Clear, moonlit Halloween evening. A newcomer to our tent is a pup - 16 days old. George is caring for him. Feeds him condensed milk on his finger. Two new crews came in. Feeling OK. Little worried about Shyrle and her anti-Semitic problem at the University. Boys had a 20 franc limit at Molesky's tent. Did not play. Drank most of a quart of cap-corse. Feeling slightly tipsy. Make french fries with coffee and bread. Brusa assisted. Returned to tent at 11:00PM. Retired 11:30PM.

NOVEMBER 1, 1944

Awoke 7:15AM. Fair morning. Interrupted night caused by our pup's spasmodic crying. Today is John Nelson's birthday. Congratulated Bob Lesser for making 2nd Lt from F/O. Rather a difficult advancement overseas. Pancakes, oatmeal, bacon, stewed prunes, jelly, grapefruit juice. Standdown on Rome trip. Received fourteen pkg cigarettes (40 francs) as part of rations. Fried chicken, fresh fried potatoes, peas, bread, butter, chicken rice soup, fruit salad. Dismal day. Played touch football. 448th played 447th. We won 32-0. Played on our field. Picked up negatives from group photo. Boiled beef, mashed potatoes, peas, bread, jelly, coffee. Cloudy evening. Had some hot rum and tea at Mike's tent. Retired 10:00PM. (As a rule I read in bed).

NOVEMBER 2, 1944

Awoke 5:50AM to the tune of GI Joe's helping.   Huka came off guard at 6:15AM. Played with the pup. Fed him, but didn't do any good. Egg pancakes, oatmeal, bread, bacon, marmalade, orange-grapefruit juice. Cloudy AM. Fairly warm. Standdown on Rome trip. This group has not flown a mission in two weeks due to bad weather over target area. Boys that went to Rome rest camp have been there for two weeks, due to weather. Only supposed to stay 3 days. Baked beans, fresh boiled potatoes, diced carrots, fruit salad, hot tea, bread, butter. Doughnuts were served by a Red Cross maiden. Had a meeting in mess hall. Captain Farwell, one of our lead pilots, is our new CO. Spoke to Captain Hargrove, liaison officer of infantry. Sized up the war with huge maps. Clear, warm day. Played touch football. Working out some of the stiffness from yesterday. Hash, lima beans, spinach, vanilla pudding, bread, peanut butter, coffee. As a rule the spinach is sour. The hash just doesn't seem to click with me. Attended a special training film at group theater dealing with enemy interrogation of our forces. Moonlit, cloudy evening. Very stiff from playing football. Raining. Retired 10:00PM.

NOVEMBER 3, 1944

Awoke 7:30AM. Raining. Whole-wheat cereal, pancakes, bacon, marmalade, coffee, tomato juice. Very windy. 35MPH. Cross wind on runway. Standdown on all flying. On detail to mountains to get stove for fireplace in club. Boiled chicken, gravy, string beans, mashed potatoes, bread, butter, fruit salad, coffee. Frenchman killed American Negro guard at QM depot last night. Two white GI's stabbed by Negroes in Bastia. Unless the guilty parties are brought to justice soon, there <u>may</u> be trouble on the island between the whites and Negroes. Ate a pork chop sandwich at 4:30PM. Captain Burke gave me jeep to visit Bergestrom who has been moved to 40th field hospital several miles north of the 340th. Bill Bishop, Charles Krauss and yours truly went. Charles Wemberly went along as far as hospital as he is going to Bastia. Bergestrom is in good condition. They intend to leave flak in. Is about the size of two 45 caliber bullets. Cement floors, tents and rest of hospital set up is bad. Visited Lozowski and Usher, had coffee and doughnuts at Red Cross. Returned base 9:25PM. Clear, windy eve. Bruno newly hired Ike who is building fireplace in club and is sleeping our tent. Retired 10:30PM.

NOVEMBER 4, 1944

Awoke 7:40AM. Clear, sunny morning. French toast, oatmeal, tomato juice, coffee. Standdown on Rome trip. Briefing for mission at 10:35AM. Put in cellophane front window for reading during the day. Creamed macaroni, fresh tomatoes, string beans, bread, butter, water. Went with Mike to 124th QM. Bakery. Showered outside. Roast beef, fresh mashed potatoes, peas, gravy, chocolate pudding, bread, coffee. Conversed with Bruno Antonio Perri, Calibro, Italy our Italian mason. Fair evening. Retired 10:00PM

NOVEMBER 5, 1944

Sun shining in cellophane window awoke me at 6:30AM. Played with "Snafu". Pancakes, stewed prunes, bacon, marmalade. Rome trip canceled. Took off to bring back those stranded in Rome. Two missions today. 100% on yesterday's Urelli RR bridge.

Milk run. Spaghetti and sauce, lima beans, spinach, fresh vegetables, salad, bread, butter, water. Went over to Red Cross and special service HQ for 321st GP. Helped crack stone for fireplace with sledgehammer. Vienna sausage, tarter sauce, fresh boiled potatoes, string beans, fresh tomatoes, fruit salad, coffee, bread. Drank Marsala at Morefields tent. He brought it back from Rome. Partly cloudy sky. Conversed with Bruno in Italian. Retired 9:30PM.

NOVEMBER 6, 1944

Awoke 6:30AM. Read in bed while. Raisin pancakes, oatmeal, coffee, grapefruit juice. Very clear and warm. Tried to be taken off of Rome rest camp trip. No dice. Commencing to housebreak "Snafu". Visited at 340th and Cecil Usher said Rudy's wife knows about his fate. God, how I feel for her. The baby was born the same week the telegram from the State Dept arrived. Every time I think of him, I fill up inside. Mail is coming through constantly. Meat loaf, gravy, mashed potatoes, fresh vegetables, salad, bread, butter, hot tea. Went up in mountains for more rocks for fireplace. Ate early chow as I am on first shift of guard. Roast beef, mashed potatoes, peas, fried onions and peppers, coffee. Clear evening. Snafu fed meat for first time. Sick at first. Bass and I pulled first taxi strip guard. He spoke about Hawthorne's dislike for the Jews. Knowing Bernard Bass as I do, I believe he agitates, very argumentative. Very starry evening. Flying lead operator on tomorrow's mission. Retired 10:30PM.

NOVEMBER 7, 1944

Awoke 6:45AM. Very restless night. Excited about mission. Slightly cloudy AM. French toast, oatmeal, tomato juice, coffee. Briefing for mission at 8:30AM. Pilot Capt Dossey, navigator Lt McKinley, Capt Joyce, bombardier. Only lead ship of formation has such, as the rest follow the lead and drop off him. Wearing complete heavy equipment. Take off 9:30AM. Target is RR bridge 25 miles NW of Venice. Cloudy and hazy. Path of IP covered. Changed axis of attack twice. Hit target 100%. Milk run. Made perfect contact with ground station (nicegirl #2). Landed 1:30PM. We are fed upon returning. Beans, hash, string beans, bread, marmalade, water. They don't prepare anything special for us --just leftovers. Anxiously awaiting presidential election returns. Dull, cloudy PM. Watched ordnance and 448th touch football game. 448th won 19-27. Very rough game. Fried spam, spinach beans, vanilla pudding, coffee. Windy evening. Drank a couple of glasses of Marsala at club. Not on tomorrow's mission. Retired 9:30PM.

NOVEMBER 8, 1944

Awoke 7:30AM. Extremely windy. Slept little throughout the night. Terrific winds from Tyrolean Sea. Threatened to blow tents during the night. Pancakes, grapefruit juice, marmalade, coffee. Roof on mess hall torn up. Gathered detail and commenced repair. Mission briefed and at ships, awaiting wind to die down as cross wind is too strong. Roasted chicken, gravy, mashed potatoes, fresh onions, beets, fruit salad, hot tea. Finished roof repair. Boiled beef, mashed potatoes, string beans, cauliflower, bread, marmalade, coffee. Wind died down. Retired 10:30PM.

NOVEMBER 9, 1944

Awoke 7:15AM. Snafu wanted to go outside. Very windy. Pancakes, oatmeal, orange-grapefruit juice, coffee. Mission took off. Corn beef hash, boiled onions, bread, butter, coffee. Mission had to land at 310th due to 50MPH crosswinds on our runway. No bombing. Taylor and Smitty over for supper. Roast beef, mashed potatoes, string beans, boiled onions and potatoes, bread, peanut butter, coffee. Attended "Gildersleeve's Ghost". Good laugh. George and I made security preparations on tent. Wind severe. Ordered to put out all stoves. Received "The Prophet" from Shyrle and a swell package from #19. Retired 11:55PM.

NOVEMBER 10, 1944

Awoke 7:30AM. Very cold but clear. Stewed prunes, fresh 1/2 grapefruit, fresh fried eggs, bread, coffee. Standby on mission 9:00AM. Latrines blew over during night. Briefing at 10:00AM. Some ship at 310th damaged from wind at our field. Target RR bridge at Ostegalia. Defended. Lt Kruse pilot. Carrying 500 lb. Take off. 11:50AM. Very cold. Fair weather. Over target at 2:00PM. Intense accurate flak. Lead ship with Capt Dossey went down. Yours truly, Peeler (bombardier) Penida (engineer) hit. Left engine shot out. Came back on single engine. Hydraulic system out. Radio out. Made crash landing at 310th. Beautiful. Everyone OK. Ship a complete wreck. Dossey and boys bailed out over Po valley. Crashed at 3:25PM. Ambulance took us back to 321st. Wounds dressed. Two other ships crash-landed. Despite the shock, everybody is OK. I received a flak face laceration. Vienna sausage, sauerkraut, tomato soup, bread, upon arriving at squadron 4:30PM. Everyone inquisitive about mission. God it's good to be back. Retired 10:30PM.

NOVEMBER 11, 1944

Awoke 6:00AM. Very cold. Very restless night due to crash landing. Clear. Grounded for a couple of days. Fresh fried eggs, whole-wheat cereal, grapefruit juice, coffee, bread. Maickewicz borrowed jeep from Mr. Snyder, Red Cross field director. Lt Churchill, Lt Zaukauptan, Pineda and yours truly went to 340th field hospital to visit James Herod. Herod was hit by flak in three places in right arm. Double compound fracture. His flying days are finished. Returned squadron 12:30PM. 9 purple hearts were issued on yesterday's raid. 100% hit. Group lost 5 ships. Met Genl Knapp yesterday. Brought liaison receiver back from our ship yesterday. Boiled chicken, gravy, string beans, lima beans, leaf lettuce, canned peaches, bread, butter. Teaching Jerry Kures to box. Walters and Griffin busted to privates for overstaying Rome rest camp. Feeling punk. Corn beef paddies, roasted sweet potatoes, peas, fruit salad, bread, coffee. Made a bookshelf. Very clear and cold evening. Retired 10:00PM. (Armistice Day)

NOVEMBER 12, 1944

Awoke 7:45AM. Very cold and clear. Pancakes, oatmeal, coffee, tomato juice. John leaving for mountains again. Probably Bruno going with them to his home at Pietra Poala 15 kilometers past 57th wing. Standdown on today's mission. Rations $2.90, 10 bottles beer, 2 cokes, 3 packages gum, 1 bar soap, 5 Hershey's, 3 cigars, 8 bars candy, 15 packages cigarettes. Hamburgers, tomato sauce, string beans, mashed potatoes, fruit salad, bread, tea. Picked up sleeping bag at Tech supply. Gave it to Mike as I have one. Raining. John and fireplace workers went to Papas for dinner. Roast beef, string beans, mashed potatoes, fruit salad, bread, coffee. Visited Taylor, Smitty and Fisher. On Rome rest camp trip tomorrow. Retired 10:30PM.

NOVEMBER 13, 1944

Take off 10:15AM. Landed 11:30AM. Littorio Airfield, Rome, Italy. Weapons carrier took us (Ben Moleski, Stewart Rockwell, Joseph Abecienias) to officer's Red Cross (center of town). Finally ended up at California Pensione by carriage. The padrone di la casa took us down via Aurora across Via Lombardia to another pensione. We have two rooms on second floor. One has three single beds, the other one bed. No telephones, running water or bath. The toilet is down the hall. Our room faces the center patio of the apartment building. From here we went to a cafe, on Via Lombardia which is down one flight to the basement. From here Otello, a waiter, showed us a popular nightspot. Cafes and restaurants open at 5:00PM and close at 7:00PM. This is an allied restriction. This bar is known as "Maria's", which is also similar to a wine cellar. Here beaucoup females come to be picked up by soldiers for shack jobs. Of the crowd my Italian is about the best. I fixed "Ebbe" up with some whore for the night for $15. $10 for her and $5 for a room. Police raid hotels, apt houses, etc. as no women are allowed on first floor. Returned to our casa at 8:30PM. Talked with Secilia awhile. She

understands no English. (Housekeeper 72 years).
Rome has some beautiful females. Retired 9:00PM.

NOVEMBER 14, 1944

Awoke 8:00AM. Raining. Had coffee and buns at Red
Cross (5 cents) snack bar. Inquired about Capt Felix
Aulisi at Red Cross field director's office but he is on
duty in Naples. Shave and haircut at Red Cross
barber shop. Met a paratrooper from Penn. Showed us
around Rome a bit. Ate at Army rest camp restaurant
(10 cents). Purchased gifts and Christmas cards.
Attended cinema "Dittatare," (The Great Dictator) (40
cents). American speech, Italian writing on screen.
Got lost in city after dark - as Rome is in blackout.
Took "hock" (horse and buggy) back to Marios. Met
Abbey's shack date from last evening. Maestro Gori is
where all the shacking couples go after leaving Marios.
They are just several blocks apart. Abby's shacking
again with Anna. Othello fixed us (Ben, Rocky and I)
up with una bottela vino and loaf of bread to bring
back to our room. We always bring some food back for
Secelia as she has little and food is scarce. She is
beginning to care for us like a mother. We have one
desk lamp. Floors are of marble-like stone.

NOVEMBER 15, 1944

Awoke 7:15AM. Comfortable night. No breakfast.
Abby didn't arrive for Red Cross tour this AM. Red
Cross tour at 9:00AM by bus with guide. No charge.
Slight rain. First stop was the Pantheon where the
bodies of kings and queens still are at rest in marble
tombs. Next was the Coliseum where vendors and
peddlers were present. Visited St Peters Cathedral
and Vatican City. We had an audience with Pope Pius

XII at 12:50PM. Swiss guards, ushers, pope bearers etc, were about. Much to the displeasure of its occupants, Rocky and I took a Limey bus back to the center of town as our bus left. Ben stayed on at Vatican City. Abby, Rocky and I ate at EM restaurant. Rocky and I attended opera "Othello" at Royal Opera house. I treated as I tried to interest him in good music. ($2.00 seats). Opera glasses. Met boys at "Gares." 10:00AM. Secilia and we boys drank wine in our room. Everyone happy. Ebbey shocking. Retired 11:00PM.

NOVEMBER 16, 1944

Awoke 7:10AM. Preparing to leave for Corsica. Littoria closed. Open only to C47's. Ate at Red Cross snack bar. Had another breakfast at a civilian restaurant. Paid $1.50 per person for two fried eggs and a few fried potatoes. All places other than those authorized eateries are off limits. Attended morning stage show featuring Jan Grey, an American songstress. Special tour (25 cents) of Forum, Mussolini's private quarters (Palace of Venice), St Paul's Cathedral and the English cemetery. Took pictures. Visited Shelly's grave. Ate at GI restaurant. The GI restaurants, which were formerly Italian, have been taken over by Uncle Sam to provide a clean eating spot for troops. Italian waiters do the serving. Aluminum utensils are used. Music is provided by Italian violinist and accordion player. Musicians and waiters depend on tips. Hours of service are from 10:30 - 1:00PM and 4:30 - 7PM. Could not attend Il Traviata as all seats have been sold. Attended Rebecca at Red Cross theater. No charge. Finest theater in Rome. Stopped at Marios for a few minutes. Ben and Abbey a bit high. Abbey shacking again tonight with a different woman, another Anna. Through conversations this whore told me a GI who slept with her last night made off with her $90.00. In the same pensione are Italian babes. When we return to our rooms, they always are a couple of floors above. Secilia told me that the girls are full of VD. They always want food. They lowered a basket and we returned it with an empty wine bottle. The girls sent it crashing to the earth. Retired 10:30PM.

NOVEMBER 17, 1944

Awoke 7:00AM. Littorio closed. Ate at Red Cross snack bar. Met Ben Molesky's friend Red from his home town, Gary, Indiana. Speaks good Italian. Met a GI at GI restaurant named Joe Choate. We purchased tickets for this evening's opera "Madame Butterfly. ($2.00) Joe is with 702nd engineers at Foggia, Italy. Attended stage show "Funa Fulla", Italian stage show (70 cents). Bar in lobby. Women are scarce - poor make up. Ate at GI caf. Very pleased with opera (Box D#22)) Changed seats as we were sitting at 90 degrees in relation to stage. Returned 9:00PM. Kibitzed awhile. Retired 10:00PM.

NOVEMBER 18, 1944

Awoke 7:30AM. Clear, sunny AM. Littorio closed. Met Clarence Butterfield on street. He is permanent at AAF rest camp. Inasmuch as we have been here a week, we are entitled to rations. Picked up some at downtown exchange. Truck to rest camp. Chow with Butterfield. The rest camp is like college dormitories used formerly to school Fascists. The 5th Army rest center was formerly a Fascist arena. At Tiber Terrace, a former wealthy sportsman's club just across the

Tiber river from the rest camp is where entertainment is provided. Ate supper at rest camp. Ben and Abbey left for Marios. Rocky and I wrote cards and listened to recordings in the music room. Saw "Sweet and Low Down". Returned 8:45PM. Cold evening. Ben kids the females every night in the next apt up. Retired 10:30PM.

NOVEMBER 19, 1944

Awoke 7:45AM. Littorio closed. Clear day. Met Roy and his other 5th Army buddies at Red Cross snack bar. Roy Laube, 425 McKinley St, Gary, Indiana. Ate dinner at RAAC. Met Jim a soldier from Johannesburg, South Africa at Jewish Soldier's Club. Jim speaks with a heavy British accent. He is 6'4" tall, lanky with a small mustache. The Jewish Club far exceeds the Red Cross. They serve all kinds of pastry. Two cents for sandwiches, four cents for pastry. Met many soldiers from Palestine. We all attended stage show "Fan Fulla". The primadonna threw Ben her rose. Jim met a babe on the street, brought her in a caf, for a couple of drinks and in less than one hour returned having been in bed with her. Paid her $2.00 for the room and gave her a $5.00 bill. Went to Marios again. On the way we met two decent girls. Took them with us, talked and danced. Invited them to our room. Spoke to Secilia first as she is particular about the reputation of her apartment. Brought sandwiches from RAAC - 10 cents apiece. Had a little party. Conversed about Fascistic days. The girls worked as librarians. Ages ran about 23 years. Today they attend school, learning English so they can work with the Americans for better positions. These were the first girls we met that didn't ask for cigarettes, candy, clothes, etc. Roy sleeping in Abbey's room as Abbey is shacking again. Girls parted at 9:00PM. Roy and Ben took them home. Ben, despite being married, goes wild about most any skirt. Clear cold night. Had Jewish incident arise on street. Been smoking a lot lately. Only drinking wine. Moderately. Mamma washes our clothes free. Aside from slight cold, yours truly feels ok. Retired 11:00PM.

NOVEMBER 20, 1944

 Addresses: Franca Serra, Via Muazio Plemente 64, Rome, Italy
             Maritza Jonadec, Via Fasalegna 49, Rome, Italy
             Jewish Soldier's Club, Piazza Polis, Rome, Italy
             RAAC Restaurant, Castaldi via del Buffalo, Rome, Italy

Awoke 8:25AM. Fair day, slightly cloudy. Lottorio still closed. Ate breakfast at Jewish Soldier's Club at 10:30AM. They always serve tea. At 11:00AM ate dinner at RAAC. Walked about main drag shopping. Visited "Stars and Stripes" building. Through the cooperation of Mr. DeEnglis, I found a printer to make tickets for the club. 2,000 for $15.00. He originally wanted $20. Boys never seem to get enough of girls. Returned to Pensione at 4:00PM. The boys visited the females on the top floor. Anna, the babe that Abbey's shacked up with last evening came to our apartment. Secilia told us that she claims she is now engaged to him. In fact she showed Secilia the ring. Yours truly happens to know that a hope in Corsica gave her that ring. At any rate I informed Secilia to forbid her entrance to our apartment. Franca and Maritza returned to our place this PM. Had manicure, shave and shine. Attended "Bride by Mistake" at Red Cross theater. Returned to Gori's after show for some spaghetti. Abbey shacking with same Anna. Our two so-called legitimate girl friends have decided to shack with Ben and Roy. Tony, Roy's friend also from the 5th army is using Abbey's room tonight. Retired 10:30PM.

NOVEMBER 21, 1944

Awoke 8:25A. Littorio closed. Captain Holloway (PRO 446th) securing transportation to take us to Targunia fighter field about 90 miles north of Rome. Waited until 2:00PM. No trucks. Spoke with war correspondent. Rocky and I went to Tiber Terrace for hot shower and chow. In the evening we attended "What's Thou Cooking" at the Argentina theater near Piazzi Venice. Cast was composed of former professionals now GI's and USO girls. Excellent. Swell theater. Free for allied troops. Returned home 9:30PM. After dark, we carry flashlights as Rome is blacked out. Secilia is cleaning and pressing my pants. Warm evening. Abbey still shacking. Money getting low. Let Abbey take $33.00 Got quite a kick out of saying goodbye to Secilia three times. Note: Rome itself is bubbling with activity. However there seems to be nothing along the productivity nature. Allied soldiers from every nation are about. Uniforms vary, but they are all neat. The Italian civilians are out to suck as much money as possible. They have no particular like for us - aside from what we can give them. The AMGOT is running a black market. In fact the fascists are still powerful. The communists are of much strength. In fact it's the only organized "ism" in Italy. Rome is a clean city with many modern conveniences. I was amazed to see so many blonde and fair skinned Italians.

NOVEMBER 22, 1944

Awoke 7:50AM. Clear morning. Packed and kissed Secilia goodbye. Capt Halloway and gang took off at 9:00AM for Targunia airfield by 1041st QM. 2 1/2 ton truck. Very rough road. Arrived airfield. 64th fighter group at 23:30PM. Ship #529. Lt Holocombe pilot took us back. Travels 92 miles by truck. Littoria closed to all bombers. Took off 2:15PM. Landed Corsica 2:50PM. Good to be back. Cooks preparing for big Thanksgiving dinner tomorrow. (Turkey). Yours truly received the DFC, Purple Heart, Air Medal and two clusters. Anxious to write home and to Shyrle. Snafu really sprouted up after not seeing him in ten days. Our group (446-445) pulled two missions over Yugoslavia. Blackard left this AM. I missed him. 8 bottles of beer missing from my frag box? John satisfied with club tickets. Walter Ruguski going home. Had mental collapse. Spaghetti and sauce, boiled cauliflower, beets, bread, marmalade, coffee. Did a bit of visiting. James Herod is finished with combat. Retired 10:00PM.

NOVEMBER 23, 1944

Awoke 7:10AM. Snafu wants to get out. Clear, partly cloudy Thanksgiving morning. Fresh boiled eggs, oatmeal, bacon, coffee, bread, apple jelly. Mission briefing at 10:30AM. Yours truly is in lead element. Briefing changed to 11:20. Standdown on mission. Only serving spam sandwiches this noon as big turkey dinner is at 3:00PM. Dull day. Roast turkey, gravy, peas, mashed potatoes, stuffing, cranberry sauce, canned pineapple, cheese, raisin pastry, coffee. On first shift of guard. Area guard. Boys really celebrating at club. Ike was taken to his tent Jackson (cook) went wild. Finally passed out. Quite a hilarious Thanksgiving night. Retired 10:00PM.

NOVEMBER 24, 1944

Awoke 7:10AM. Fair AM. Pancakes, oatmeal, 1/2 grapefruit, meat, marmalade, coffee. Boys have big heads this AM. On today's mission. Briefing 10:50AM. Been thinking a lot about home lately. Standdown at briefing. Meat loaf, string beans, fresh sweet potatoes, fruit salad, bread, butter, coffee. Cleaned guns on B37 - some joke. Picked up new flying fatigues at Tech supply. Attended airplane recognition class at group briefing hut. Roast beef, potatoes, tomatoes, and bread, chocolate pudding, coffee. Attended "Louisiana Hayride", left in middle of show, sad. Retired 8:40PM. Feeling very nervous.

NOVEMBER 25, 1944

Awoke 7:30AM. Fair AM. Fried eggs, sausage, hot cereal, coffee, bread, jelly. On Plan B mission. Briefing 10:00AM. Plan A Standdown, Plan B standdown. Rations this AM $2.20 - 6 beers, 2 cokes, 3 cigars, 4 Hershey's 1 box gumdrops, 14 pkgs cigarettes, 1 pkg gum. Hash, fresh fried potatoes, string beans, canned tomatoes, canned sliced peaches, bread, coffee. Attended aircraft recognition class. Markewicz and I hitched to the 310th. Visited Clarence Pratt from gunnery school. Our squadron is far superior. Returned 4:30PM. Taylor and Smitty came over. Smitty made Staff. Taylor, buck. Smitty grounded for bad ears. Roast beef, gravy, string beans, fresh boiled potatoes, pickled tomatoes, vanilla pudding, coffee, bread and jelly. Markewicz and I visited 1985 engineer fire fighters. Fellow doing the pictures of our crash landing. Wrote letters at club. Met Pat who visited Bergestrom in Naples. Flak has been removed and he is doing nicely. Retired 9:00PM.

NOVEMBER 26, 1944

Awoke 7:00AM. Read awhile. Fair AM. Fresh fried eggs, sausage, bread, jelly, coffee. On plan B mission. Carrying incendiaries. A & B standdown. Stew, fresh boiled potatoes, carrots and peas, chocolate cake, bread, butter, cocoa. Attended airplane recognition class. At "War Room" attached to S-2, met Lt McKinley and Zaucaupt who bailed out over Astiglia near our lines. Dossey is in Florence. The other four are unaccounted for. Probably prisoners of war. Been raining all afternoon. Corn beef hash, tomato sauce, coffee, bread, fruit salad, butter, fresh boiled potatoes. Attended meeting at 6:30 at club. Lt Wyman spoke on GI Bill of Rights. Retired 9:15PM.

NOVEMBER 27, 1944

Awoke 7:50AM. Drizzle. Pancakes, hot cereal, bacon, tomato juice, jelly coffee. On Plan B mission. Standdown on Plan A & B. Raining. Spaghetti and meatballs, peas, string beans, bread, butter, sliced pineapple, tea. Markewicz obtained Red Cross jeep from Mr. Snyder. Drove to 310th. Rained all the way. Gas can in stove exploded in my face. Momentary blindness and singed eyebrows and lashes. Dispensary treatment. Excused from aircraft recognition. Stew, string beans, chocolate pudding, bread, butter, coffee. Wrote letters at club. Snafu is really growing. Retired 9:15PM.

NOVEMBER 28, 1944

Awoke 6:55AM. Read in bed until 7:40AM. Drizzle. Dreary AM. Pancakes, oatmeal, jelly, coffee. On B. Standdown on A & B. Raining. Fried chicken, mashed potatoes, peas, bread, butter, coffee. Attended aircraft recognition class. Raining. Roast beef, gravy, fresh boiled potatoes, peas, vanilla pudding, bread, jelly, coffee. Finished "The Brothers Ashkenazi" by IJ Singer. Wrote at club. Two Tom Collins. Retired 9:00PM.

NOVEMBER 29, 1944

Awoke 7:15AM. Very chilly and clear AM. French toast, jelly, oatmeal, coffee. Standdown on mission. Area very muddy. On detail to mix cement in officer's area. Goofed off. Canned pork, lima beans, string beans, fruit salad, bread, butter. Attended aircraft recognition class. Attended GI stage show at group theater. All colored cast. OK. Replacement came in (18) Lewis Martin (8th Airforce England and Edward Vanderberg. Pork chops, beans, string beans, bread, jelly, coffee. On first relief of guard. Area guard #2. 447th came over. Spent most of guard duty in club. One Tom Collins. Clear, Cold night.

NOVEMBER 30, 1944

Snafu awoke me at 7:0AM. Clear, cold AM. Pancakes, bacon, apple butter, coffee. Going to QM with Mike to weight in. May go to Rome to box Escobar and I fought three, two-minute rounds. Did a bit of roadwork. Showered and rubbed down. Mission had a milk run. Hit target. Clear, warm day. Wrote letters

at club. Retired 9:15PM. Lights not working. (payday
- 5800 francs)

DECEMBER 1, 1944

Awoke 7:00AM. Didn't fall asleep until almost
1:00AM. Excited about Rome boxing bouts. Fair
morning. Scrambled eggs, oatmeal, stewed prunes,
grapefruit juice, coffee. GI Joe LaBella, Hojanache,
Escobar and yours truly went by jeep to the 57th to
use ring. I fought two rounds with Escobar, two with
Hojanache, one with LaBella. Wind fair, endurance
fair. Took sulfa bath (10 francs). Huge stove tubs
with hot and cold running sulfa water. Complete rub
down. Meatloaf, peas, tomato soup, fruit salad, coffee.
Went down to "Prune Faces" with Abbey to have my
OD's cleaned. Had a couple of 3 ounce glasses of Cap-
Corse. Whenever I exercise that old stiffness about the
left side of my chest arises. Slight headache.
Standdown on A. Roast beef, gravy, string beans,
diced beets, bread, jelly, beans, coffee. Williams who
went down with Capt Dossey over Po Valley returned
today. Sent $160 to Merriam. Clear evening. On
"Weather Ship" tomorrow. Retired 11:00PM.

DECEMBER 2, 1944

Sgt of guard awoke me at 4:30AM. Breakfast in
kitchen. Coffee and fried eggs, bread. Taking pack
lunch. Take off 6:25AM. Purely a radio operator's
mission. Flew to Venice staying over Adriatic. Fair
contacts. No side tone. No RF on trailing wire. All
CW operation. Weather OK. Landed 10:15AM. Stew,
peas, bread, butter, canned tomatoes, fruit salad,
coffee. James Royce (radio) and I installed new
transmitter in #481. Clear, warm day. Mission

successful, milk run. Creamed spaghetti, Vienna sausage, coffee. Clear evening. Retired 8:30AM.

DECEMBER 3, 1944

Awoke 6:30AM. CQ blowing whistle. Still dark. Cold on mission. Carrying 500 lb incendiaries. Briefing 8:50AM. Lt Tetlow,, pilot. Flying four ships , evasive action. Headquarters and barracks at Bologna. Defended target. Take off 10:15AM. Target 10/10 coverage. Did not drop. Milk run. Landed 12:50. Very nervous on mission. Carried "chaff". Really beginning to sweat them out. Ed Vanderberg pulled his first mission today. Creamed chicken, peas, boiled cabbage, mashed potatoes, cherry pie, coffee, bread, butter. Applied for driving license. Expect to leave for Rome tomorrow. Clear, warm day. Stew, string beans, peas, bread, butter, coffee. Attended "Information and Education" meeting at club. Cpt Opitz, chairman, S/Sgt Waldo, speaker. General discussion on deciding on topic for next week. On incendiary mission tomorrow. Retired 10:30PM.

DECEMBER 4, 1944

Awoke 7:30AM. Clear day. Fresh fried eggs, sausage, oatmeal, bread, hard-tack, 1/2 grapefruit, coffee. Fought three rounds with Hojanache. Ran 1 mile. Fair shape. Early chow 11:00AM. Creamed macaroni, string beans, soup, bread, potatoes, coffee, cauliflower, butter. Take off 1:10PM. Same target as yesterday. Lt Ivory, pilot. Target closed in. A bit air sick. Did not drop. 25th mission. Landed 3:50PM. No developments on Rome trip. Nice day. Roast beef, mashed potatoes, peas, gravy, vanilla pudding, coffee. Fair evening. Retired 9:00PM.

DECEMBER 5, 1944

Awoke 7:30AM. Cloudy, warm AM. On incendiary mission. Briefing at 12:00PM. Hard boiled eggs, oatmeal, bacon, hard tack. Sending out laundry with "Toddie" to mountains. Standdown on all three missions. Goofed off detail. Wondering about Shyrle and the folks at home. God, how I'd like to be home. Hash, fresh sweet potatoes, string beans, cake, bread, butter, tea. Clear, windy day. Van, Lewis, George and I gathered wood for tent in weapons carrier. Roast beef, fresh boiled potatoes, peas and carrots, sliced peaches, bread, butter, coffee. Received a package from #19 dated Sept. 8th. Attended "Barbary Coast Gent." Beaucoup laughs. Very clear, but windy evening. On tomorrow's mission. Retired 10:15PM.

DECEMBER 6, 1944

Awoke 7:30AM. Drizzling. Oatmeal, pancakes and apple butter, 1/2 grapefruit, coffee. Briefing at 12:00PM. Standdown on all missions. Attended aircraft rec. class. Dull, cloudy AM. Hash paddies, string beans, mashed potatoes (fresh), tomato soup, sliced pineapple, bread, butter. Briefed new radio operator. About 5 new crews came in this past week. Pork chops, lima beans, peas, fruit salad, bread, apple jelly, coffee. Since the truck generator has been removed, our lighting system hasn't been too good. Cloudy evening. Christmas parcels beginning to come through. At 7:00PM I was unexpectedly called for guard. 1st shift. Halloway sick. More parcels came in. Picked up telegraph set from Bruce to practice code. Retired 11:00PM.

DECEMBER 7, 1944

Awoke 7:00AM. Partly cloudy sky. Feeling great. Fried eggs, oatmeal, bacon, 1/2 grapefruit, coffee, bread, marmalade. On incendiary mission. Briefing 11:45AM. Boxing trip to Rome canceled. All missions standdown. Prepared parcel to send home. Gifts for all. Baked beans, string beans, fruit salad, bread, butter, coffee. Very warm PM. Attended Aircraft Recog. Commenced building punching bag rack. Had supper with Taylor and Smitty at 445th. Doctor (Captain) Smith, flight surgeon of 445th spoke on first aid. Attended "The Merry Monahans." Waldo asked me to speak at I and E program this Sunday evening. Clear evening. Huka and Vanderberg always like the tent extremely hot. Retired 10:30PM.

DECEMBER 8, 1944

Awoke 7:35AM. Very windy, slight rain. Pancakes, oatmeal, marmalade, grapefruit, coffee. The chow line is longer at 8:00AM than it is at 7:30AM. Everyone waits until the last minute. Briefing at 11:45AM. Doubt this mission will take off. Standdown. Hash paddies, string beans, mashed potatoes, tomato sauce, fruit salad, bread, butter, coffee. Attended aircraft recog class. Finished backboard for punching bag. Getting colder. Left over pork chops, sweet potatoes (fresh) string beans, vanilla pudding, coffee. Visited Lt Wyman. Visited new combat men. Chilly night. Retired 10:30PM.

DECEMBER 9, 1944

Awoke 7:30AM. George pulled last shift of guard and had fire started when I awoke. Clear, cold AM.

Mountains are heavily covered with snow. Pancakes, whole wheat cereal. Marmalade, orange-grapefruit juice. Briefing for mission 11:35. Same as yesterday. Edward Vanderberg, 8233-255th Street, Long Island, NY (Floral Park), a new combat man who I knew in the states is OK. Likes to kid about, but does his share of work. Standdown on mission, but nickeling. Corn beef hash, tomato sauce, string beans, potatoes, apple pie, coffee. Received rations this PM. - cost $2.80. 14 pkgs cigarettes, 6 bottles beer, 2 cokes, 1 can juice, 3 Hershey's, 3 pkg Necco wafers, 1 can peanuts, 3 cigars, 3 chicken dinners, 1 bar soap. Fair day, chilly. Taylor cut my hair at 445th. Took over John Gray's job as barber. 20 francs. Disposed of light carton of cigarettes at - per carton. Nickeling mission flew at 19,000 feet. No credit. Peas, beans, Vienna sausage, tartar sauce, diced beets, bread, apple jelly, coffee. Energizer out of commission. No lights, burning candles. Met Ben Molesky's brother, Joe. Joe Moleski is with the UNRRA. Retired 10:20PM.

DECEMBER 10, 1944

CQ blowing whistle at 6:30AM for first mission. Up at 7:30AM. Briefing 8:25AM. French toast, wheatena, syrup, coffee. Very cold, clear AM. On incendiary mission. Take off 9:50. Very cold. Over target 11:30. Dive-bombed gun emplacements. Could see 500 lb GI mission catching hell. Our target was at Bologna. Yours truly threw out chaff. Milk run. Landed 12:50. Hit target. Boiled chicken, string beans, gravy, bread, sliced pineapple, coffee. Van and I are saving combat liquor together. Punching bag. Roast beef, gravy, peas, fruit salad, bread, butter, coffee. Yours truly was main speaker at I and E program this evening. Spoke on GI bill of rights. Joe Moleski, Ben's brother, spoke about the UNRRA. Meeting a success, well accepted. Clear evening. Retired 10:15PM.

DECEMBER 11, 1944

Awoke 7:55AM. Very cold. Powdered eggs, whole-wheat cereal, bacon, coffee. Standdown of mission. Attended aircraft recog. Class. Cloudy AM. Received a swell package from home. Canned pork, string beans, fresh boiled potatoes, fruit salad, soup, bread, butter. Completed shelf for radio and books. Yesterday's pictures I took came out fine. Feeling OK. Spoke with Lt Bechtle. Jim Herod's arm is going to be OK. Articles of War read by Lt Mose at OM club. Retired 9:20PM.

DECEMBER 12, 1944

Awoke 6:45AM. Raining, cloudy, but warm. Pancakes, oatmeal, bacon, applebutter. Standdown on mission. Went on detail to Shisonaccia to pick up logs for orderly room stove. Macaroni, string beans, beets, canned apricots, bread, butter, tea. Stood 321st group formation and presentation at 448th football field. General Knapp presented me with the DFC, Purple Heart and Air Metal. Quite a thrill. Fair PM. Roast beef, potatoes, peas, gravy, bread, butter, coffee, fruit salad. Pulled 1st shift of guard. Clear, starry night. Kibitzed with Negro runway guards. Retired 11:00PM.

DECEMBER 13, 1944

Awoke 7:20. Clear AM. Briefing 8:15AM. Fried eggs, bacon, whole-wheat cereal, bread, apple butter, coffee., orange-grapefruit juice. Target is in Brenner Pass. Take off 9:30. Mission called back. Land 10:00AM.

Immediate standby. Early chow. Fried chicken, string beans, boiled potatoes, bread, butter, tea, peach roll cake. Briefing for another mission at 11:20AM. Standdown. Langley, Atherton (new man) and yours truly cleaned guns this PM. Attended first aid lecture by Capt Marshall at EM club. Indirectly pointed out yours truly for doing a good job on Bergestrom. Took final test in aircraft recognition. Enderlee and I sort of pulled together. Slight rain. Macaroni and chicken, string beans, bread, butter, coffee. Ben Moleski returns from Barry and Naples, where he went for several days with his brother Joe. He brought back beaucoup whiskey and a swell sweater for me. Yours truly has quit smoking. Feeling great. Had a bit of cognac at Ben's tent. Clear evening. Retired 10:30PM.

DECEMBER 14, 1944

Awoke 7:10AM. Clear, cold AM. Fresh fried eggs, oatmeal, 1/2 grapefruit, coffee, bread, apple butter. Briefing at 10:05AM. Carry 1000 lb GP's. Target bridge at Brenner Pass. B17's snafu-ed up so we are out to get the bridge. Take off 11:30. Flying at 10,500 feet. Not too cold, about 0 degrees. In vicinity of target at 1:25. 10/10 coverage. Returned to base. Landed 2:50PM. Pilot Lt Roseneau. I am now assigned to 037. Flew left wing lead today. Chow at 3:15PM. Creamed chicken and noodles, string beans, canned tomatoes, canned pineapple, bread, jelly. Attended USO show at group theater. Good show. Clear, warm day. Did not go to evening chow. Had toasted cheese sandwiches and hot chocolate in tent. Same mission for tomorrow. Retired 8:45.

DECEMBER 15, 1944

Awoke 6:10AM. George coming off second shift of guard. Very cold AM. Heavy frost. Briefing on mission changed from 8:10AM to 10:10AM. Fresh fried eggs, bacon, oatmeal, bread, jelly, orange-grapefruit juice, coffee. Clear AM. Lt Roseneau, pilot. Same crew as yesterday. Take off 12:10PM. Weather clear, Weather over primary target 9/10. Flew at 10,500 feet. Some ground activity. Target of opportunity bombed. Hit a bridge and blew up oil storage. Landed 3:30PM. No dinner. Waited until supper. Roast beef, gravy, sweet potatoes, string beans, ice cream, bread coffee. Warm, fair. 067 fell out of formation with oil leak, right engine. 652 fell out, could not bring up landing gear. "Gerry" had flak guns in Red Cross area. Made toasted cheese sandwiches and drank tomato juice and orange-grapefruit juice. Retired 10:30PM.

DECEMBER 16, 1944

Awoke 7:20AM. Restless night. Snafu slept in the large pocket at the front of my bedroll. Hard and soft boiled eggs, oatmeal, bread, coffee, orange juice. Briefing at 8:10AM. Standdown on mission. As a rule we are almost finished at the briefing but at group and dressed. Then they standdown the mission. Fairly cloudy. Mailed parcel to Shyrle today. The administrative inspector from wing highly commended on our squadron area. George brought in another load of roots for firewood. Baked beans, peas and carrots, sliced pineapple, bread, butter, tea. George, Van and I dug roots in airfield area for another load of firewood. The water for the showers is heated and there is a stove in the shower shack. 721 returned from Catania today. Turned in khaki class A's today (2 shirts, 2 pants). Received wool pullover sweater with collar. Cloudy PM. Abrecunas and Hawthorne are grounded for one month for leaving their guns loaded in the ship. Corned beef hash, tomato sauce, fresh sweet potatoes, peas, sliced lettuce and vinegar, coffee, bread, jam. Slight rain. Retired 10:30PM.

DECEMBER 17, 1944

Awoke 7:20AM. Briefing 10:05AM. Cloudy AM. Foggy. Fresh fried eggs, bacon, whole-wheat cereal, coffee, bread, jam. Standdown on mission. Mock mission. Stew in hash form, tomato sauce, string beans, cauliflower, sweet potatoes, sliced pineapple, bread, jelly, coffee. Were unable to have target practice as group requests a permit to carry firearms off squadron area. This came about as a result of a landmine exploding on the beach killing and injuring several officers. Clear, sunny PM. Did a bit of bag punching. Mailed parcel to Merriam, including handkerchief. Boiled chicken, gravy, sweet potatoes, string beans, cauliflower, bread, butter, coffee. Capt Hargrave, infantry GLO attached to 321st GP spoke at the I and E meeting tonight. He spoke about our present war fronts. Well received. As a rule we have a bull session before retiring at night. It's best to read around 10:30PM as everyone has retired and the lights become brighter as there isn't so much pulling on the energizer. Retired 11:00PM.

DECEMBER 18, 1944

Awoke 6:45AM. Had to go. A bit of the GI. Dark, cloudy AM. Briefing 9:25AM. Fresh fried eggs, sausage, whole-wheat cereal, hard tack, coffee, 1/2 grapefruit. Standdown of mission. Raining. Stew,

peas, cauliflower, fruit salad, bread, jelly, coffee.
Raining. Raining. Read "The Robe" by Lloyd Douglas.
John and Ryan left for Adjaccia. Roast beef, gravy,
string beans, cauliflower, fruit salad, bread, butter,
tea. Worked on Lisson radio and wiring in tent.
Retired 10:30PM.

DECEMBER 19, 1944

Awoke 7:20AM. Cloudy, drizzly AM. Briefing for
mission at 9:25AM. Fresh fried eggs, whole-wheat
cereal, bread, jam, grapefruit juice, coffee. Danny
Hurley came in last night and we shot the bull until
lights went out at night. Feffer and Gallagher came
after keys for club last night. In fact they made a
second trip about 1:00AM. Celebrating at Ike's tent.
Mike Green leaving for states. Snafu is now off limits
in our tent. He watered the pocket of my bedroll where
I usually let him sleep. Standdown on mission.
Boiled, creamed chicken, fresh boiled potatoes, string
beans, bread, butter, coffee. Boys are doing a lot of
drinking this PM as weather is halting all operations.
Finished "The Robe". Commenced reading from the
bible. Roast beef, diced beets, string beans, lima
beans, gravy, bread, jam, coffee. Still raining.
Energizer very weak. Have to use candles in addition.
Van, Lewis and I had a few at the bar. Feeling a bit
tipsy. Retired 10:30PM.

DECEMBER 20, 1944

Lights awoke me at 6:20AM. Raining. Rained hard all
through the night. Briefing 9:45AM. Pancakes,
bacon, oatmeal, syrup, coffee, tomato juice. OD
caught guard asleep last night. Standdown on
mission. Raining. Roast beef, gravy beans, tomato

soup, canned tomatoes, bread, jam, coffee, fruit salad.
Van Order gave me a wet cell this PM. Cut into
Cunningham's energizer. Lisson radio working swell.
Meeting of combat crews. Volunteer crew to go on IS
to 12th Airforce headquarters. No dice for yours truly.
Canned pork, kidney beans, bread, butter, coffee,
sliced pineapple. Enjoying the radio. Van, Lewis and I
had a couple of drinks at club. Retired 10:30PM.

DECEMBER 21, 1944

Awoke 8:00AM. Rained hard all night. Still raining.
Standdown on mission. Fried eggs, oatmeal, bacon,
grapefruit juice, coffee, bread, apple butter. Beaucoup
drunks as there is nothing to do during rainy weather.
Hamburgers, string beans, fruit salad, bread, butter,
cake, coffee. For the past four days it has rained
almost continually. The mud is terrific. Lights burn
all day on such days. Rivers, creeks are swollen.
Roads and farms are under water. Eating early chow.
On 6 to 10 guard shift. Stew, gravy, string beans,
beans, beets, bread, jelly, coffee, fruit salad. Raining
all the time on guard. Very miserable night. Retired
11:00PM.

DECEMBER 22, 1944

Awoke 7:40AM. Turned cold during night. Pancakes,
syrup, bacon, coffee, grapefruit juice. Standdown on
mission. Attended meeting at EM club on gun
malfunctions. Richard Farwell featured. Rice and
canned chicken, string beans, bread, butter, fruit
salad, coffee. Clear, cold day. Rockwell and I worked
on heavy punching bag stand. Frank Varga (185 lb)
and I fought four rounds with the gloves. Martin and
Vanderberg argued about sex. Roast beef, gravy,

mashed potatoes, fruit salad, coffee. Clear night. Van, Len and I had drinks at club. Club smartly decorated for Christmas. Cold. Retired 9:00PM.

DECEMBER 23, 1944

Awoke 6:40AM. Still dark. Built fire. Briefing 8:00AM. Corn fritters, bacon, jelly, coffee, orange-grapefruit juice. Raining. Standby for two hours on mission. Capt Neprook gave me about ten (10) shots of Corsica. Standdown on mission. Macaroni and tomato sauce, string beans, beets, fruit salad, bread, butter, tea. Cloudy, cold day. Haven't received mail in some time. Van and I cut legs 6" off metal stool supporting stove and added another piece of stovepipe. Powering the stove provides more warmth. Van constructed a speaker for the radio. As a rule on days of standdown, we hang around, read, sleep, kibitz, clean guns, work on details, etc. Usually I work out about 1/2 hour every other day. Still burning roots. Safe and cleaner than gas. Corn beef hash, rice, hot tomatoes and sauce, kidney beans, fruit salad, bread, jam, coffee. Over at club for a few drinks. Spoke with Lew awhile, trying to straighten him out a bit. Very miserly and overcautious. Retired 10:00PM.

DECEMBER 24, 1944

Awoke 7:30AM. Briefing 8:35AM. Powdered egg pancakes, oatmeal, orange juice, coffee, bread, jam. Raining. Standdown on mission. Rations - 3 beers (canned) 2 cokes, 12 pkg cigarettes, 3 Hersheys, 3 cigars, 3 gum drop packages, 1 carton gum drops, 2 pkg cheese tidbits ($2.20) Meat loaf, fried onions, beets, bread, jelly, tea, fruit salad. Had quite a party for about 50 Corsican children in the club. Everybody contributed part of their rations. Roast beef, gravy, rice, fruit salad, coffee, bread. Boys are commencing to drink heavily. Atherton, my tail gunner went berserk, drew his 45 pistol, but was quelled by the boys. "Doc" gave him a shot of morphine and a couple of the medics put him in a straight jacket. Drunks all over the area. Van and I went over to club about 8:00PM. Captain Farwell donated a case of cognac to the EM club as a Christmas gift. Yaw bought $10 worth and Lawless bought $25 - for the boys at the bar. Van and I took Joe Critter back to his tent as he was just about ready to pass. Up he pops back to the club. Mike Kocis staggered about. Van and George supporting him. Bob Peiffer did a swell job in decorating the club and mess hall. His brother a 1st lieut. with the 338th infantry of the 85th division with the 5th army is visiting him at the present. Trigler, Marrich, helping John at bar. Glasses are being broken on a wholesale scale. Several of the young Italian KP's are drunk. Critter and Isledyke are both out. Yours truly is having a few but with moderation. My pilot Lt Roseneau, Lt Riley, Copes and Norris came over to club, all plastered. Cooks are preparing all night for a big Christmas dinner tomorrow. Singing GI's are all over the club. John is mixing special drinks for George, Van and me. Retired 11:30PM. Raining - standdown for tomorrow. At 12:30AM, John came in and cleared up day's business at bar. About 12:45AM Leo Gallagher, bartender at officer's club, staggered in with two bottles of cognac. At 1:00AM, Koscis wobbled in after Van and George thought they put him to bed. Mike bunked himself on George's cot and dozed off. Bob Pieffer came in with quite a load, but his brother is sober. Gallagher popped the cognac and the boys had a few. After 3:00AM, the boys finally left. Nike was a special case. Finally dozed off at 3:30AM.

DECEMBER 25, 1944

CHRISTMAS

Awoke 7:20AM to let snafu out. Hit the sack again until 9:30AM. Showered in ice cold water. Boys are at it again. Drunk. Everybody wishing everybody else a Merry Christmas. Koscis brought over a dozen eggs, a loaf of bread and Van made scrambled eggs and yours truly made toast. Dull, cloudy AM. No mission. Big dinner at 3:00PM. Roast turkey, dressing, mashed potatoes, string beans, cinnamon rolls, cranberry sauce, mince pie, coffee, bread, butter. Van, Lew and I brought our meal over to tent. Everybody getting drunker. Colonel Smith and his dame (Janie of the Red Cross) came over to the club. Taylor and Smitty came over. Got Crisp and Fisher to come over to 448th. Drinks were on the house. Got a half bottle of rum and made drinks at the tent. Looked for Danny Ivory. Had beaucoup food and guys at our tent, then we roamed from tent to tent. About midnight, things broke up. Someone broke in club. Ike has three bottles from a suspect. Nelson and Ike located thief. A fellow recently arrived here from the 8th did the job. Also drunk. Ike hit him several times. Sgt of guard put him under arrest. Removed his pistol from hook just in case. Woke him out of a sound sleep. This incident spoiled my whole Christmas. Finally hit the sack. Retired 1:30AM.

DECEMBER 26, 1944

Awoke 7:50AM. Feeling tired. Partly cloudy AM. Cold. Briefing 9:55AM. Pancakes, oatmeal, jelly, tomato juice, coffee. Jim Herod, radio operator, who

had a severe wound from flak over Astiglia, came to
the outfit for a visit. Arm still in a sling. Still swollen.
Pieffer's brother returned to his outfit with the 5th
Army. Briefing pushed ahead to 11:40AM. Ate early
chow - macaroni, kidney beans, tea, bread, butter,
fruit salad. Take off 1:00PM. Lt Roseneau pilot.
Mission in Northern Brenner Pass. Heavy intense and
accurate flak. Very nervous. Did not bomb. Flew as
cameraman. Ran into flak three different times.
Terrific evasive action - landed 5:40PM. 1 hole in tail.
Muffins, kidney beans, gravy, fruit salad, coffee.
310th band playing at our dance at EM club tonight.
Females coming from surrounding country. Retired
10:00PM. No mission up.

DECEMBER 27, 1944

CQ blowing whistle at 6:20AM. Thought I might get
up and investigate mission board. Woke Van who is
first mission. Yours truly on second mission. Briefing
9:10AM. Cameraman. Lt Lyons pilot (918). Fresh
fried eggs, oatmeal, bread, jam coffee. Target is San
Ambroglio - north end of Brenner Pass Tunnel. Take
off 10:20AM. Over target 12:15PM. Lesser,
bombardier, did not drop. Glass clouded up on
bombsight. Medium flak. Very cold. Incendiary ship
went in first to knock out guns and disperse chaff to
throw off radar. Didn't feel a bit nervous today.
Landed 1:50PM. Pork chops, soup, applesauce, bread,
butter. Very tired. Roast beef, mashed potatoes,
beets, bread, jelly, coffee. Cloudy warm PM. Meeting
in EM club of all EM combat men. Capt Burks and
Farwell chewed us out. Piss poor bombing and
formations. One ship lost formation and landed in
Marseilles. Retired 11:00PM.

DECEMBER 28, 1944

Awoke 7:55AM. First thought that struck my mind was Elliott's 32nd birthday. Not on mission. 2 missions going up. Fresh fried eggs, wheatena, bread, jelly, orange-grapefruit juice, tangerines. Cloudy, damp AM. Lew and Van on mission. La Bella returned from Rome. Went on group ship. Biscuits, cheese, stew, beets and onion, jelly, coffee, white radishes. 10 new officers, 10 new EM's came in this AM. Corn beef hash, tomato sauce, boiled cabbage, fruit salad, bread butter, coffee. Attended "Sensations of 1945" Received box of cigars and book from the folks. Clear, starry night. Snow-covered mountains show up picturesquely in moonlight. Commenced "Porgy" by DuBose Heyward. Retired 9:30 PM.

DECEMBER 29, 1944

Awoke 7:30AM. Clear, cold AM. Briefing at 9:10AM. Fresh fried eggs, whole-wheat cereal, bread, applebutter, coffee, orange-grapefruit juice. Feeling tired. Carrying 1000 lg GP's. Bridge at Brenner Pass. Flying right wing lead element. 2nd flight. Take off 10:12AM. Clear weather. Over target 12:10PM. Flak, heavy, intense and accurate. No holes. Slight chills. Lt Autrey, pilot. Little nervous. Gunner in 445th wounded. John Carruthers parachute saved his life. Landed 2:00PM. Meat loaf, peas, tomato sauce, bread, butter, coffee, oranges. Colored band from 41st engineers arrived by plane from Bastia.   S/Sgt Dave Crowley Jr took photos of Seward and myself for Yank magazine. Pork, Boiled cabbage, fruit salad, kidney beans, coffee. Called a meeting of all newly arrived combat radio operators. Flew 31st mission. Band sounded swell tonight. Very windy. Retired 10:20PM.

DECEMBER 30, 1944

Awoke 7:50AM. Very cold. Van and Lew leaving for briefing on first mission. Yours truly on second mission. Scrambled eggs, whole-wheat cereal, bread, applebutter, orange-grapefruit juice, coffee. Colored band stayed overnight in squadron. Just a handful of girls were at dance. Briefing postponed to 11:40AM. 1st mission postponed until 10:30AM. Early chow for our mission. Hash diced beets, rice pudding and fruit salad, mixed bread, butter, coffee. Lt Bard, pilot. Flying lead - 081. Take off 12:45PM. Target is RR bridge at Crema, Italy. Over target 2:42PM - 100%. Milk run. Landed 4:00PM. Lead crew is always escorted in by command car. Colonel spoke with me. Weather is cold and cloudy on Corsica. Ate early chow as on 1st shift of guard. 6 to 10PM. Stew, boiled cabbage, chocolate pudding, bread, butter. Very cold on guard (tech supply). Received letter from Gerry with clipping from paper awarding DFC to yours truly. Retired 11:00PM.

DECEMBER 31, 1944

Awoke 7:25AM. Very cold night. Ice in the lowlands for the first time. Clear, cold AM. George had fire built as he was on 2 to 6 guard shift. On 2nd mission. Briefing 9:40AM. Hard-boiled eggs, bacon, whole-wheat cereal, bread, marmalade, coffee, orange-grapefruit juice. Martin on 1st mission. Carrying 1000 lb GP's. Right wing of 1st element. Lt Autrey, pilot. Ship 530. Target is RR bridge at Padua north. Take off 10:43AM. Over target 12:45. 100%. No flak. Very cold. Gunner shot out antenna on lead ship. Yours truly took over radio traffic. Landed 2:30PM.

Fried chicken, bread, butter, fruit salad, coffee. Paid
$116.00. Abecunas and Hueler paid off. Lew and
Vanderberg did also. Didn't go to chow. Wrote letters.
Kibitzed. Received my first letter from Dad while
overseas. Retired 10:00PM.

JANUARY 1, 1945

Awoke to the new year at 7:40AM. Light blanket of
snow on ground and flurries in the air. Briefing
9:40AM. Fresh fried eggs, whole-wheat cereal, tomato
juice, coffee, bread. Briefing changed to 11:05AM.
Flying wing spare. Lt Autrey, pilot. #530. Carrying
1000 lb GP's. Fuel dump at Pavia. Flew until we
sighted enemy territory. Returned at 1345. Take off
12:04PM. Very cold. Christened showers at 3:00PM.
Barney Goldman deserves Legion of Merit for such
construction. Waited until boys returned from mission
before going to chow. 100% hit. Slight flak. Light
snow flurries. Turkey, gravy, dressing, cauliflower,
mince pie, oranges, bread, butter, coffee. Excellent
meal. Wood for stove getting low. Considering
burning gas. Retired 8:30PM.

JANUARY 2, 1945

Awoke 8:00AM. Fair day. Very cold. Briefing at
9:10AM. Fresh fried eggs, bacon, whole-wheat cereal,
bread, coffee, tomato juice. Standdown on mission.
Called out to line for ditching lecture. Raining. Roast
beef, gravy, bread, butter, canned peaches, coffee.
Attended lecture on escape and evasion at 4:00PM at
EM club. Lt Richter who just came back through the
lines spoke. Lt Moose of 5-2 also spoke about late
"poop" from intelligence. Roast beef, gravy, kidney
beans, fruit salad, bread, butter, coffee. Showers

caught on fire about 6:45PM. Three shots fired by guard warned us. Sgt Isledyke almost suffocated in attempt to extinguish blaze with carbon tech. 1985 firefighters arrived with CO2 cylinders. Immediately put Ike in gas mask this time. Fire truck tore down wire for lights. Installed gas in tent. No luck. Explosion. Removed gas line and went back to wood. Retired 10:30PM.

JANUARY 3, 1945

Awoke 7:45AM. Clear and warmer. Briefing at 9:10AM. Fresh fried eggs, whole-wheat cereal, bread, coffee, orange juice. Lt Autrey (530) carrying 1000 lb GP's. Bridge in northern Italy near Austria. Take off 10:45AM. Right wing last element. Colonel Smith, pilot of lead of our element. Clear and warm (-2 degrees). No flak. Missed target at 1:22PM. Colonel Smith very rough as pilot. Landed 3:45PM. Showered. Missed dinner. Supper - spaghetti, beans, fresh small onions, chocolate cake, coffee. Burning a can of gas in stove. Cold evening. Retired 10:30PM.

JANUARY 4, 1945

Awoke 7:10AM. Very cold and frosty. Briefing 8:05AM. Fresh boiled eggs, bacon, oatmeal, coffee, bread, tomato juice. Lt Autrey (530) carrying 1000 GP's (1-24 hour delayed action). Target is RR and road bridge at Calliano in Brenner Pass. 10/10 coverage all the way in. Heavy fleecy and thick overcast. No flak until 30 seconds before bombs away. LaBella hit in face, but went back to station and dropped bombs. No. 2 ship 2nd element 2nd flight. Flew at 13,000 feet. Cameraman. Good photos. First mission I've flown in some time that I can honestly say I was not nervous.

Broke away from formation over coast and high-tailed for home due to LaBella's injury. Landed 1:30PM. First time I checked bomb bays over enemy territory. Boiled and fried chicken, rice, bread, butter, coffee, fruit salad. Still have GI's (diarrhea), no cramps. Hit the bag a bit. Gill (8th Airforce), who is drunk per usual had a fight with another newly arrived combat man. Drew pistol. Gill to be court-martialed. Boiled beef, potatoes, fruit salad, bread, butter, coffee. Attended "Step Lively". Light rain throughout movie. Retired 10:30PM.

JANUARY 5, 1945

Awoke 8:00AM. Rushed to make chow. Met a big line. Standdown on mission. Raining. Today is a regular run of the mill. Chow isn't too good. Just hanging about reading. Gossip is concerning a possibility of our moving. Van is on guard. Quiet peaceful evening. Retired 11:00PM.

JANUARY 6, 1945

Awoke 7:45AM. Briefing 10:20AM. Raining and windy. French toast, bacon, oatmeal, coffee, fruit juice, jelly. Enjoying "Canal Town" and "Turnabout". Standdown on mission. Raining. Usual run of poor chow. GI's still bothering me. Gill awaiting court martial at stockade. This will make his 3rd court martial since entering the army. It was told to me on the QT that I am making T/Sgt this month.

JANUARY 7, 1945

Awoke 7:45AM. Terrific cramps. Still have GI's. Fair AM. Feeling a bit empty. Been moving my bowels about six times a day. Briefing 10:10AM. Scrambled eggs, whole-wheat cereal, bread, coffee. Plan "A" Standdown. Briefing changed to Plan "B" 11:15AM. Plan "B" also standdown. Slight rain, heavy overcast. Twelve ships mock formation and bombing. Roast turkey, stuffing, peas, fruit salad, bread, butter, coffee. Commenced reading "Genesis" from the Holy Scripture. Took dose of Paregoric for GI's. Gets very boring just hanging around. Rations $2.10 - 12 pkg cigarettes, 3 cigars, 1 beer, 2 cokes, 1 bar soap, 1 pkg pretzels, 1 can peanuts, 1 Hershey bar, 3 Baby Ruths, 2 Butterfingers. Took another dose of paregoric. Roast beef, gravy, beans, fruit salad, bread, butter, coffee. No appetite. Still running. Retired 11:00PM.

JANUARY 8, 1945

Awoke 7:45AM. Van had stove going full blast. Cold and clear. Briefing 10:10AM. Fresh fried eggs, oatmeal, fruit juice, bread, coffee. Plan standdown "A" (cancels incendiary ship). Plan "B" also standdown. Chow is regular run of the mill. Very windy. Slight rain. Longing for mail. Ever since arriving on Corsica my thoughts have always been with #19, #8, #636. I don't believe I've ever retired one single night when I haven't longed to be with them all. I hope God grants me such good fortune. On first shift of guard 6-10PM (tech supply). One guard at 310th to look after three of our planes that landed there due to heavy gusts of crosswinds at our field. Still taking medicine for my GI's. Retired 11:00PM.

JANUARY 9, 1945

Awoke 7:45AM. Briefing 10:15AM. Pancakes, whole-wheat cereal, jam, coffee, fruit juice. Windy, cloudy.

Plan "A" Standdown. Plan "B" in effect. Briefing
11:20. Early chow. Cheese, spam, bread. Carry 1000
lb GP's. Some delayed action bombs. Lt Stromberg
pilot (530). Take off 12:45. Filled in right wing lead.
Made landfall over friendly territory. Very heavy cloud
formations. Flew for awhile at 14,000 feet. 28 degrees
below zero centigrade. Official announcement of
making T/Sgt. Fairly clear. Landed 2:30PM. No
mission. Van and John had a run in. Did not go to
chow. This is my ninth consecutive day of GI's Taking
bismuth and paregoric. Attended "My Pal Wolf" - fair.
New theater nearly completed. Slight snow flurries.
As a rule we make toast every night.

JANUARY 10, 1945

Awoke 6:45AM. Van had stove going full blast.
Briefing 8:15AM. Hard and soft boiled eggs, hot
cereal, fruit juice, coffee, bread. Carrying 1000 lb
GP's. Marshaling yards at Roverstrom. Defended. Lt
Lee (530), pilot. All ships awaiting take off.
Standdown on mission. Clear and warm. Usual run
of the mill chow. Still have the GI's. Van, Lew and I
carried gas from trailer to 50-gallon drum for stoves'
supply. Retired 9:15PM.

JANUARY 11, 1945

Awoke 6:15AM with cramps. Commenced fire. Corn
fritters, hot cereal, coffee, fruit juice. Briefing 8:15AM.
Standdown on mission. Capt Farwell gave Markewicz,
Wald and me permission to go wild boar hunting. Left
squadron at 9:30 with carbines. After a several hour
climb, we set foot on some Frenchman's property and
were invited in . Ate dinner and drank beaucoup vino.
Fireplace heated the room. Very hospitable. Left our

overshoes there. Gave them candy and cigarettes. A bit drunk. No boar, rabbits, etc. Returned squadron 4:30PM. Very tired. Met some boys down from the 340th. Clear PM. Snowing the morning. Retired 7:45PM.

JANUARY 12, 1945

Awoke 7:10AM. Feeling OK. Awoke 3:15AM. Had cramps and the GI's. Stove kept going all night. Briefing 8:25AM. Fresh fried eggs, oatmeal, fruit juice, coffee, bread. Partly cloudy AM. Same target as we have been trying to bomb for almost two weeks. (Rovereto, Marshalling yards). Carrying 1000 lb GP's and some delayed action bombs. Lt Lee, pilot (530). Still wing spare. Standby in area until 11:30AM.

At 10:50AM. Standdown on mission. Canned cornbeef, tomato sauce, lima beans, sliced beets, coffee, bread, fruit salad. Went out to line. Weiss gave me instruction on Norden Bomb Sight, also cut a scarf from a parachute. Having heavy punching bag made at 341st service squadron. Raining. Spaghetti and sauce, lima beans, sliced beets, fruit salad, bread, butter, coffee. John went to mountains for potatoes??? Raining, snowing and hailing. Retired 10:30PM.

JANUARY 13, 1945

Awoke 7:30AM. Cramps. Still GI's. Ground covered with ice and snow. Briefing 9:50AM. Dismal looking sky. Fresh fried eggs, hot cereal, bread, fruit juice, coffee, apple butter, bacon. Dressed and all set for mission. Standdown. Hamburgers, tomato sauce, mashed potatoes, beets, fruit salad, coffee, butter, bread. Took off for mountains with Vanderberg and

Markiewicz. Went to look up a bella senorina
Markewicz is always raving about. Spoke in Italian to
old man of house. Said she left for another village.
Her baby died and husband is in French army in
Algeria. Returned to squadron to hear my name being
paged over PA system. Major Knieval told me I am to
leave for Florence, Italy. S-2 told me I am to be
featured in a broadcast from the AEF station about my
set over the Galliate raid. Leaving Tuesday AM. Pork
chops, fresh mashed potatoes, beets, cold canned
sauerkraut. Noticing a change in George Huka lately.
Used to be very congenial and friendly. I believe the
change is due to John Nelson's influence. I try to be a
regular guy. Everything has a limit. Cloudy night.
Retired 10:00PM.

JANUARY 14, 1945

Awoke 8:00AM. Raining fiercely. Standdown on
mission. Fresh scrambled eggs, oatmeal, fruit juice,
coffee, bread, apple butter. Had a very disturbing
dream last night. Dreamt John tried to knife Van and
shoot me with 45 caliber pistol. I finally disarmed
him. Lightning and thunder throughout the night
terrific. Very odd to hear this time of year. Sgt Scott
called for me at 9:30AM. Went over to group photo lab
for picture that Dave Crowley took. (Got him out of
bed). Picture is in accordance with radio broadcast
scheduled for this Tuesday. Scotty writing script.
Macaroni and tomato sauce, carrots, boiled potatoes,
fruit salad, coffee, bread, apple butter. Still working
out about 1/2 hour a day. Boiled beef, beans, carrots,
chocolate pudding, coffee, bread, apple butter. Taking
sulfa guanidine for GI's. Took 7 pills at 5:00PM.
Clear, starry night. Retired 10:00PM.

The True Diaries of Irving J. Schaffer

JANUARY 15, 1945

Awoke 7:45AM. Fair AM. Briefing 9:50AM. Fresh
fried eggs, oatmeal, bread, apple jelly, fruit juice. Area
guard fired three shots about 1:00AM last night which
awoke me to the cry of 'fire'. Supply tent in flames.
1985 fire fighters on the job. Ammunition exploding
all over the place. Van and I stood guard over our tent
to protect it against sparks. Target is marshaling
yards at Rovereto, Italy (Po Valley). Lt Lee, pilot (530)
wing spar. Take off 11:45. Filled in as right wing. 1st
element, 2nd flight. Temperature at 11,000 feet was -
10 degrees Celsius. Over target 1:45PM. Light
inaccurate flak. Weather clear over target. Landed
3:30PM after having a malfunction in releasing our
nose wheel. Warm day. Retired 10:30PM.

JANUARY 16, 1945

Awoke 7:30AM. Raining hard. Rained all night.
Fresh fried eggs, oatmeal, jelly, bread, coffee, fruit
juice. Scotty called for me at 8:10AM with carryall.
Went to 57th Bomb Wing. Picked up orders at wing
HQ area and left for flight line at 310th. C-47 on field.
All flights canceled because of weather. Water rising
in all streams. Returned to squadron at 9:30AM.
Commenced reading from book Elliott sent me "Stories
of the Great Operas and Their Composers" by Ernest
Newman. (Read Mozart's "The Marriage of Figaro")
John, Wesley, Huka and Lt Bosick left for Bastia.
Fresh fried chicken, fresh boiled potatoes, gravy, fruit
salad, bread, butter, coffee. Raining continually.
Water getting in our gas supply. Covered it with half
shelter. Corn beef hash, tomato sauce, kidney beans,
dehydrated carrots, chocolate pudding, coffee.
Attended meeting at 8:45PM at EM club. Capt Farwell
(CO) spoke about fire hazard in area and immediate

check up on clothing as records were destroyed in fire that destroyed supply tent. Still raining. Capt Leonard checked our tent. Retired 11:00PM.

JANUARY 17, 1945

Awoke 7:30AM. Cloudy. Rain ceased during the night. French toast, syrup, oatmeal, fruit juice, coffee. Scotty and I left for 310th. Courier going to Florence but not Rome. Returned to squadron 10:30AM. Van off on mission. Macaroni and meat balls, gravy, sliced beets, chocolate pudding, coffee. Attended USO camp show at 2:30PM. Enclosed theater almost complete (hangar). Show was fair. Showers caught on fire again resulting from a short circuit. Slight damage. Mission returned 4:00PM - very rough. Several of our ships badly shot up. No injuries. 447th radio operator killed and tail gunner wounded. Target was way up in Po Valley. John returned from Bastia (shacked up). Cloudy PM. Roast beef, gravy, dehydrated potatoes, sliced beets, chocolate pudding, coffee, bread, butter. Retired 10:30PM.

JANUARY 18, 1945

Awoke 7:30AM. Left squadron area at 8:30 with Scotty by jeep. Took off from 310th on #479 which is a 57th SW ship. Lt Scully, pilot. Landed Ciampioni Airfield, Rome 11:00AM. Field quite muddy. Sun shining. ATC bus took us to town. (Command car). Went to MAA - PRO headquarters. Script censored. Passed OK. Made recording for broadcast at Radio Rome. (4:30PM) Very successful. Scotty and I hired apartment at California Pensione.$1.00 per person. Radio, piano, bathroom, etc. Dominic, padrone of apt remembered me from last November. Developing a bad chest cold. No heat in building. Spent very uncomfortable night.

JANUARY 19, 1945

Awoke 9:00AM. Room very cold and washing water the same. T/Sgt Sam Levine, HQ Sq 57th bomb wing and Cpl James L Madden of same, out with Pat Fred Allen of the 310th bomb group are staying in same apt building. Capt John Gilluly of the 310th bomb group was also on broadcast. Ate chow at GI restaurant. Did some shopping. Prices are very high. Spasmodic rain throughout the AM. Went to the Jewish soldier's club and enjoyed a breakfast of pastry and coffee. (incidentally I met Lobley and Tony (5th army) at Mario's bar last night. Also seen usual run of prostitutes. Fixed the boys up with females for a good night's sleep. After that we went to Gori's - favorite eating spot where all these wenches bring their soldier boys. Retired 11:30PM. After kibitzing with Anna (landlady) and her tall, blond good-looking daughter.

JANUARY 20, 1945

Awoke 9:10AM because Lobley was urging us to get up. Ate chow at GI restaurant. Bid Lobley and Tony so long and checked out of our apt. Went out to airfield. 442nd at field - pilot in town. Waited at field until 5:30PM. (Field closes) Lt Huggan, pilot of ship went and goofed off in town. Registered at rest camp after a lot of hustling about (9:00PM). Dilly, dallying around due to inefficiency of man in charge. Spoke with Clarence Butterfield. Attended dance at Tibre Terrace. Negroes attend same as whites. Very aggravating. Our quarters at rest camp very warm.

Ate midnight chow. Retired 1:00AM. Cold is slightly better.

JANUARY 21, 1945

Awoke 7:30AM. Fair weather. Ate chow at rest camp. Checked out. Met pilot at officer's billeting. Hung around airfield for three hours waiting for engineer (shacked up). Took off 12:50PM. Landed 310th at 1:40PM. 57th BW command car took us to 321st. Mission out. Pilot in 447 killed - very rough. Glad to be back. Cold about the same. Rations: 6 bottles beer, 2 cokes, 14 pkg cigarettes, 3 pkg gum, 3 cigars, 10 candy bars, 1 cake soap, 1 bar Fig Newtons, 1 can peanuts. Vanderberg awarded air medal and also made buck Sgt. Feeling very tired. Didn't do a thing. Retired 8:00PM.

JANUARY 22, 1945

Awoke 7:30AM. Clear, cold. Briefing 9:00AM. Pancakes, oatmeal, fruit juice, jelly, coffee. Target is Povis RR bridge in Brenner Pass. Carrying 1000 lb GP's. Defended (726). Lt Autrey, pilot. Flying with 16 mm movie camera as PRO from group. Take off 10:15AM. #2 ship, 3rd element, 2nd flight. Italy completely covered with snow. Over primary at 12:50PM. Lead bombardiers' bombsight froze up. Did not bomb, scant flak. Bombed alternate target at Crema RR bridge (100% hit). Very cold and clear. 28 degrees below Celsius. Landed 3:15PM. Very tired. Supper - roast beef, gravy, beans, ice cream, bread, jelly, coffee. Clear, cold evening. Lt Autrey came over and we killed a quart of champagne I brought back from Rome, plus some combat whiskey. Retired 11:45PM.

JANUARY 23, 1945

Awoke 7:15AM. Briefing 8:35AM. Fried eggs, bacon, oatmeal, coffee, fruit juice, bread. Same target as yesterday. Take off 9:55. Standdown. Flew local T for one hour. Landed 11:15AM. Cloudy. Meeting of all radio operators at 1:15PM at operations. Capt Burke spoke about groups complaint about bad photography. Yours truly submitted suggestion regarding a plexiglass panel over camera hatch which is to be used. Lt Bennet, engineering officer taking over matter. Raining on first shift of guard, 6 to 10. Was put on motor pool. Fair evening. After guard, attended a brief chow at Scotty's tent. Very tired. Retired 12:00AM.

JANUARY 24, 1945

Awoke 7:30AM. Nelson calling me. Briefing 9:50AM. Sunny AM. Cream of wheat, pancakes, bacon, fruit juice, coffee, jam. Standdown on mission. On detail at supply. Called out for local flying. (927) Lt Smith, pilot. Local bomb range. Flying as photographer. Take off 10:30. Shot 24 photos. Zero degrees temp. Landed 1:30PM. No chow. Ate buttered toast. Clear warm day. Evening meal regular run of the mill. Donald Bergestrom, fellow I took care of on Galliate raid back in squadron for a spell. Awaiting to go home. Looks, fair. Poteet leaves for home tomorrow. Fire in officer's area at 9:00PM. Lt Wimous' tent burned. Retired 11:00PM.

JANUARY 25, 1945

George awoke me at 7:45AM. Clear, sunny AM.
Briefing 10:10AM. Van coughed all night (bad cold).
Pancakes, syrup, wheatena, fruit juice, bacon, coffee.
Standdown on mission. War progress looks very good.
Fried chicken, mashed potatoes, canned tomatoes,
stewed apricots, bread, coffee. To fly on bomb range
as photographer. Local flying canceled. Went out to
line to clean guns (530). Engineering to adopt my
suggestion on camera. Clear, Warm day. Salmon,
lemon potatoes, fruit salad, peanut butter, coffee.
Attended "Mrs Pinkerton". Excellent movie. Cloudy
evening. Capt Farwell (CO) made major today. Retired
10:30PM.

JANUARY 26, 1945

Awoke 7:356AM. Clear AM. Scrambled eggs, oatmeal,
bacon, fruit juice, coffee. Standdown on mission. Left
for Bastia with Jerry Kures and Vandenberg at
11:00AM. Arrived 1:00PM. Drank beaucoup Cap-
Corse. A bit drunk. Van and Jerry got fixed up. Left
Bastia at 5:00PM. Conversed with Nazi prisoners for a
few moments. Decrepit and sad looking soldiers.
Arrived squadron 7:15PM. Ate canned sardines sent
from home. Retired 9:00PM.

JANUARY 27, 1945

Awoke 7:10AM. Briefing 9:20AM. Pancakes, hot
cereal, jam, fruit juice, coffee. Clear, warm AM.
Target is Louis RR bridge in Brenner Pass. Carry 1000
lb GP's. Target defended. Take off 1:00PM. Very
rough. Flying right wing third element (911). Lt
Autrey. Weather bad - unable to get into either

primary or alternate target. Hit terrific wind pocket.
Threw ship into confusion. Yours truly hit in head
with loose armor plating. Jettisoned loose plating.
Bomb hung in bay. In fact two are hung. Hydraulic
system damaged. Pumped down wheels, flaps. Lt
Autrey made fine landing at 310th. Very narrow
escape. Feeling nervous. Pork, kidney beans, string
beans, custard pudding, bread, butter, coffee. Autrey
and Langley released hung bombs. Autrey came over
to tent. Drank a bit. Retired 12:00AM.

JANUARY 28, 1945

Awoke 7:10AM. Feeling very tired. Pancakes,
oatmeal, bacon, tomato juice, coffee, canned butter.
Not on today's mission. Fair weather. Much warmer.
Laid in sack and read. Usual run of the mill for chow.
Picked up pictures at photo lab. Horsed around area.
Finishing heavy punching bag. Capt Marrick
(adjutant) back from states. Married. Clear, windy
day. Mission pretty badly shot up. Beaucoup flak
souvenirs. One man hit in 446th (leg). Retired
11:00PM.

JANUARY 29, 1945

Awoke 7:30AM. Heavy overcast. Snowed during
night. Cold AM. On 2nd mission. Briefing 9:25AM.
Very restless on retiring last night. Leg muscles felt
very tense. In fact my whole body still feels taut.
Chest still bothering me from the Astiglia raid. Eggs in
form of pancakes, hot cereal, bread, army butter
spread, fruit juice, coffee. Target is Louis Marshalling
yards. Carry 1000 lb. #3 ship, 3rd element. Lt
Autrey (538). Take off 10:45AM. Weather bad.
Weather fine over Italy. Very rough flying.

JANUARY 30, 1945

Awoke 7:00AM. Very cold and clear AM. Briefing
9:25AM. Pancakes, oatmeal, bacon, stewed prunes,
fruit juice, coffee. There has been much talk about
our moving to Italy. Rumors are plentiful, but that's
the way of a rumor. I can notice that when spitting,
that when drawing from the lungs, a black color
saturates the spit. In all probability, this is due to the
burning of gas. 321st won the championship of the
Island in the touch football league. Ike, Danny and
Jerry played. Will wait until I return to the states
before securing a gift for the folks for their anniversary
next month. Flying (530). Lt Autrey, pilot. Target is
Rovereto RR bridge. Carry 1000 lb GP's delayed
action. #2 ship, 3rd element, 2nd flight. Autrey very
skeptical about our ship. Smoking engine on take off.
Take off 10:45. Made landfall over enemy territory at
Sestri-Levonte. Turned around after fifteen minutes of
flight. Heavy, blinding storms. Landed 12:45PM.
This made my 40th mission. Cloudy skies. Vienna
sausage, tartar sauce, diced beets, canned sliced
peaches, bread, butter, soup. Visited Taylor at 445th.
Ate supper there. Clear, starry evening. Autrey, pilot,
complained about #530. CO giving us different ship
tomorrow. Retired 9:30PM.

JANUARY 31, 1945

Awoke 6:45AM. Clear morning. Briefing 11:35AM.
Van on first mission at 9:30AM. Fresh fried eggs,
bacon, stewed raisins, hot cereal, bread, peanut
butter, coffee. John left for the mountains again. Ate
early chow at 11:00PM. Carry 1000 lb. Target is
Pescenza RR bridge. Temporary standby. Take off

1:30PM (#927). Lt Autrey, pilot. Circled near enemy territory twice awaiting fighter escort. Finally went in and bombed alternate target. 100% hit. Landed 4:20PM. #2 ship, 3rd element, 2nd flight. Yours truly to go to Capri Rest Camp tomorrow. Canned pork, sweet potatoes, cabbage salad, canned pears, bread, jelly, coffee. On first shift of guard. Motor pool. Retired 11:00PM.

FEBRUARY 1, 1945

Awoke 7:30AM. Departed Corsica 9:30AM. Arrived Rome 10:30AM. Dropped off Lt Gardner. Departed 10:45AM. Arrived Naples 11:15AM. Billeted at Rest Camp Hotel. Ate dinner at black market restaurant (small steak, french fries, salad, wine). Also had a meal (15 cents) at GI restaurant downtown - not so hot. Walked about Naples. Followed a couple of kids who propositioned us regarding some women who promiscuously engage in love. Climbed about the city to what seemed like a village all of its own. Many winding and narrow alleys. Made entrance to a very small, cold, poorly furnished several rooms where 2 young girls, 1 older woman, a man and us made it eight. Jim did the honors. Yours truly still maintains himself. Jim paid her $3.00. Disposed of carton cigarettes and sweater. Ate at private home (also black market). Our room in the Rest Camp Hotel has 5 cots, no mattresses, three blankets. Not too chilly on 6th floor. No elevators. Naples still in blackout. Civilians are still begging and trying to buy anything. Many vendors selling products at exorbitant prices. Retired 11:00PM.

FEBRUARY 2, 1945

Awoke 8:00AM. Missed breakfast. Slept quite well.
Ate breakfast at black market Restaurant. Been
drinking quite a bit of wine. Mostly Marsala. Checked
out of hotel. Secured tickets etc for the Isle of Capri.
Boarded boat at 2:30PM. Met a couple of Wacs also
going to Capri. Billeted at Hotel Pagano Vittoria.
Regular hotel. Private room (2 beds). Running water -
similar to American hotel. Chow served in dining room
by Italian waiters. 4 piece orchestra provides music.
Italian waitresses also on the job. American Red Cross
girls are in charge. Bar just off lobby. Very clean.
Attended dance at "Seaside Club". Met Nappy, ARC
worker who used to attend Skidmore College. The
weather is quite warm in comparison to Rome or
Corsica. Retired 11:30PM.

FEBRUARY 3, 1945

Awoke 8:00AM. Very sunny. Ate breakfast. Instead
of taking Red Cross tour to the Blue Grotto, Jim and I
hired a smart, clean looking lad to row us there. This
boat is home made. Before the war its construction
costs 99 cents. Today $20.00. Sea quite calm. The
Blue Grotto is a subterranean cove which is immense
inside but its opening barely permits a row boat. In
addition to paying our boy Gino, it costs another 35
cents apiece to enter. In the afternoon we met Gino
again and we hiked up to the Tiberian ruins. Took
pictures. Very educational and interesting. Capri is
very compact - population is about 10,000 - 6 1/2 x 1
3/4 miles. Paid Gino $4.00 for day plus several bars
of soap. Began to rain. About 4:30PM. Jim retired.
Ate supper by myself. Picked up emblems, ribbons
etc, that I had made at gift shop. Retired 9:00PM.

FEBRUARY 4, 1945

Awoke 7:30AM. Ate breakfast. Jim and I hired automobile (open touring) and guide. Ascended upper most peak of Capri. Visited San Michele with all its historical remembrance. Especially the hand sculptured busts of many Roman notables. Visited the ruins of former German and Italian forts overlooking the Tylrennian Sea. Saw the better part of the interior of Certosa (monastary). Monk acted as guide. Every spot we visited signs requested donations. Paid driver of car $5.00 and guide $3.00 and 1 pkg cigarettes. Returned hotel 11:30AM. Can plainly see Mount Vesuvius, Sorrento. Met a young lady from NYC who is a secretary for UNRRA while touring Ana Capri. Not much to look at but very pleasant. All civilian bars and restaurants are "off limits". Water shortage on island. Attended dance at Seaside Club. Met UNRRA female and Nappy there. Italian band (OK) playing all popular American tunes. Jim doesn't dance, but spends most of his time at the bar in hotel. Retired 11:30PM.

FEBRUARY 5, 1945

Awoke 6:30AM. Packed and ate chow. Jeep took us to pier at 8:00AM. Boat left at 8:30AM. Wacs, Red Cross, civilians, etc. on boat. Porpoises followed bow of boat. Naples full of freighters and one American light cruiser. Cloudy sky. Coffee and cookies served on boat. About 2 hours by water from Capri to Naples. Trucks carried us to airfield. No ship from 448th. Wing ship (442). Lt Duggan, pilot. 12 men on ship - only 9 chutes. Saw B-25 crash land on runway at Naples. Took off 3:00PM. Stopped at Rome. Took off

4:00PM. Landed Corsica 4:30PM. Hitched to 448th. Fair chow. Van also returned from Rome today. Standdown of moving. New field in Italy (near Ancona) strafed. Retired 10:00PM.

FEBRUARY 6, 1945

Awoke 7:45AM. Clear, sunny AM. Briefing 10:00AM. Had a difficult time sleeping last night. Very nervous. Combat is commencing to creep up. Oatmeal, fried eggs, bread, jelly, coffee. (40) Lt Autrey carrying 1000 lb GP's. Target is at Roveretto (Brenner Pass). Defended. Take off 11:15AM. Clear and cloudy. 11,500 feet. Beaucoup enemy fighters. Over target 1:59PM. ME109 made a pass. Accurate flak. Yours truly dispersing chaff. Pilot and co-pilot hit. Left formation at Sestri-Levante. Landed 3:45PM. 447th last lead ship. Lt Sam Barile (co-pilot) had three stitches taken in left eye where he was hit. Autrey slight facial plexi-glass wounds. Roast beef, lima beans, peas, fruit salad, bread, jelly, coffee. Feeling fair. Received beaucoup mail. Clear, starry evening. Retired 10:00PM.

FEBRUARY 7, 1945

Awoke 7:00AM. Van had radio and lights on. Briefing at 7:35AM. Yours truly not flying. Lewis going to Rome Rest Camp. Clear sunny AM. Pancakes, syrup, oatmeal, coffee, fruit juice. John Nelson involved in selling rations and government equipment. More or less a barter deal. MP's pick up him and Gardner up in an off limits area in the mountains. Had rations in a jeep. Did not answer detail call today. Canned corned beef, rice, tomatoes, cake, bread, butter, coffee. Pick up gloves at tech supply. Clear, warm day.

Mission went to Lavis (Brenner Pass). Very rough. 1 ship missing. Lt Sheffield (P) Lt Saunders (CP) Laskow (E) Sevier (R) Reeves (B) Brentar (G). Ham, mashed potatoes, peas, apple sauce, bread, butter, coffee. Capt Burks returned from France. Clear evening. Retired 11:00PM.

FEBRUARY 8, 1945

Awoke 7:45AM. Sunny AM. Feeling fair, but somewhat nervous. Martin went to Rome Rest Camp yesterday. Fresh fried eggs, hot cereal, bacon, fruit juice, coffee, bread, marmalade. Briefing 10:25AM. Carry 1000 lb. (721) (90) Lt Autrey, pilot. Target is Calliano RR bridge in Brenner Pass. Six anti-flak ships and fighter escort. Take off 11:30AM. Partly cloudy sky. Over target at 2:05PM. Using K-1. Heavy intense and accurate flak. 918 (82) hit on bomb run. Broke away and disappeared in mountains. Many ships in distress. Our bombardier hit in head. Flak helmet saved his life. Lead navigator and bombardier injured. Lead bombardier in 447th killed. Powell engineer severely wounded in left knee. Landed 3:00PM. 100% hit on target. Lt Berkhead, Lt Saunders, S/Sgt Ratcliffe, S/Sgt Hawthorne, T/Sgt Randall, Sgt Hoverka went down with 918. No word yet from Lt Sheffield's ship. Canned pork, dehydrated potatoes, canned corn, vanilla pudding, bread, jelly, coffee. Colored band from Bastia playing at club tonight. Marks the second anniversary of this group being overseas. Free beer and food. All the boys are down in the dumps tonight. Miss our buddies. Clear, starry night. Retired 10:30PM.

FEBRUARY 9, 1945

Joe Ryan came storming in about 7:50AM. Clear, sunny AM. John got quite stinking from drinking. Fresh, fried eggs, oatmeal, bacon, bread, jelly, fruit juice, coffee. Chow is the general run of the mill. Weather is fair. Mission bombed alternate at Mantua. 100%. No Flak. No Fighters. Feeling fair. Been thinking a lot about the folks and Shyrle. Nothing special took place today. 1st shift of guard.

FEBRUARY 10, 1945

Usual morning arising chow etc. Abecunas and I left for 340th. Visited Lozowski and Usher. Both are OK. Saw Thomas and Gifford in the 487th. The boys have to fly 70 missions. Saw Alley Baine. Flying #4 bombardier. Returned squadron 5:00PM. Rode part of the way back in truck loaded with freshly cut trees. Clear sunny day.

FEBRUARY 11, 1945

Awoke 6:15AM. Briefing 8:25AM. Fresh fried eggs, oatmeal, bread, fruit juice, coffee. Standdown on missions. Van and I went out to line to take pictures. Windy. Capt Furey assigned to group as assistant operations officer. Major Newman left for home after completing 75 missions. Nothing special happening today. Reading "God's Little Acre" by Erskine Caldwell. Clear, starry evening. Retired 10:00PM.

FEBRUARY 12, 1945
Awoke usual hour. Standdown on mission. Nothing special happening.

FEBRUARY 13, 1945

Awoke 6:00AM. Briefing 7:10AM. Carry 500 lb GP's. #84 (Autrey, pilot) Lovis Rail Diversion. Lead 2nd element. Over target 10:15AM. Moderate accurate heavy flak on first pass. Did not drop. Similar flak on second pass - 100% although someone dropped stray bombs. Air is always rough in Brenner Pass. Jerries also threw up phosphorous bombs. P-47 cover. Partly cloudy weather - warm weather. Autrey doing swell. Landed 12:00PM. Stood formation for presentation of medals by General Knapp. Waited on the old boy for two hours. Lt Bard and Zinhand made captain today. Lt Cannon insisted on my drinking Paul Jones with him.

FEBRUARY 14, 1945

Awoke 7:10AM. Cloudy AM. On nickeling mission. Other mission going back to Lavis. Fresh fried eggs, hot cereal, bread, fruit juice, coffee. Target is in Florence-Bologna area. G-46 (94) Lt Zakopscan, pilot. Autrey co-pilot. Checking Zakopscan out. Following left wing third element. Dropped at three different release points. Take off 11:00AM. Landed 1:00PM. Over enemy territory for about 10 minutes. Mission to Lavis made out OK. One incendiary ship came back with 82 holes. No one injured. Another was hit in the bomb bay on the bomb run. A phosphoric bomb caught on fire. Bombardier (Qualls) went in bomb bay and finally got rid of bomb. Smoke and fire was extremely dangerous as both gas tanks were hit and leaking. Weather is warm. Feeling OK. Punching bag again. Commenced reading Wagner's "Faunhaueser." Retired 9:30PM.

FEBRUARY 15, 1945

Van awoke me at exactly 8:00AM. Briefing 9:50AM. Heavy overcast. Target is Dogma RR bridge several miles from the Austrian border. Slightly defended. At ships for an hour. Standdown. Attended "Winged Victory." Only fair. Autrey and Atherton came over. Fairly warm evening. Retired 11:00PM.

FEBRUARY 16, 1945

CQ blowing whistle awoke me at 6:40AM. Fairly light. Heavy overcast. General Cannon (2 star) to present group with "Battle Streamers." Briefing 7:45AM. Target is same as yesterday. Co-pilot (Lt Beekman) found huge gash in our right tire. Engineering went to work immediately changing it. Awaited several hours at ship finally a standdown. Did not attend formation. Group is on the alert again - to move. Retired 11:00PM.

FEBRUARY 17, 1945

Awoke 6:45AM. Cloudy AM. Briefing 8:45AM. Target is Dogma town RR bridge. Hung around ships until 10:46AM. Engine time. (530) Lt Ivory - pilot. Take off 10:55AM. Heavy overcast until we reached Elba. Met fighters at Rimini at 12:35PM. Primary weathered in. Bombed alternate at Pernome at 1:26PM. Milk run. Beautiful fighter escort. Vapor trails all over sky. Landed 3:15PM. New men arrived today. Attended "Saratoga Trunk". Good picture. Retired 10:00PM.

FEBRUARY 18, 1945

Awoke 8:00AM. Briefing 9:50AM. Target is Bressarone, Italy. Northern Brenner Pass. Over enemy territory about 456 minutes. Clouded in. Did not drop. Cloudy mission (#47). Preparing for trip to Cairo tomorrow.

FEBRUARY 19, 1945

Steve Bernschi (CQ) woke me at 5:00AM. Still dark. Early chow - eggs and coffee. Take off in 529 at 7:55AM. Capt Grady and Bard - pilots. S/Sgt Law, S/Sgt Magyar, S/Sgt Markiewicz, T/Sgt Bruse, T/Sgt Qualls, T/Sgt Beek. Carrying K20 taking pictures en route. Stopped at Bergesi to refuel and eat. Saw the harbors and cities of Tunis, Tobruk, Bergasi and Cairo. Weather en route fair. Landed 5:55PM. Changed lire to piastres at finance. 1 pound ($4.13) 1 piastre (.04). Staying at Hotel Adelphi tonight. Ate a fine meal including strawberries and cream. All the Egyptians are money crazy. Retired 12:00AM.

FEBRUARY 20, 1945

Awoke 9:30AM. Ate breakfast at New Star Restaurant. Ali Babi as our guide and protector calls himself, is dressed in regular night gown Mohammedan style. Purchased Cairo boots. Hired Taxi - went to bazaar (poor business section). Purchased Chanel #5 perfume at $4.00 per ounce. Visited pyramids, sphinx and saw King Farouk's new home in the making. Ate supper at Sphinx. Fried chicken and all the trimmings. Took pictures. Fairly warm - women dressed in all black and half veil covering the face. Very common. Spending most of our time with officers.

Very few GI's. Mostly British. Ate supper again at the Star Restaurant. Had a fine manicure, shave and haircut. City is very modern and the food is excellent. Attended night club. Saw good floor show. Ate in night club. Took a hack back to hotel. Ate again. Evenings are fairly cool. Guide to pyramid's name is Moses. Preparing to leave for Tel-Aviv tomorrow. People still follow ancient customs and speak many languages, especially French. Five of us sleeping in one room. (45 piastres each per night). Feeling fine - retired 1:00AM.

FEBRUARY 21, 1945

Awoke 9:00AM. Ate a very heavy breakfast. Eggs, cheese, tomatoes, bread, butter, french fried, etc. Very sunny and warm. Said so long to Ali Babi and Moses. Take off at 2:20PM. Took shots of pyramids with K-20. Saw Suez Canal. Landed Lydda Field, Tel-Aviv at 3:30PM. Warmly received. Picked up rations. Called Mrs. Fish. Accommodations at American House. Very clean and modern hotel. Also eating meals there. The people are very friendly, intelligent and speak English. Brusa and I went to night club at the beach facing the Mediterranean Sea, known as the San Remo Cabaret. Met Capt Grady and Bard. Had to shake a civilian. Fair floor show. No rye or scotch. Drank brandy. Cover charge for soldiers 40 mills. Anxious to date a decent girl. No begging, fighting. Women or the like on the streets at night. Mrs. Fish is formerly of Brooklyn, New York.

FEBRUARY 22, 1945

My nights aren't exactly restless, but I awoke often during the night. Very sunny, but windy. We are eating out. Brusa and I separated from the rest of the boys. Roaming the business section. Registered with British CMP (Corp of Military Police). Every person entering Tel-Aviv must do similar as every guest!! whereabouts must be known. The ocean is very rough. The streets, buildings, etc. are all exceptionally clean. Made the acquaintance of a very attractive British WAC of the ATS (Auxilliary Territorial Service). Took her to dinner. Her home is in France and in on leave from her base in Alexandria. Started out making the rounds. Many of the night clubs are occupied by private parties. Brusa, Lili and I got quite drunk and we didn't behave too well. Sometimes one brandy does things to one. However, we did no harm to Lili. We traveled by taxi most of the evening. Lost Brusa at the oceanfront for a spell. How I ever managed Brusa and myself is something I cannot understand. Retired 11:40PM.

FEBRUARY 23, 1945

Awoke 9:15AM. Feeling OK. Still waking the way I always do - off and on. Mrs. Fish changed our room from #21 to #16. Now we have a private shower. Went out to Telewinsky airfield and picked up our rations. Uncle Sam runs regular GI bus service. Strong winds and rain. Eating at the American House. As a rule we have steak, chops, or chicken. Turkish or American coffee is available. American scotch or rye is to be had from 3 1/2 pounds and up. Been having shaves and facials and shampoos regularly. Anxious to meet some nice girls. Those that I have seen are most attractive and decent. Prices on most everything are very steep. Seems almost impossible that 30 years ago this place was nothing but desert. Refugees from all over Europe are located here as well as military personnel. Eating fine steak and chicken dinners prepared by Mrs. Fish. Magyar and I attended "Road to Frisco" at theater in square. All cinemas are in English. Movie was OK. Still raining. Took a cab home (200 mills). Retired midnight. (Talked with Mrs. Fish).

FEBRUARY 24, 1945

Markewicz awoke me at 6:15AM. All of us left for tour this AM (350 mills). Went by GI truck. Strong wind and rain. Visited Jerusalem, Bethlehem and absorbed many of the sights with a guide. We ascended about 2700 feet and it was snowing. Countryside very beautiful. Visited the Church of the Nativity, Cavalry Hill, Galilee, Tomb of Christ, Virgin Mary and many other sites. Ate dinner at the YMCA in Jerusalem. Very cold and rainy. Trip was about 100 miles round trip. Returned to Telewinsky Field at 4:30PM. Ate at the American House. "Z" invited me to party at Miss Eliza Shoham, 27 Hasmal St. Stayed several hours. Listened to American music, danced a little. Had a fair time. Retired 12:00AM.

FEBRUARY 25, 1945

Awoke 9:00AM. Cloudy AM. Feeling tired but enjoying myself. Did a bit of shopping. Bought a book for Shyrle by Leopold Stein. Bought several watches. Very modern and heavily stocked shopping district. Boys went out and made the bars. Had supper at the Yarden Hotel as the guests of Capt Grady and Bard. Chamber music while eating. Steak dinner. We all adjourned to the Bohemian club for a bit of night life. Drank white wine. Got a bit tight. Retired 1:30AM.

FEBRUARY 26, 1945

Awoke 9:15AM. Showered. Noticed red dry blotches
on my shoulders and arms. First developed these in
Cairo. Drinking a lot of orange juice and eating fruit.
We all went horseback riding this afternoon at
Gordon's riding academy. Had a swell time. Rode
through the orange groves. Very fast and smart
looking horses. Attended the Eden cinema. Saw
"Swiss Family Robinson". Poor theater - poor facilities.
Brusa and I walked out in the middle of the show.
There are many coffee shops about Tel-Aviv. Capt
Brady and Bard were over for supper. Everyone was
pleased. The boys went out for a few drinks, but yours
truly remained at the hotel to write a few letters.
Retired early.

FEBRUARY 27, 1945

Awoke 9:00AM. Resting most of the day and relaxing.
Being Purim, everyone is celebrating and the children
are masquerading as we do during Halloween. Brusa
and I attended RAF band concert at the Services Club
at the waterfront. The waterfront is where all the night
clubs are located and has a good reputation. Band
was excellent and played all American popular dance
tunes. Brusa and I sat up and talked until 2:00AM.

FEBRUARY 28, 1945

Markewicz awoke me at 7:30AM. We are leaving for
Alexandria today. Heavy rain. Paid my bill which
came to 9 1/2 pounds ($36.00) Had great difficulty in
starting the ship. Finally took off at 12:45PM. Landed
Cairo, gassed the ship and purchased a few gifts at the
PX. Landed Alexandria 5:50PM. Staying at American

Red Cross club #4. Formerly home of a very wealthy Syrian. Very clean quarters and meals are OK. 7 of us in one large room. This house entertained five kings. Attended dance at Red Cross club #3. Very smart club. Met Jeanette, Red Cross girl from Savannah, Georgia. Retired 11:30PM.

MARCH 1, 1945

Awoke 8:30AM. Slept very comfortable. Took in tour of city from 10 to 12. Visited ruins of Pompeii, etc. Picked up case of Ringer's ale for Van. Visited waterfront. Very clean. Attended "Up in Arms" at the Rio theater. No cushions on seat. American talkie with French and Hebrew on side slides. Excellent weather. Retired 12:00AM.

MARCH 2, 1945

Awoke 8:10AM. Good chow. Took off noon. Gassed up at Benghazi. Landed Tripoli 4:30PM. Saved 1 hour on time. Staying overnight at ATC hotel. Majority of people are Jewish. Attended "Cargo of Innocents" at Union theater. City in blackout. Very clean and many park areas. All of the many places we visited have many Negroes, Arabs and the like. Nothing like dear old America. Retired 11:30PM.

MARCH 3, 1945

Awoke 9:00AM. Ate at caf, on the main drag. Picked up our PX rations. Raining. Exchanged our Tripolian lire for Italian lire. Purchased coke and beer (6.00) Take off 2:15PM. Ran into several storms. Plane flies like a top. Went to 12,200 to override storm. Landed Corsica 5:45PM. Very clear. Boys have been telling us about some rough missions. Woody Sheffield and crew landed in Switzerland and are on their way to the states. Lew Reeves is in hospital up there. Was wounded in the arm. Sorta glad to be back - yes and no. Packages and beaucoup mail were waiting. Retired 11:20PM.

MARCH 4, 1945

Awoke 7:10AM. Finding it more difficult to sleep as the days progress. Very sunny AM. Briefing 9:10. Lead spare. Filled in as left wing last element of 446th. Target is Ala rail bridge in Brenner Pass. The lead of our element was a sad pilot. Flew at 11,500. Very clear but cold. One burst of flak. Hit target. Take off 10:30AM. Landed 2:30PM. Autrey stopped in tonight to tell me of the good news. He is leading a flight of six. Clear, starry night. Major Knieval is in hospital in France. Retired 11:30PM.

MARCH 5, 1945

Awoke 7:00AM. Standdown on mission. Read Il Traviata. Can't seem to get used to the food after being in Cairo and vicinity. On first shift of guard. Entrance guard. All guards on the alert as a German prisoner escaped from the Bastia prison camp. Retired 11:30PM.

MARCH 6, 1945

Awoke 7:00AM. Briefing 8:10AM. Target is Campo RR Bridge in Brenner Pass. This target is where an 88 mil. shell exploded in the nose of a 445th ship. Blowing nose completely off. Lt Autrey leading second box of six. Primary closed in. Bombed alternate in Po

Valley. Missed target. Lt Cannon, bombardier. Took off 10:18AM. Landed 12:45. Feeling very nervous and upset. Do not feel as though I can fly required number of missions. Clear, starry evening. Retired early.

MARCH 7, 1945

Awoke 7:00AM. Briefing 8:10. Flying lead spare. Lt Autrey, pilot. Lt Stout, navigator, Lt Cannon, bombardier. Filled in lead of last element. Primary is at Longarone in Brenner Pass. Primary weathered in. Hit alternate 100% (East Mantua Rail Bridge). Feeling quite nervous on missions.

MARCH 8, 1945

Awoke 6:00AM. Clear sunny AM. Briefing 7:20AM. Pilot is Lt Bechtle. Target is Roveretto RR bridge. Flew right wing. Lead element. Group CO Lt Colonel Cassidy flying co-pilot in lead ship. Weather was bad and why the formation did not turn around was because of impressing the colonel. At IP, weather broke and was clear over target. 100% hit. Our right engine was hit and sprang an oil leak. Lost about four gallons of oil on way back. Made it with feathering. This was my 51st mission. Still punching the light bag every day. Finished "This is Your War," Ernie Pyle. USO show at group theater. But who wants to go several hours in advance in order to get a seat. Retired 11:00PM.

MARCH 9, 1945

Awoke 7:40AM. This is a day off for the 448th. Very clear and warm. Commenced "Show Me a Land," Clark McMeekin. Had a short meeting at NCO club.

Lt Stevens, newly arrived observer from states, in charge. Attended movie strictly for the 448th. Pertained to the indoctrination of combat life of an army Chaplain. Attended nightly movie at group theater "Meet Me in St Louis". Slight showers toward late evening. Retired 10:30PM after downing a few drinks at club.

MARCH 10, 1945

Awoke 7:40AM. Clear, sunny AM. Briefing 9:30AM. Pilot Autrey (82) 112. Leading last element of first flight. Target is at Stoz in Brenner Pass. Rail junction. Take off 10:30. Over target at 12:30PM. 100% hit. One hole in our left tail. Right wing ship badly shot up. Escorted it home. Sculley is pilot (87) 538. Crash landed at our field. No one injured. All the boys are complaining about flying 70 missions. Feel it is too many. Put in my 52nd mission. Very nervous. Pray constantly. Clear evening. Retired 11:00PM.

MARCH 11, 1945

Awoke 7:15AM. Clear sunny AM. Briefing 8:50AM. Flying 112 (82). Target is in Brenner Pass. Defended. Lt Autrey, pilot. F/O Rutz, bombardier, F/O Lang, navigator. Leading second box of six. Primary was hit by first flight. We did not bomb because of turbulence and lack of altitude. First flight missed target. Spitfire escort. Made two passes at alternate. Pissicotore RR Bridge. About seven miles from Piscenza. 100% hit. Lt Crisp, lead of 446th almost collided with us in forming mission over field. Flak was heavy, moderate accuracy at primary. None at primary. One 88mm shell went directly through right wing of Ruben's ship.

Two ships had hung bombs. Qualls down in bomb bay again. Retired 11:30PM.

MARCH 12, 1945

Today is a day of rest for the 448th. Other squadrons in the group are out on missions. Very warm and sunny. Pulled 1st shift of guard. Clear evening. Retired 11:30PM.

MARCH 13, 1945

Briefing 8:40AM. Flying lead with Capt Lyons. Leading group. Altitude 12,000. Throwing out chaff. Target is Rail Bridge at Avio in Brenner Pass. First time we hit the target. Milk run. Clear, sunny day. First day I haven't worn heavy boots and pants since last fall. 100% hit on target. Lt Gardner, bombardier, Lt Steely, navigator.

MARCH 14, 1945

Briefing 8:20AM. Flying 82. Lt Autrey, pilot, Lt Sutton, bombardier, Lt Stout, navigator. Target is at Campo RR Bridge. Supposed to be very hot. Nine incendiary ships. Over target at 12:00PM. Flak is inaccurate. 100% hit on target. Yours truly very nervous. 55th mission. Very indifferent attitude toward Autrey lately. I Don't know whether flying lead has gone to his head or just what's happened.

MARCH 15, 1945

Capt Marshall, flight surgeon, took me to field hospital for x-rays. Back and chest has been bothering me more than ever. Resulted from Galliate raid. I seem to be getting weaker as the days go on. However I do not want to quit flying. Very nervous, cannot sleep. Stood formation for presentation of awards by Major General Cannon and Brigadier General Knapp over at 445th last night. Retired 10:00PM. 321st celebrated 2nd year in combat.

MARCH 16, 1945

Target for today was to be at Mulhdorff. Standdown. Feeling weaker and weaker. No sleep. Attended "Dark Waters."

MARCH 17, 1945

Briefing at 8:50. Target is Ora - Brenner Pass. Nine incendiary ships. Lt Autrey, pilot, Lt Sutton, bombardier. Primary socked in. Sweated out the mountains. God, I can't seem to control myself. Made two passes at alternate. 100%. Retired 10:00PM.

MARCH 18, 1945

Very restless night. Feeling nervous. Very bad dream about ditching. Briefing 7:35AM. Target is Ora - Brenner Pass. Target area is covered. Alternate also covered. 57th mission. Doctor Marshall grounded me temporarily.

MARCH 19, 1945

Not on today's mission. Hung around all day. Wrote a few letters. Very nervous. Pains in chest constant.

MARCH 20, 1945

Taking codeine to sleep. Very nervous. Spasmodic
sleep. Awoke 6:00AM. Briefing 9;50AM. On Shoran
mission. Bombing by radar. Target is Spilimbergo
ammunition dump. Felt very nervous and on several
occasions I wanted to leave the ship. Made three
passes at target. Did not drop. Spitfire escort. Carry
10 lb GP's. Spoke to Lt lee to be taken off tomorrow's
mission. Doctor Marshall has not been in all evening.

MARCH 21, 1945

Routine day. Very sunny and clear.

MARCH 22, 1945

Routine day. Very sunny and clear.

MARCH 23, 1945

Routine day. Very sunny and clear. Boys are
bombing Austria. Yours truly has been doing a bit of
drinking lately. Sorta helps me to sleep. Reading "So
Little Time" - John P Marquand.

MARCH 24, 1945

Clear and sunny. Went to 15th field hospital with Lt
Autrey and Cpl Denby as blood donors for Sgt Powell
who was seriously wounded FEBRUARY 8th over
Lavis. Wounded in right thigh. This made his second
blood transfusion. He is going to be OK. Had a haircut
by wing barber. Longing to get home more than ever.
It's sure going to be wonderful to see the family and be

with Shyrle. I only hope I haven't changed. My lost weight can be regained. My chest still bothers me.

MARCH 25, 1945

Cloudy and windy. Donald Weeks (tentmate) and I started hitching to 340th. After waiting several hours to get a ride, we returned to the squadron.

MARCH 26-30, 1945

These five days are compacted as nothing special has happened. I have been grounded by the flight surgeon. Aside from reading which I have done very little lately, I only sack it up. Evenings are usually spent at the bar. I am very restless. No appetite. Sleep little. Getting ready to move to our new field at Folkenara, Italy. Some parts of our group are getting ready to move. Visit Taylor quite regularly. Weather is beautiful. My longing to be with Shyrle is stronger than ever. Not observing Passover. However, each man of the faith was allotted two boxes of Matzos. Prepared by Goodman and distributed by the Jewish Welfare Board to fellows overseas. 321st Mitchell bombers are doing fine in the basketball league. After winning island championship, they next defeated all contestants at Naples. At Florence, they defeated the Navy team from Oran but were beaten by the Aviation engineers. Bombers defeated the A's, colored team from fifth Army. Tonight they defeated the Aviation engineers - 35 to 27. Slightly polluted from a champagne party at 445th. To see Major Farwell tomorrow.

MARCH 31, 1945

Presentation of awards canceled again as the "Wheels" are attending the championship basketball game at Florence. Orders to start tearing down tents.

APRIL 1, 1945

Easter Sunday. Nothing special happening. Beginning to tear down tents, etc. Burning everything we are not taking with us. Not giving anything to Corsicans. GI's giving beaucoup candy and stuff to kids that roam through area.

APRIL 2, 1945

Area guards posted to keep civilians out of area. Loading C47's and B25's as transports to our new field at Talkenara, Italy. Invested a few dollars with Don Weeks in crap game. Lost. Weather is cloudy but warm. Very anxious to get home and to Shyrle. No official word pertaining to my being grounded. Haven't flown in two weeks. Very restless. Unable to concentrate or read.

APRIL 3, 1945

B-25's and C47's continually hauling stuff to new base at Falconara, Italy. Yours truly helping to lead. Burning lumber and unusable material. Officers eating with enlisted men as the officer's mess hall is down. LT's at Bastia to form convoy and haul equipment not portable by plane. Land at Leghorn and travel 365 miles overland to Talkenara. Mountainous country. Don't have any desire to eat or sleep. Extremely nervous. Weather is excellent.

APRIL 4, 1945

Loaded plane in AM. Pulled 4 hours area guard in the PM. Keeping out civilians and guarding against fires. Had to ask a couple of pretty females to vacate the area. Touch luck. Been visiting Taylor at 445th quite often. Disposed of some personal articles. Sent home $90.00 Was paid $100. Been trying to get an appointment with Major Farwell regarding my being grounded. Ike unable to make appointment as Major is extremely busy with move and nightly social events.

APRIL 5, 1945

Ripped up floor of tent. Fires burning all day. Advanced echelon moved. Hanging around area - goofing off. Missions have been milk runs lately. Primary is always closed in. Alternate used. Seward, Vick, Magyar left for the states.

APRIL 6, 1945

Departed for Falconara at 1:30PM. Nine men per plane. Nine ship formation. Very nervous in flight. Bad weather. Landed 4:30PM. This base was formerly operated as a Fascistic airfield. The British took over with the advance of the Eighth Army last AUGUST and now we are taking over. All types of American and British planes operate from this base. From this time on the majority will be B25's. Our quarters are within a compound. In fact the entire group is a wide corridor flanked on either side by eight large doorless rooms which hold about 300 men. The buildings are of stone and cement and are always chilly and damp inside. The officers are in tents. The field is about a mile from the compound. One taxi strip handles the traffic of the group. A narrow steel matted runway suffices for the present. 7000 feet. Running water and Italian type toilets are with the building. However hot water is not available. The officers and enlisted men will continue to eat together until mess hall facilities are completed. Our quarters are cleaned by Italians. Retired 10:30PM.

APRIL 7, 1945

Awoke 6:45AM. Slept OK for the first time in many weeks. Commenced reading Leo Tolstoy's Anna Karenina. Went out to line to watch mission take off. Briefing hut was formerly a theater. Very comfortable setup. Weather is excellent. Feeling the best I've felt in many weeks. Regaining appetite. Van and I walked to Falconara. Were propositioned by an Italian civilian regarding a female. Wanted $5.00 and two packages of cigarettes. Walked about town sizing up the situation. Quite warm. Railroad (main line) runs along seashore. All the boys buying champagne. Gets dark about 8:30PM. We are about 80 miles from the front lines. Met Raymondo, Italian professor on way back. Teaches at Ancona - a former Italian naval base and second largest seaport on the Adriatic. Accompanied him to his house. Lives with his brother in his parish attached to the church. The priest showed us the church and we were invited to the house. Met his elderly mother and young sister (bella). Drank wine and promised to return Monday night. Wants to fix us up with women. Left at 10:00. Church is about 1/4 mile west of field. Very pleasant people. Retired 11:00PM.

The True Diaries of Irving J. Schaffer

APRIL 8, 1945

Awoke 7:00AM. Slept well. Reading in sunlight. Food seems to taste better over here. At present our mess hall is on the rear porch and center of the two wings of our quarters. It is open air. The kitchen is in a large room, one side being exposed for serving. A Neissen hut with a cement floor will be used upon completion. Officers and GI's are sweating out chow lines. British quarters are to our right and to our left are British showers which are quite welcome until ours are put up. A ten foot wall surrounds the compound. All the 321st group is within the compound. It is quite spacious and enough open space to play ball as we do. The original Italian latrines remain and they are indeed uncomfortable. A supportless squat is required. Just a few yards away a British mobile army laundry cares for the clothes of the Eighth Army boys. Steam as well as electric trains run just across the way from camp. Mussolini's body is on view in the square in Milan. Rumors are circulating to the effect that Hitler is dead and Himmler is to accept unconditional surrender.

APRIL 10, 1945

CQ (Kures) blowing whistle at 5:00AM. Briefing 5:40AM. Didn't sleep well. Read until 1:00AM. Ship #77. Capt Lee, pilot, Major Farwell, co-pilot. Lead ship, lead group. Carrying 500 lb bombs. 48 ship. Target is at Longostrino, Italy supporting the ground troops. Hit target. No flak. Gun positions (artillery). Warm. Not nervous. Take off 7:45. Over target 9:00AM. Landed 9:45AM. (59th mission). Briefing for PM missions 12:50PM. Capt Leonard, pilot. Lead flight. Carrying frags (#77 ship.) Target is reserve German troops in front line area. Clear, warm weather. Take off 2:45. Target time 4:00. Landed 4:45. Flak. Did not drop due to malfunction in bomb sight. (Lt Brink, bombardier). Did not have any trouble on transmission on either mission. "Jerry" tried to block me out (60th mission). Feeling tired but OK. Moved to right wing of bldg into bay #8. Combat and group men separated. Retired 8:30PM.

APRIL 11, 1945

CQ (Tip) blowing whistle at 5:30AM. Briefing 6:50AM. Ship #86. Lt Autrey, pilot. Lt Colonel Young, co-pilot. Lt Armstrong, bombardier. Carrying frags. Lead. Take off 8:00AM. Over target 9:15AM. Flak. Landed 10:00AM. Did not drop. Wire from invervolometer to bomb bay burned. Feeling OK but tired. Been trying to write to Shyrle for three days. Feeling pretty good. Eating better. Taking Atebrine. Spoke with Doc about finishing at 65. No definite answer.

APRIL 12, 1945

Awoke 7:00AM. Briefing 8:20AM. Carrying 1000 lb GP's. Target is 3 open railway bridges at Martobor, Yugoslavia. Heavies lost five ships over target yesterday. 40 x 1000 ft. Heavily defended. 12 phosphorus ships. Tail end Charlie. Lt Akers, pilot #17 Over target 11:30AM. In flak for approximately five minutes. Several holes in radio compartment. Missed target. Yours truly did get photos. Carrying K20. 446th lost ship over target. Some bombs dropped in city. General Tito says bridge is a must. Wasn't a bit nervous. Seem to be enjoying chow. Van and I went to Ancona to meet Raymondo. Found Doctor Occipinti at home. Via Goito K - 4 P2V. Met his two daughters, Georga (24) Oga (22) and son Alberto (17) and wife. Very pleasant people and nice home. The doctor was a Captain in the medics of the Italian army. Drank some wine, batted the breeze awhile. Stopped in at the YMCA for a snack. Mostly British. Hitchhiked back to camp (8 miles). Walked about three miles. Clear, starry evening. Curfew in town 10:00PM. Very heavily bombed. Raymond left before we arrived.

APRIL 13, 1945

Standdown on mission. Reading Somerset Maugham's "The Razor's Edge." Getting a slight sunburn. Officers constructing tents. Visited the Padre with Van. Made appointment with Raymondo for Monday night in Ancona. Van and I have been contributing to the kitty of the church. Noticed disgusting habit of Raymondo spitting on floor in his home. Retired 11:00PM.

APRIL 14, 1945

Mission taking off awoke me. Partly cloudy. Hanging around most of the day reading, writing, etc. Received a book from Shyrle named "Hello Man". Written by a Unitarian minister who Shyrle has heard on several occasions. Chatted for a while with an English guard. Irish and Scottish lads. Pulled first shift of guard 7-11PM in area.

APRIL 15, 1945

Sleeping quite well lately. In fact I'm feeling good. Briefing 7:05AM. Major Farwell, pilot. Lt Armstrong, bombardier. Lt Steely, mavigator. Leading group. Carrying 1000 lb GP's. Target is bridge at Steineck, Austria. Mountains still heavily covered with snow.

Seemed good to go by the Brenner Pass for a change
rather than to go over it. Primary closed in. Fairly
cold. Hit alternate at Ostiglia, Italy bridge. Ran into
some rough weather on way back. Rather liked the
mission. Milk run. Take off 10:00AM. Landed
2:30PM. Played softball. Visited Raymondo. His
sister did Van's laundry. We always bring them
something. Met three English soldiers at Raymondo's.
One, a very boastful and talkative chap bent my ear.
Yours truly and Van just listened and departed early.
65th mission.

APRIL 16, 1945

Awoke when boys got up for briefing and got up at
7:45 as the roar of our B25's taking off made me fully
awake. I haven't mentioned our diet for many weeks
as it continues the same and still does today. Cloudy
all AM. Spoke to Major Bursks about finishing up.
Grounded me and said he would talk to Major Farwell.
Laying about in the sun.

APRIL 17, 1945

Sleeping a little better than usual. Played a little
softball. Hazy weather. God how much I want to get
home and see the folks and Shyrle.

APRIL 18, 1945

Usual run of the day. Developed infection in my left
big toe. Lt West, Lt Beckman, Van and I went to the
home of some people whose acquaintance we
previously made. Dinner was delicious - spaghetti,
wild duck, rabbit, fresh salad, bread and beaucoup
wine. Hitchhiked to and from camp. Money was out

of the question. The home is in a small stone structure typical of European peasants. Many of these people were Partisans.

APRIL 19, 1945

Major Burks spoke with the CO and the decision is left in my hands as to whether I fly or not. Want my answer tomorrow. At first I thought I might continue on, but my luck is about ended. Will give a negative answer tomorrow. German pilot landed on crash strip this evening at our field (ME 109). Sick and tired of war. It was a strip down reconnaissance job. Little stiff from playing ball several nights back.

APRIL 20, 1945

Regular run of day. Commenced "War and Peace" by Tolstoy. Went over to 446th with Taylor. Capt Kimball, Baird, Abecienos, Taylor and yours truly commenced drinking in Capt Kimball's tent. Gin, Italian whiskey, wine, combat whiskey and what not. Later on Capt Crisp. Lt Fisher, Lt Schneitzer and quite a few of the other boys we trained with in the states came over. Quite a drunk party. Still don't remember how I got home.

APRIL 21, 1945

Awoke with sore throat and feeling punk in general. Been soaking my infected toe. Finally opened up and beaucoup pus came out.   Just loafing around, reading, sun bathing, etc. The group has been flying 2 and three missions a day. Many replacements are coming in and many are finishing up. New men seem fairly decent.

APRIL 22, 1945

Van flew again today, making it his 65th. We visited the doctor in Ancona. Had a very enjoyable evening. Walked about the residential district of town. Most of the city is pretty well bombed out. Women are quite attractive and dress well. Many Fascists still are about. Women want nothing to do with soldiers. After light afternoon showers, the weather turned very cool. Took GI truck back to base.

APRIL 23, 1945

After breakfast I retired to the sack again. Spent the PM in the sun. Jim Morefield injured over Roveretto returned from hospital. Finished flying. Played ball. Taylor, Van and I attended "To Have or Not to Have" with Lauren Bacall, Humphrey Bogart at group theater. Midnight snack - sardines, cheese and Mrs. Peshind's cookies.

APRIL 24, 1945

Laying about reading, writing etc. Van and I went to Ancona. Visited ack-ack positions covering city. 40 and 90 mm American guns but are manned by British. Ancona supplies the Eighth Army. That is perhaps the reason for so heavy defenses. Walked throughout the higher hills looking over radio and radar equipment. British sailors and American colored MP's almost got in a brawl. Some "limey" tossed a bottle through the nigger's club front door window. Returned to camp 10:15PM. Midnight snack.

APRIL 25, 1945

Slept like a log last night. Getting back to my old self.
Rained in the PM. Went to supper in Falconara.
Woman who works for British laundry unit and who
also does my laundry invited Van and I to supper.
Spaghetti with chopped meat. Beef, bread, wine,
finoccio. Decent meal. Two sons are American
prisoners of war in Tunisia. They live in lower three
rooms of a three story apartment house on main drag.
All the homes are cold and unheated. Her husband
works in the compound, cutting hair, shining shoes,
etc. In the evening he works at his pre-war
occupation, tailoring. It is not permissable to allied
troops to eat or drunk in civilian cafes or houses. So
what. Van and I departed 9:30PM.

APRIL 26, 1945

Sleeping pretty well, eating fair and feeling better than
I have felt for a long time. Worked on ration detail
about 1 hour. Sweated out evening show from 8:00PM
until 9:45. "Uncertain Glory" - fair. Our new chow hall
is a Venetian hut - painted white and olive drab.
Rigged up showers.

APRIL 27, 1945

After breakfast I retired back to the sack until
11:00AM. Standdown on mission, due to bad weather.
Partisans captured Genoa, Milan, Turin and other
industrial cities. Goering resigned from Luftwaffe due
to heart trouble. I'd have the same if I were in his
shoes. Attended lecture on new evasion and escape on
Adriatic side of Italy. PI boats to be at rendezvous
points certain night hours to rescue airmen in enemy

Irv's crew from flight school before leaving the USA.

Irv's Distinguished Flying Cross (left) & Air Medal (eventually 5 Oak leaf clusters added for various acts of bravery under fire while flying).

Irv (holding machine gun) and his bomber crew in Corsica

Irv's primary job was radio operator, but he was also trained as an aerial photographer and gunner

Irv's aircraft after a crash landing in 1944, note the lack of landing gear.

Irv's fraternity brother (shown above in two pictures from the 1934 Senior Yearbook) from the Wilbur J. Lynch Senior High School's Alpha Beta Gamma fraternity, Izzy Demsky. Izzy was from the poor part of town and later wrote a book called, "The Ragman's Son," he is now better known as actor Kirk Douglas.

Irving J. Schaffer receives medals from General Knapp, the Distinguished Flying Cross, the Air Medal, and a Purple Heart.

Irv took Shyrle boating one afternoon in 1945 and, proposed to her.
Guess what she said.

territory. Presentation of awards by General Knapp. Becoming a little restless again. My orders have not gone in as yet. I imagine due to finishing on 65, I'll have to hang around awhile. Truthfully I don't mind too much as I'm getting back to my old self. However I do long for Shyrle and the folks.

APRIL 28, 1945

Weather has been the cause of the last four standdowns. Very few targets are remaining. From all aspects, the war should cease momentarily. Partisan uprisings are popping all over. Mussolini has been shot as well as his mistress and other important Fascists. They were captured at Como near the Swiss border and shot. Enjoying Tolstoy's "War and Peace'. Also read "Hamlet". Saw "Uncertain Glory." Fair. Feeling good, eating well and relaxing plenty. Usually play ball every evening. The boys left for the Cairo rest trip.

APRIL 29, 1945

"Lady" gave birth to six pups (1 died) in the barber shop. Mother and five pups doing fine. "Baby" also was due. Doc chloroformed her as she was infected with ticks. Buried her by the motor pool. Group order claims all dogs must be done away with. The boys sorta become attached to the mutts and they to the GI's. Anyone out of uniform is quickly chased from the base by the dogs. Pulled 6 hours of day guard at motor pool wall entrance. Been enjoying my pipe and an occasional cigar. No cigarettes. No more liquor. Still feel back pains. As a rule I generally retire 11:30PM. Read until the sandman sacks me in.

Lights out midnight - no noise after 10:00PM. Some joke.

APRIL 30, 1945

Hitchhiked to Ancona. Carried #116 camera. Shot the harbor, bombed building, etc. Warm partly cloudy day. Returned to camp 5:00PM. Pay call (148.00). Captain Autrey purchased several sets of sun tans for me at officer's PX ($10.00). Attended "Marriage is a Private Affair." All sexy shows are liked by GI's. Beaucoup card games going on as today is payday.

MAY 1, 1945

Sent $300 to #8. Cloudy day. Nothing special happening. War is all over in Italy. Just doesn't seem real to know the Brenner Pass is undefended. Used the inside of my sleeping bag for the first time. Saw "Summer Storm" at camp theater. Fair. No more missions to be flown.

MAY 2, 1945

Although I constantly think of Mother's Day, I keep postponing my greetings. However I did send a gift. Bob Edexer and I took a stroll about the beach and British oil and fuel dump as well as their Marshalling Yards. Took photos. Watched Italian women rolling empty 50 gallon oil drums. Many were barefoot. The photos came out quite well. Sent a parcel to #19 of personal effects. I wonder if this parcel is recensored, if it will get by. Enjoying "War & Peace."

MAY 3, 1945

Cloudy day. Stayed in the sack and read until noon. All local T canceled due to gas shortage. Brought beaucoup laundry to Falconara so as to have all clean clothes on leaving for home.

MAY 4, 1945

Rations today (1:00) Basked in the sun all PM. Van and I visited the Accipintis in Ancona. Had a little chow. Had some very delicious Italian cheese. We are to have a little private dance at their home Sunday night. We always bring them something in the line of sweets, gum, cigarettes, etc. It's very difficult to acquaint oneself with the females. Fortunately we made connections. Missed squadron truck so we caught a ride at British pick up point.

MAY 5, 1945

Flew local T for 2:20 min. Shot four landings. Basked in sun all PM. Feeling pretty good, although was quite nervous while flying. Boys returned from Cairo.

MAY 6, 1945

Regular run of the mill.

MAY 7, 1945

Peace declared. Unconditional surrender. Everyone restricted to base. This is due to a possible disturbance in and about Ancona, Falconara, etc. Flares from pistols being shot all over the place. Cassidy made full Colonel.

MAY 8, 1945

Still restricted to base. Doc Smith and his Mitchell
Airs played for one hour on base. Orchestra is
composed of group musicians. Seems like the whole
barracks is drunk. Ever since arrive at this base it's
been impossible to retire before midnight.

MAY 9, 1945

Visited Anna Maria at her home. Van and Don
accompanied me. Very smart, fine apartment. Met
her family and a few other acquaintances that stopped
in. Very pleasant people. Afterwards we went to the
Doctor's home and dined with the family. We tried
drinking some of their civilian milk. What a terrible
taste - like lozenges - smoke. Pulled morning wall
guard - 7 to 11.

MAY 10, 1945

Landed on my face resulting from a back flip. Sprained
my right hand, neck and bruised my nose. Weather is
excellent. Varga left for the states. The chow is very
good. Chicken, steak, beef, etc. are constantly being
served. Ice cream, cake, fruit, bread.

MAY 11, 1945

Been doing a lot of sunbathing and swimming in the
Adriatic. Ate supper at the Aceppenti's. Nothing
special.

MAY 12, 1945

Rations today ($1.20). Sun bathing and swimming. Attended "The Great Moment." Fair.

MAY 13, 1945

Orders came to go home. Leaving tomorrow morning. Van, Skip and I went swimming with Vincent (doctor's son) at Ancona. Very rocky coast. Afterwards we went to Anna Maria's and danced. Ate supper at the Aceppenti's. Bid them all farewell. Had a marvelous time. Promised to write and extended invitation should they ever come to the US.

MAY 14, 1945

Bid adieus to all the squadron. Left Falconara 10:15AM. Arrived Naples 11:25. Sweated out the ride. Assigned to 290th com. 22nd Bn. Sleeping in duplex building. Set up OK. Expect to be here about 10 days. Arms are sore from 3 shots I got yesterday. Weather warm and sunny.

MAY 16, 1945

Being processed and orientated. We are the first unit in the 290th co, 29 Bn. Approximately 50 of us are housed in a duplex house. Men from all walks of the Army are with us awaiting shipment to the states. Officers in charge as well as non-coms were front line troops. Our location was an intended World's Fair site for 1940. In fact it was almost completed by Mussolini. The outbreak of the war put the clamps on it.

The True Diaries of Irving J. Schaffer

MAY 17, 1945

Finishing processing. Oswald Habeck (T/S) of the combat medics and I took off for Naples without a pass as until processing is completely finished, no passes are permitted. Walked about town. Ate at GI café. Met a lot of buddies from the 321st in town. Dropped in at Soldier's Park and watched the Armed Forces struggle with the senorinas. An Italian band blaring out American tunes tried to provide music. Admission is 25 lire - females gratis.

MAY 18, 1945

Drew PX rations and clothing issue. Abrecunos, Ray, Jim, Ossie and I visited Magnolia, a small town about a mile from camp. A little Italian boy took us to some home and we drank vino. A younger daughter (17) was most attractive in a ladylike manner. Natural and without make-up. Per usual most of the Neopolitan women are shack jobs. On returning to camp several females were outside the gate propositioning the boys ($3). Abrecunios took her in the shrubs. It was a mean job but we put a flashlight on the two of them. Embarrassing moments. As a rule we retire around 10:30. Reveille is 6:30AM.

MAY 19, 1945

Spent all PM in the pool. Attended "National Barn Dance." Walked out. Went across the tracks with the boys for a drink and to have some clothes washed. Some of the boys disposed of some garments. Females still hanging around gate. Abrecunos did it again. Habeck a little sore from sunburn. Sleeping under mosquito netting - but no Atebrine. Weather is very warm.

MAY 20, 1945

Today is Sunday. Passes are permitted. Coke rations. Commenced "Leaf in the Storm" by Lin Yutang. Warm, sunny day. Beaucoup men are coming in every day. Our company at present has about 350 men. Ossie and I went to town. Did a bit of drinking.

MAY 21, 1945

Swam in pool all PM. Getting very tan. Ossie and I went to town. Visited the "Power Dive" and the PBS club on Via Roma. Met a couple of Ossie's old female friends. Had quite a time. As a rule we have been going to town on phony passes. Returned to camp next AM at 7:30.

MAY 22, 1945

Emergency rotation commencing to be alerted. Swam in pool. Vandenberg, Turney, Martin and boys from 448th arrived today. New order that first three graders are duty free sounds OK. Attended a bull session across the tracks.

MAY 23, 1945

More fellows being alerted. Ossie, Habeck and Jim Gentre alerted. Going by ATC. Infantry boys a little nervous about flying. Attended "The Glass Key".

The True Diaries of Irving J. Schaffer

MAY 24, 1945

Hanging around reading, swimming and eating well. Food is OK.

MAY 27, 1945

On alert C592-2. Pulled customs inspection. Illegally passing through my diary. Had lire exchanged for that dear old American currency. What a fine feel it has ($50). Still carrying $10 in Traveler's Cheques and $5.00 bill when I left the states. Only permitted B-4 and musette bag. Boarded "James Barbour" Liberty Ship at Naples pier. Loaded 299 veterans from all branches of the Army. The ship is sailed by a Merchant Marine crew. (1 stacker). We are situated in the aft - upper hold. Our bunks are four deep and of the navy type. While awaiting assignment to the hold, K rations were passed out on deck. An Air corps Lt Colonel and Major are troop commanders. Both are good Joes. Marty Chauncy, Carl Daniels (447th) and Oliver King, finance clerk (448th. Make a foursome for pinochle. Fresh water is available three times a day for two-hour periods. Only salt water showers. Watched the sky and sea before retiring. Thinking how very wonderful it is going to feel to be with the family and see Shyrle. I wonder if I've changed. Retired 10:00PM.

MAY 28, 1945

Awoke 8:00AM. Slept surprisingly well. Chow hours are 8-9, 12-1, 5-6. The ATS (Army Transport Service) provides its own kitchen and facilities for troops. Entirely separate from ship's crew. We are divided in groups. Each group works 1 day on rotation set up.

Not bad at all. All this bunk about returning troops eating fresh fruits, vegetables, meats, milk, etc, is a lot of bunk. Same old chow. Chow lines are long and so is the washing lines for messkits. Despite it all, every last guy is tingling with the thought of going home. Played pinochle and hearts. Drew PX rations. Cigarettes, candy, peanuts, etc. Always have to sweat out a line. The gun crews are still alerted as submarines are still about. Our ship makes 12 knots and will probably take 18 days to port. Commenced "The Apostle" by Sholem Asch. Rained the better portion of the day. Hold very stuffy. Put $40.00 in ship's safe. The enlisted men have the forward portion of the deck and the officers the aft. The crew has separate quarters. Their chow is excellent. Steaks, chops, etc. Retired 10:30PM. Feeling OK.

MAY 29, 1945

Awoke 8:15AM. Imagine eating hard boiled eggs for breakfast. C'est la guerre. Skipper came aboard via Italian craft. Got underway at 11:20AM. Goodbye to Naples and Italy and Europe. Calm sea. Slightly bumpy due to no load. We are supposed to be the first victory troops arriving via water. Clear, sunny PM. Retired 10:00PM.

MAY 30, 1945

Awoke 8:40AM. Missed most of breakfast. Played several games of chess with Harold Phares. Feeling a bit seasick. Changed from bow to amid-ship (burping). News of Japanese bombing of some US city by balloons. Passed southern tip of Sardinia. Clear, windy, cool. Decoration Day. Retired 10:00PM.

The True Diaries of Irving J. Schaffer

MAY 31, 1945

Awoke 8:10AM. Sleeping fairly well. Ship jounces about due to empty holds. School of porpoises following boat. Two stacker passed us about 2 miles away going in opposite direction. Warm, sunny day. Food is fair. Crew painted port side of upper deck. Assemble canvas over upper forward hold - sort of a tent affair. Sun is too strong for some. Did a bit of calisthenics. Sunset at 9:30PM. Retired 11:00PM.

JUNE 1, 1945

Awoke 8:25AM. Rather a restless evening. Turned watches back one hour. Spotted southern coast of Spain. Should pass the Rock of Gibraltar sometime this evening. On detail with group four. Lost two games of chess to Harold Phares. AM very clear and sunny. Rather a calm sea. Boys are discussing what they are planning when they return to the states. Some have lost fathers, mothers and sisters, brothers in battle. Others are getting a divorce. Some are going to be very, very happy and others very disappointed. As for yours truly I will wait and hope and pray. Retired 10:30PM

JUNE 2, 1945

Awoke 8:15AM. Turned watches back another hour. Passed Rock of Gibraltar at 2:00AM. Been on board one week and sailing five days. The Atlantic is considerably rougher. Some are seasick. Yours truly is keeping his fingers crossed. Brought my blanket on deck. Slept all PM. The hold is too stuffy. Wind is beginning to whip up a spray. Everything on board is orderly. Gun crews really keep their "Babies" in

shape. Played hearts most of evening. Retired
11:00PM.

<u>JUNE 3, 1945</u>

Awoke 7:25AM. Ship tossed around quite a bit last
night. Breakfast hours have been changed from 8-9 to
7-8. Partly cloudy AM. Sunbathing per usual.
Becoming quite a pinochle player. Fresh chicken for
supper (cold storage). Feeling OK. Getting anxious
about my homecoming. It does strike the sentimental
side. Ride has been exceptionally smooth. Hope the
folks aren't worrying.

<u>JUNE 4, 1945</u>

Awoke 8:00AM. Big chow line. Found out clocks have
been turned back another hour. Rather cloudy PM.
Keeping out of sun today. Feel like I might be getting
sun blisters on my lips. Had a terrific pinochle
session. Slight drizzle. Beautiful rainbow. Can see
beginning and end. Should put into port next
Wednesday. Retired regular hour.

<u>JUNE 5, 1945</u>

On detail with group #4. Did nil. Rained most of day.
General idea of chow on our liberty ship: Breakfast -
powdered eggs (unfinished) with almost baked bread,
GI coffee, sometimes dry cereal with powdered milk.
Dinner: Vienna sausage, dehydrated potatoes, diced
canned beets, GI soup, that unfinished bread again
and, oh yes, butter sometimes or jelly or peanut
butter. Coffee goes with every meal. Supper - as a
rule about the same as dinner. Unfortunately if one is
not desirous in trying to digest these victuals, one

162

must take the desperate way out - starving. Wow - how wonderful it is going to be to once again have access to the comforts of the dear old USA. Finished "The Keys of the Kingdom" by AJ Cronin. Commenced "The autobiography of Benjamin Franklin" associated with Carl Van Dorn. Nights are becoming restless.

JUNE 6, 1945

Clear, sunny day. Sunned on deck. Crew is dropping cables and painting top side. My daily exercise consists of about fifteen minutes of PT. I notice I'm about the only individual doing such. However, I feel not a bit self-conscience. For the first time the sea has commenced rolling - nothing rough. Been doing a lot of thinking lately. Marriage, army, folks, etc. Deep within I know I'm in possession of certain qualities that will show great promise. However I can't seem to surface my unknown. Been seriously considering a life of solitude away from all my previous surroundings. Returning to my previous environment is disadvantageous. I must also consider the folks. What about Jerome?

JUNE 7, 1945

Awoke 8:00AM. Clocks were set back another hour last evening. Cloudy AM. Immediately up being furloughed - phone calls and roses are in order for mother and Shyrle. Engine was cut for two fifteen-minute periods enroute today. Watched the flying fish off the port side. Many of the boys are sleeping on deck. As yet I haven't found the hold too stuffy. Made out quite well (Marty) in pinochle. A once over every other day consists of my bathing. Brush my teeth regularly. For the first time since reading it I have enjoyed Benjamin Franklin's autobiography. Retired 10:30PM.

JUNE 8, 1945

Awoke 6:55AM. Clear, sunny morning. This entry is being made at 8:07AM on deck. Passed another freighter going in opposite direction. Ship had inspection. Franklin's autobiography very dry. Marty and I took it on the chin again in pinochle. Feeling OK aside from the fact my breastbone is always sore especially when I exhale or contract my upper body. Retired 11:00PM.

JUNE 9, 1945

Awoke 7:25AM. Very windy, cloudy. Quite a choppy and rolling sea. On group #4 detail. Helped in latrine. Read "Red" by Sommerset Maugham. Also "Gambler Road," by Oppenheim and "The Prince of Jems," by Michael Arlen. Not so hot. Ran into a slight squall. Had to close up hold. Very close even with vents working. Turned clocks back another hour. Retired 10:00PM.

JUNE 10, 1945

Awoke 7:00AM. Very rocky night. Semi-clear morning. 5 more days to USA. Beaucoup rumors about. Conversed with a chap from New York most of the AM. Was studying journalism at NYU before the Army snagged him. Was a teletype and wireless operator with AFHQ in Africa and Casserta. Sea somewhat choppy. Ships radio beginning to pick up direct broadcasts from America. Played pinochle with Harry, Red, Marty. Lost. Retired 11:00PM.

JUNE 11, 1945

Bulletin says 4 more days to port. PX rations. Fair day. Passing lots of seaweed. Beat Harold two games of chess. One draw. Took a shellacking in pinochle. Calm sea.

JUNE 12, 1945

Today is Oliver King's 32nd birthday. What a good guy. Calm sea. Harry and I made out quite well in pinochle. Chest still bothering me. It's an odd situation. X-rays and examinations show nothing. Can't keep complaining. Will have to carry on.

JUNE 13, 1945

Turned watches back another hour putting us on good old USA ET time. About 48 hours from land. Oliver passed out this morning. Reoccurrence of malignant malaria. I shall assist him all I can. Doctor placed him in sick bay. Short arm this AM. Partly cloudy. On detail with group #4.

JUNE 14, 1945

Regular run of the mill. Oliver is feeling much better. Spotted buoys off coast of Virginia. Sea lanes. Chicken for supper.

JUNE 15, 1945

Dropping of anchor awoke me at 6:00AM in harbor. Hampton Roads. Pulled alongside dock at 9:30AM.

Small army band. Left ship at 11:30. Red Cross served doughnuts and lemonade. Our group comprised a 14 army bus convoy escorted by motorcycle MP's. Boys really gave the female civilians an awful going over. Arrived Camp Patrick Henry about noon. Marched to auditorium. Talked to by Colonel adjutants about camp rules. German and Italian POW's do all the chores. Rather a small looking group of prisoners. Very orderly. Our first meal was terrific. Steaks, celery, olives, mashed potatoes, all the milk you could drink, etc. Everything was tops. Supposed to ship out tomorrow noon. Called dad. Pop was all choked up. Tried to call Shyrle - lines all busy. Will try again tomorrow.

JUNE 16, 1945

Called Shyrle and I fairly shook with excitement. So near to me yet so far away. Time will tell. Orders canceled until tomorrow for departure. Chewed out by a colonel of the 9th airborne for not saluting. Rather pleasant reprimanding. Everything is nice about Camp Patrick Henry.

JUNE 17, 1945

Departed Patrick Henry via 18 car troop train at 10:15. Band in accompaniment. Trip took us 12 hours. Very hot and train was filthy. C'est la guerre. Billeted in barracks #10 at Dix. Showered and hit the sack at 2:30AM. Wow am I tired.

JUNE 18, 1945

Just hanging around. Called Geraldine. Golly it sounded and felt wonderful. Missing my screening.

Screened and up for discharge. MOS 757. 106 points.
Too good to be true. Now that such is the case, I must
see Shyrle - find out our relation - see how the folks
are doing and really buckle down. In the event
matrimony is out of the question, I MAY push off for
South American lands. There are so many angles.
Attended "Thrills of Romance" - OK. Theater #5.
Imagine no interruption of film - real seat. Stopped in
at service club dance. Just moseyed around.

JUNE 19, 1945

Dull cloudy AM. Waiting to be transferred to
"Separation Area." Sent home before bag and
equipment.

JUNE 20, 1945

Moved over to separation center.

JUNE 21, 1945

Attended USO show and boxing matches. Fair. First
day of summer. Still waiting to be put on orders.
Everything seems to be snafu-ed at this camp. Harry
Snauely (friend I met on way across) and I moved into
a room upstairs barracks 36 - 22nd co.

JUNE 22, 1945

Still not on orders. Rained hard during the night.
Cool, cloudy AM. Went through breakfast line twice.
Getting beaucoup rest. Feeling OK. Attended "Out of
this World." A bunch of laughs. Found Elliott waiting
for me when I returned. Surprised. He looks very

good. Waited almost three hours for me. Sent me two
telegrams and no dice on phone connections. Spoke
at length about the family and our future plans. He is
pushing off for Charleston, SC where his ship the
"Action" will do air-sea rescue. Took him to main gate
or should I say he took me. He knows more about this
place than I do. Departed at 1:30AM. Sure felt
wonderful to see him. Cloudy day.

JUNE 23, 1945

Still not on orders. Elliott might possibly call or come
again. Read Ernest Hemingway's "The Sun Also
Rises." Stunk. The barracks and camp set-up is
similar to Scott Field. However at this point of the
game, we are not subjected to what one might call
discipline. Snafu-ing up will only mean a delay in
discharge. Commencing to activate my stalemated
knowledge of current events. Elliott did not come.
Retired 10:00PM after a session of PT.

JUNE 24, 1945

Still not on orders. Read "Commodore Hornblower" by
CF Forester. OK. Very hot and clear day. Had a
nightmare while taking a nap this afternoon. Dreamed
plane was going to crash. Couldn't get out. Attended
Ernie Pyle's "GI Joe". Much better than the book.

JUNE 25, 1945

Put on 26-43 orders today. God how very wonderful.
To be discharged tomorrow. Very warm. Processing.

The True Diaries of Irving J. Schaffer

JUNE 27, 1945

Claim disability veteran's pension - left arch, knee, back. Passed physical OK. Final discharge at 5:45PM. Went to NYC. Called the folks. Stopped at Hotel Latham for the night. 4th and 28 East ($2.50 - both). Took 12:01 to Schenectady. Met Gerry. Quite a welcome. Home by bus at 6:00PM. Folks look OK. Very surprised to learn of Geraldine's operation and Dad's illness. Mother looks good. House looks excellent. Dona, Ken, Hermanie, Margorie, etc. were over. Glad to be back. Merriam and Dicky were waiting also. The grounds look excellent. The interior of the house has been somewhat remodeled. Mrs. Marikew passed away last Saturday. I was so anxious to see her. Mr. Plunkett has been bed ridden for almost 6 months.

JUNE 28, 1945

Awoke 7:45AM. Dicky slept with me. What a wonderful child. Gerry made appointment for me with Dr Salvatore for tomorrow at 9:00AM. [Incidentally that is this AM.) Rode down with Mr. Lewellyn and Miss Dorothy Passera. Very pleasant company. Changed one filling at my request. Teeth in perfect shape. Going to have a cap put in. Paid balance of Geraldine's bill. Notified draft board #383 of my honorable discharge and had it recorded with County Clerk. Miss Harriet Coates (very charming) took care of same. Merriam drove me to rationing board where I secured my ration books. What a lot of bother. Jack same down at 5:00PM. Looks good. Merriam expecting another youngster. Not before late next winter. Met Morry Plender at the house. Looks good. Took me down to the Greenspans and met "Goody's" wife. Golly, how his sisters have grown. Younger

brother Louis degreed in engineering and is in the
Navy. Retired midnight.

JUNE 29, 1945

Awoke 7:00AM. Had breakfast with the family. God,
how very wonderful it all seems. I needn't make
entries about the food because such delicious chow is
easy to remember. They are sure trying to fatten me.
Dressed and went downtown. Mailed an airmail
special to Shyrle. Settled an old account with the
Book of the Month club ($3.12). Elliott sent me a swell
metal watch band. Had my usual at Hills. Mr Hill
looks quite well considering his illness this past
winter. Gerry brought over Walt Maine's wife, Louise.
(Rutland VT) Very pleasant. Retired 11:00PM.
Commenced AJ Cronin "The Green Years."

JUNE 30, 1945

Awoke 7:45AM. Feeling OK. Clear, sunny AM. Visited
and shopped a bit downtown. How very wonderful this
peace and quiet is. Longing to see Shyrle. I wonder
what the outcome of our very fine and decent
friendship will be.

JULY 1, 1945

Geraldine and I missed the 10:50 bus so we made the
11:50, which was 15 minutes late. Jack, Merriam and
baby met us in G'ulle as it commenced raining.
Arrived Sacondaga about 3:00PM. Beach very
crowded. Meeting lot of faces I haven't seen in some
years. Don't particularly care about being with a lot of
people and answering questions. Not much of a young
crowd. Most all my old crowd is married. Ate at Frank

Izzo's. Converted his place into a nice restaurant.
Drove up to "Sac" again in the evening and we all went
to the Adirondack Inn and danced. Don't think I was
very good company. Perhaps too quiet. Had a few
drinks at the bar. (Scotch and soda). Kibitzed with a
discharged flight instructor. All banged up from a
crash. Merriam dances excellent. Retired 1:30PM.
Slept off "Dicky's" Room.

JULY 2, 1945

Awoke 9:10AM. Dicky asking me to get up. Cloudy
AM. Merriam keeps her home immaculate. They have
an ideal home in every way. Left for Amsterdam at
11:20AM. Met young Stone from the 7th Army. His
brother-in-law, Dick Petril killed in France. Visited
about downtown. Raining. Mom's food is wonderful.
Went down to Bill's on market St with Ken and
Hermanie. Doing as little visiting as possible. God,
how tiresome, annoying and embarrassing it is to have
people ask questions. It seems so stupid of our own
American public not to understand campaign ribbons.
Sleeping well.

JULY 3, 1945

Having my Carl Zeiss camera repaired. Took out "The
Nazarene" from the public library. Have to stop and
kibitz with many people. Morry Olender and I invited
to house party at home of Beverly Glickman in Albany
NY. Yours truly to have blind date. Party tonight.
Morry used his brother, Joe's car. 5 couples, 3 sailors
from Scotia navy depot and Morry and I and my date
Mary Rosen. Swell girl. Works on staff of
Knickerbocker News in Albany. Slightly on the stocky
side, but well packed. We got along excellently.

American liquor is OK. Stayed overnight at Beverly Glickman's, where party was thrown. This girl is very fond of Morry.

JULY 4, 1945

Didn't go to bed at all last night. One of those all night parties. Took the girls out to dinner. Headed for home about 2:00PM. Morry picked up his family in Amsterdam and we proceeded to the Sacandaga Park. Met many people on the beach. Had an invite to Teddy Blitze's place. We visited the Cramers and had some more food. Drove over to Briar's summer home in Northville. Beautiful spot. Well-kept grounds. Mrs. Carter (Mayor's wife), Mrs. Vollmer and Miss Harriet Coates were over. A merry time. Morry and I went over to the Inn. Band playing in Circus Grill. Met Gerry, Mildred and Perry. It makes me feel quite bad when I see sister Geraldine undated. She is a marvelous dancer. Sat at a table with the newlyweds of the past years or so. Danced with Lee Newert (Mrs. Richard Grey). Beautiful daughter (8 mo.) Lee looks great. Like her husband. Doesn't seem to be the crowd of old. God how very tired I am. Arrived home 1:30AM.

JULY 5, 1945

Awoke 10:45. First time I slept so late in the long time. Days don't seem to be very sunny. Commenced Sholem Asches "The Nazarene." Called Shyrle. Just couldn't wait any longer. Her voice sounded wonderful. Retired 1:30AM.

The True Diaries of Irving J. Schaffer

JULY 6, 1945

Awoke 10:45AM. Feeling OK. Made arrangement to have Dick Steward, golf pro at Municipal Golf Course to give me lessons. Starting Monday, 5:00PM. Sun bathed a while. Mike (Mary) Rosen, called me from Albany wanting to know if I were coming to Albany Saturday night. Yours truly does not knock himself out anymore. I've always wanted to be on the reserved side, classically and I am beginning to achieve such. Dana was over. Expects to join her husband in several weeks. Read, Retired 12:00AM.

JULY 7, 1945

Phone ringing awoke me at 9:25AM. Basked in sun most of day. Read "Cannery Row" by John Steinbeck. Play the recordings Shyrle sent to Geraldine. Lynne Fontaine's recitation of The White Cliffs of Dover. Supposed to have date in Albany. No dice. Can't see it. Ken and I went out and made the rounds. Pretty stinko. Retired 2:00AM.

JULY 8, 1945

Morry called from Albany at 7:10AM. To meet the gang in Schenectady. No dice on hitchhiking. All met at Evelyn Bailin's home, 1765 "A" Avenue. Left in two cars. Mrs. Bailin also came. Very fine and decent person. Yours truly dated Mary (Mike) Rosen. Picnicked at Bolton's Landing, Lake George. Swam, canoed, had a swell time. Stayed over in Schenectady.

JULY 9, 1945

Returned home. Dentist's appointment 9:00AM.
Doctor Salvatore preparing my bridge. Drilled on me
about an hour. Made another appointment for noon
today. Want to get fixed up so I can leave for Madison
soon. Visited Geraldine at Sears. Hitchhiked home.
Took golf lesson from pro (Dick Steward) at Municipal
course. Taking series of 6 lessons.

JULY 10, 1945

Hitchhiked to Schenectady for dental appointment.
Hitched back in the rain. Always seems to be a truck
that picks up soldiers. 2nd golf lesson at municipal
course. Purchased set of 7 used clubs from Joe Gray.
Dick Steward (pro) satisfied with my progress. Gerry
and I attended "Enchanted Cottage." Ice cream at
Hills. She also gave me a rumba and samba lesson.
Retired 11:00PM.

JULY 11, 1945

Went to Gloversville on 9:50AM bus. Merriam, Dicky
and I went to Robinson and Smith to get my clothes
out of storage. Sure looks good to see civilian clothes.
Dinner at Foxford Terrace. Another golf lesson this
PM. Clear, cool, windy day.

JULY 12, 1945

Eating, sleeping and feeling good. Slight stomach
disorder. May be due to readjustment to civilian life.
Shyrle is most considerate in her correspondence.
Leaving on JULY 20. Another golf lesson. Pro said I

am coming along OK. Complete relaxation. Having my usual at Hills. Ice cream and syrup.

JULY 13, 1945

Clear, sunny AM. Doctor Salvatore fitted my bridge today. Comfortable. Paid in full. Took Gerry out to dinner. Enjoying the radio immensely. House very quiet and peaceful. Mother offers a special prayer every Friday night for Grandma and Grandpa. Have my usual ice cream at Hills every evening.

JULY 14, 1945

Sunbathed until rain commenced. Morry Olender and I hit the road as in pre-war days. Annette Goldblatt, Mary Sue Rosen (yours truly) traveled to Albany. Went to Herberts. Danced and had a few drinks. This is the third date I've had with Mary (Mike) and I believe she is quite fond of yours truly. She is a very pleasant girl and a most enjoyable date. At present she is employed by the Knickerbocker News in conjunction with the sports editor. Several years at Russel Sage college. Natural intelligence. Returned home 2:30AM. Read for awhile.

JULY 15, 1945

Awoke 11:15AM. Read and played recordings and listened to the radio most of the day. Dull, rainy day. Now that the time is approaching for my much longed for visit to Shyrle, I am ever so anxious. Folks are really trying to fatten me. Yours truly might be hurting them but I don't enjoy being pampered, so to speak. Readjustment will come - gradually. Gerry worked at Sears today. Gerry and I attended "Knob Hill" at the Rialto. Fair. Enjoyable evening. Rained.

JULY 16, 1945

Played golf (9 holes) at municipal course. Partner Mort Guttenberg. Sad score. Purchased rain coat and sport jacket at stores. Paid in full. Bought some haberdashery at Mortons. Ken, Hermanie and yours truly guzzled a few in the evening. New spot called "Yells" on Perth Road. Used to chauffeur for Frank Morris. Retired 1:30AM.

JULY 17, 1945

Quite excited about my visit to Shyrle. Wonder how things will materialize. Been thinking more than ever about my future. What to do - college, work and college, etc. Jack, Merriam and Dicky came down. Left check ($100). Merriam expects another youngster this coming winter. Getting that old nervousness. Played 18 holes of golf with Sam Weisman. Sad score. Reading John Hersey's "A Bell for Adano." Not so hot. Purchasing odds and ends for my trip west. Muggy and cloudy.

JULY 18, 1945

Gerry calls me every AM before she leaves for work. Played 9 holes of golf with Mort Guttenberg. Getting better. Rainy AM. Medals engraved. All set for trip to see Shyrle.

The True Diaries of Irving J. Schaffer

<u>JULY 19, 1945</u>

Dad saw me off at station. Caught 4:24 PM west. 30 minutes late. Became acquainted with traveling engineer of the General Electric Co. Apologizes for having liquor on his breath. Apparently where I offered him some gum, he must have thought I was aware of the fact. In fact at the time I would have enjoyed a drink myself. Soldiers and sailors dominate the travelers. Train was not the least crowded. Advanced four cars at Buffalo. Ate in dining car. Cool and comfortable. Been thinking lots about Shyrle. Rather a definite situation, this thing called marriage. Arrived Chicago 8:20AM the 20th. Made up time during night. Sent #19 and Shyrle telegrams. Showered and cleaned up in Chicago at WVSA. Very pleasant women. Ate dinner at Marshall Fields. Took "Hiawatha" out for Milwaukee at 1:00PM. Beautiful train - struck up conversation with a young sailor who claimed to be quite a guy including the son of the president of Vanderbilt University. Changed to a 680BC coach at Milwaukee for Madison. Arrived Madison 4:08. As I stepped off the train, Shyrle was there. Yes, I took her in my arms. God how very wonderful. She looks wonderful, neat, trim and as packed full of personality as ever. The manner in which she received me could not be improved. Hotel accommodations at the Lorraine were all set at #408. Very decent and comfortable hotel. Supposed to be the hotel of Madison. Changed immediately to civilian clothes. Sport clothes. Shyrle and I walked to the university, up to Bascom Hall. Visited the Elizabeth Waters Hall. Met some of Shyrle's friends. Seem very decent. It seems so wonderful after the many months of doubting my safe return. The old man has treated me like a favorite son. Dined in the Rathskeller, a quaint little spot. Spaghetti and meatballs. Danced at the Union on the outdoor patio. Friday night is late leave night (12:30). Shyrle and I found ourselves very much concerned in each other. In fact we are both looking for the same thing. We are so relaxed in each other's company. We have known each other for such a very short time, yet it doesn't seem so. Retired 1:00AM.

JULY 21, 1945

Called Shyrle at 8:10AM. Still snoozing. Imagine and she is the early bird. Joined her at the Union for a wonderful day. Swimming and canoeing all afternoon. She certainly cuts a beautiful figure in a bathing suit. Swims well. Canoed to picnic point. Attended "Moor Born" at Union Hall. A play put on by the Wisconsin Univ players. Here it is Wednesday and I am just making Saturday's entry. Sorta miss up on certain things. Having a wonderful siesta. Shyrle has something that other girls seem to lack. Habits are very clean as well as her person. Always say goodnight beneath a certain tree in front of the dormitory.

JULY 22, 1945

The days become more enjoyable. We seem so very relaxed in each other's company. Played classical recordings - Peer Gynt, Nutcracker Suite, Evening Star - at Eliz Waters Music Room. Dressed for dinner. How very stunning Shyrle looks. Ate at Hofbrau with friends of Shyrle's. Excellent T-bone steaks. Very nice spot. Jim, one of the party, absolutely refused to let me pay any part of bill. What a guy. Met some more friends of Shyrle's (Ernie, Texas and Cherry). Went speedboat riding and later dancing at the Hollywood across Lake Mendota. Beautiful moonlight evening. Shyrle is wonderful. Very lady-like and not the least embarrassing.

JULY 23, 1945

Went to Radio Workshop Class in Studio B with Shyrle. Mr McGlicky (in charge) also played the part of Branwell in "Moor Born". Met Miss Coucher, teacher, traveler and writer. Middle age lady. Very charming. Ate dinner at Union main dining room. Old English style. Very pleasant surroundings. Fine food. Attended "Pillow to Post" at Orpheum Theater. During the movie Shyrle requested my arm about her. Hesitatingly I refused. I know she felt hurt. It made me terribly upset. I so want to always make her happy. I guess yours truly is still and always will be respectful of his female company in public. We certainly do loads of walking and we do enjoy it greatly. We seem to find more in common every day. She seems very understanding about my position. I truthfully believe she is willing to make great sacrifices. I believe we are deeply in love.

JULY 24, 1945

Met Shyrle at Union at noon. Taxis are somewhat expensive but very convenient. City of Madison is ideal. People are decent. City is very clean. Canoed and swam. Over to picnic point. Listened to Tchaicowsky's #5 in E Minor. Had dinner at Park Hotel. Air-conditioned. Enjoy dining with Shyrle.

JULY 25, 1945

Mailed birthday card to Gerry. Met Shyrle at Union at noon. Canoed. Very rough lake. Shyrle and I are talking very seriously about the future. Thoroughly explained my position to her. Seems to be willing, but needs time to think. Dined at the Hotel Loraine.

JULY 26, 1945

Today is Gerry's birthday. Met Shyrle at 11:00AM to attend music appreciation class. Mozart's #5 Symphony. Took Shirley, Shyrle's room mate to lunch with us at the Wooden Bowl. Swam most of the PM. Shyrle spoke frankly of a mood that suddenly seized her. Sorta fell out of love. We walk lots and seem to always talk seriously. God if only I could shake myself out of my trance or call it what you may. It doesn't seem so very long ago that I used to have so much fun, so many laughs. Perhaps were I to babble out with my war fears. I'd loose that tension. But I know it just won't come out. Went dancing over at the Hollywood. Took cabin cruiser with other patrons. Always have a grand time with Shyrle. Late leave 12:30AM.

JULY 27, 1945

No doubt Gerry has received Shyrle's gift. Shyrle and I picked out a gift for mother. Everything we do finds us thinking alike. I sometimes wonder if everyone can find enjoyment in the little things as we do.

JULY 28, 1945

Shyrle and I, Steve and Natalie are all going out this evening. Shyrle and I walked to picnic point. Shyrle

180

packed a dandy lunch. Once again we romped off on serious talk. It was wonderful being alone with her on so wonderful a sunny afternoon. We dressed for dinner as we usually do. Attended "Arms and the Man" at the Union, through the courtesy of Shyrle. Enjoyed it very much. Natalie and Steve unable to make appointment. Steve has an ailment in the mid-section. Hired taxi and went to the Chanticlair nightclub five miles outside Madison. I believe it was here Shyrle really began to understand and feel my love. It seems that everything happened all at once. I don't want to hurt her. Spent several hours at Vivian's with Shyrle.

JULY 29, 1945

Shyrle called and I am to meet her at Eliz Waters Hall. Our arrival was simultaneous. Tomorrow I am departing and we are first commencing to understand our love. Dined at Eliz. Waters Hall. Very enjoyable. We are talking and making future plans for our marriage. Swam and took pictures. Postponing my departure one day.

JULY 30, 1945

Shyrle came up and helped me pack. We are both blue about my leaving. Tonight it was difficult saying goodnight.

JULY 31, 1945

Took 10:00AM to Chicago but telegram to Shyrle. Boarded Water Level Limited for Schenectady. Met Herbert Kaiser of Poughkeepsie. Soldier on furlough from the West. Traveling in uniform. Dinner on train.

Comfortable trip. Train not overcrowded. Had my ear bent several times.

AUGUST 1, 1945

Arrived Schenectady 9:33AM (1 hour late). Bus to Amsterdam. Stopped in to see Dad. Wrote Shyrle. Folks gave me a nice reception home. Just had to call Shyrle. My how wonderful it was to hear her voice. We expressed our love. Gerry spoke to Shyrle for the first time. In the afternoon, Merriam and Dicky came down. Perhaps one day we shall have a youngster like Dicky.

AUGUST 2, 1945

Dad awoke me by unnecessary loud talking. Gerry and I went downtown. Dad and I visited the bank. Purchased several music albums. Played nine holes of golf with Joe Gray. Game is really improving. Dined at Stones. Very enjoyable evening. Cloudy, muggy day. Received two letters from Shyrle. I love her deeply. Retired midnight.

AUGUST 3, 1945

Took 10:45 bus to Gloversville. Staying at Merriam's home for weekend. God how I adore Dicky and the family. Merriam, Jack and Dicky and I ate at Tower Hotel in Northville. Steak dinner. Dicky sick. Returned home 9:00PM. Wrote Shyrle.

The True Diaries of Irving J. Schaffer

AUGUST 4, 1945

Wrote Shyrle. Anxiously waiting to get home so I can read letters from Shyrle. Finishing "The Nazarene." Merriam cooks well. Spent some time at Myer's Park in Gloversville. Kibitzed and retired 9:30PM.

AUGUST 5, 1945

Enjoying the quietness and solitude. Dicky not feeling very well. Youngster is my favorite and when I imagine him ill it worries me. Jerry Rubin staying with Merriam while his folks visit their oldest son Fred at Bryant Lake. Jack drove me to Fonda. Made 3:20PM bus for Amsterdam. God how anxiously I read those letters from Shyrle. It makes me feel proud, ambitious and happy when I learn of her love and plans. Lord, I shall make her very happy. Today I longed for her very much. Gerry and Lester Shore (Doctor Selbert, optometrist, brother-in-law) sunbathing on back lawn. Invited Les to dinner. Jean Chapman came over and we all went down to Hills for ice cream. Visited with Mr and Mrs Chapman and Aunt Blanche. Retired 11:00PM. Started Richard Wright's "Black Boy."

AUGUST 6, 1945

Gerry woke yours truly at 7:15AM. Took bus to Schenectady. Interview with Mr. Thompson (discharged veteran) bldg #1. Unable to make IGE. Requires engineering degree. Old job back at CAP at inspection if desired. Interview with Mr. Gerling of bldg #56. Inspection personnel. Very patient and understanding. I am not discouraged but I certainly will try to achieve a position promising advancement. To see Mr. A Sanborn at CAP tomorrow. Took bus direct to Gloversville. Dicky is better. Picked up my raincoat. Very drizzly, dreary day. Arrived home 6:15PM. Also purchased two beautiful pair of gloves for Shyrle. I miss my darling very much. Today a letter came from the Madison dead-letter office in which was enclosed a letter from Shyrle. She forgot to spell out Amsterdam. That's my gal and I love her. I only hope my job will be sufficient. She is very consistent.

AUGUST 7, 1945

Interviewed by Mr AP Sanborn, assistant general foreman of inspectors. My old boss. Yours truly can have his old job back but in doing so someone must be removed. I don't exactly like the idea, but it's survival of the fittest. Spoke with Charley Diaz, assistant general foreman of production. Would very much like to have me with him. Charge of 'green room.' Returned to bldg #1 and again spoke with Mr. Thompson, also Mr Upton. When I travel to Syracuse for the family reunion, I shall also have several letters of introduction and recommendation to work in the Syracuse plant. It's where opportunities for advancement are best. Personally, I believe yours truly will eventually end up in business. Information released on "Atomic Bomb" bombing of Japan. Long to have Shyrle with me. Mother, Dad, Gerry and I attended "Valley of Decision." Good.

AUGUST 8, 1945

Played golf with Mort Guttenberg. Yours truly shows some improvement. Mailed Shyrle's birthday gift. Returned Richard Wright's "Black Boy." Reading Joseph Gastrow's "Keeping Mentally Fit." (A guide to

The True Diaries of Irving J. Schaffer

everyday psychology) Small family quarrels and indifferences upset me very much. Only the 'old man' knows I shall do my best never to quarrel and always maintain happiness in Shyrle's and my life. Consistently thinking and debating over various jobs and positions open. I shall not bring Shyrle to Amsterdam. I definitely want her to get her degree. Gerry and I always walk to Hills in the evening for our daily soda and sundae. We always bring a cone home for mom, pop and his evenings are about the same. He isn't too well.

AUGUST 9, 1945

Not feeling too well this AM. Grippe. Played golf with Mrs. Stone, Mrs. Grossman and Peter caddied. Fair game. Beautiful day. Called Mr. Thompson, Bldg #1, GE and canceled my appointment until 9:00AM tomorrow. Received very nice letter from #308. Such recognition makes all the difference in the world. Very fond of Shyrle's parents. Attended fathering of ABG fellows at Morry Olenders home.

AUGUST 10, 1945

Folks received a swell letter from Shyrle. We are all going to be very fond of each other. Folks sent a letter of invitation to #308. A bit formal but at the outset it's OK. Counseled with Mr. Smith, manager of the Sears Roebuck store in Schenectady. Yours truly to contact Mr. Janes, personnel head of New England area. Office in Boston. Clear, warm day. Picked up letter of introduction and recommendation for use with Syracuse division of General Electric. Interested in attending Syracuse University. Would also be a practical setup for Shyrle. Gerry and I have our usual at Hills almost very night. Mom always rates a cone.

AUGUST 11, 1945

Visited Mrs. McGibbon with George Van Buren. Mom and dad left on 1:40PM for Syracuse. Family reunion. Geraldine and I went by bus to Gloversville. Staying at Merriam's home overnight. Gerry and I ate at Pedericks. Gerry is very enjoyable company. Retired early.

AUGUST 12, 1945

Started via automobile for Syracuse at 8:00AM. Pleasant trip. Jack drove all the way. Stopped outside Utica to stretch. Arrived Syracuse 11:30AM. Everyone there. Everybody looks fine. Missed those that passed away so recently. Union at Aunt Evelyn's home on Cambridge St. Aunt Bea had a nose operation. Looks fine. Mrs. Schaffer (my mom) still looks the best of the sisters in all respects. Mom is always a lady. Buffet luncheon. Self-served affair. Clear, warm day. Unveiled stone oat cemetery for Grandma Belloff. Yours truly did not attend. Dicky was quite the center of attraction. He is a very well behaved lad. Reunion broke up about 8:00PM. Mother and Dad motored home with Merriam, Jack, Gerry and Dicky. Yours truly remaining at Evelyn's. Aunt Bea, Lil, Bob and I went to the Hotel Syracuse to wine and dine and await Lil's latest, Lester. Very decent fellow. Man about 40. Lil is very serious about him and contemplates marriage providing he can get a divorce. Aunt Bea has a boyfriend in Boston named Cy (Seymour). Not particularly fond of my Aunt's behavior outside the house. Enjoy the company of my cousin, Bob Stolz. A clean, decent gentleman. Enjoy the company of Aunt Evelyn and Uncle Louie. Slept in Bob's room. Shyrle's 21st birthday. Retired 2:30AM.

AUGUST 13, 1945

Awoke 9:30AM. Made appointment with Mr. McQueen (personnel) for 2:30PM. Aunt Evelyn drove me out to Thompson Road, plant of General Electric (7 miles from heart of city). McQueen referred me to Mr. Barrett who in turn referred me to Mr. Debrawere after listening to my set up. (Debrawere and I became very well acquainted). Next Mr. Gangberg came into the picture. Formerly with the Schenectady works and a personal friend. Discussed my position with him but refused any assistance due to our previous personal relations. Finished with Mr. Gangberg 5:00PM. Mr. Debrawere drove me to town. Very pleasant and a gentleman. Attended St Lawrence University and knows Dewitt Benjamin. To return for additional interviews tomorrow. Aunt Bea, Bob and I dined out at some German restaurant. Very cool and clean. Food excellent. Rest of the folks dined at the Persian Room. Met them all at home. Talked for a while. Retired 11:00PM.

AUGUST 14, 1945

Awoke 8:00AM. Interview again at GE. Lil and Lester returning to Boston by car. Aunt Bea by train. Bid them adieu. Taxi to plant. Met Bob Stolz for a few minutes. Mr Debrawere referring me to Mr. Blyler at Wolf St plant. Mr Blyler referred me to his boss, Mr. Bennet. Dinner at Sandwich Bar in Wolf St plant. Converted car barn. Mr Blyler and Mr. Bennet both interviewed yours truly. The job Mr. Bennet has open for me is too large an assignment. Perhaps after a stiff training period I could undertake the job. It is strictly a post war setup in sales, which will involve sales amounting to 3 to 4 million dollars. Expressed myself regarding the fact that at present it would be quite impossible for me to fill this job. However there is a possibility that I may be a number 2 or 3 man which may later find me going up when Mr. Rainey and Mr Bischoff return the Syracuse office. Shall notify me for an interview. Bid adieu to all the folks. Made the 6:15PM train. Air-conditioned. Learned of V-J day when we stopped in Utica. Arrived home 9:00PM. No transportation. Mr. Robinson (bank) gave me a lift home. Susan and Gerry arrived home about 10:30PM. Bad accident in front of Hover's home about 11:30PM. Two women (intoxicated) driving a coupe hit the tree on Hover's lower lawn. Bleeding quite badly. God how very weak it made me. Finally got them to hospital. Police and ambulance arrived. Retired 1:00AM.

AUGUST 15, 1945

Awoke 8:30AM. Wrote a long letter to my darling. I certainly wish she were with me. Clear, windy AM. V-J parade 3:00PM. All stores and industry shut down. Cousin Susan and I walked. I am very fond of her. Very domestic and refined. Gerry, Sue and I attended "Anchor's Aweigh". Enjoyable.

AUGUST 16, 1945

Kissed Susan goodbye. To catch the 11:33 out of Schenectady. Went with Gerry. Went downtown. Photos of Shyrle, Ma and Pa came out swell. Mrs. Stone invited me to go to Lake Luzerne with her and sons. Took Lester Shoen along also. Very enjoyable day. Swimming and canoeing. Had dinner at

Goldsmeds in Corinths. Think Mrs. Stone is a
remarkable lady. Dicky quite ill with asthma.
Returned Amsterdam 8:00PM. Les, Bob (nephew) and
I attended "Diamond Horseshoe" (enjoyable). Les is
very much in love with Annette Nathan. Unfortunately
I don't believe she realizes such. Spoke with me about
it very confidentially. Wants to leave Amsterdam and
he cannot bear to see her everyday and know she
doesn't belong to him. Very serious fellow and very
decent. Perhaps I shouldn't have but I told him to give
the situation a fair trial. Retired 1:00AM.

AUGUST 17, 1945

Cleaned out some drawers for mother. Met Dad
downtown and spoke with Alphonse DiMezza regarding
a diamond. Shyrle shall have the best. Had lunch
with Dad. Mailed premium to VA on my policy. Clear,
sunny day. Listened to several new music albums
Gerry gave me for my birthday. Oscar Levant's
recording of Rhapsody in Blue and Tchaicowsky's
Symphony #5 in E Minor. Helped mother about the
house. Visited Ken and Hermanie for first time in over
a month. Met Mr and Mrs Gingold (relatives of the
Grossmans). My love for Shyrle is stronger than ever.
However, I shall let things take their natural course.
Nothing synthetic shall be done to temporarily
strengthen our love. It must be forever as it is now.
We must accept each other as we are. That I am sure
we will. Reading "The Life and Death of Enrico Caruso
by Dorothy Caruso. Miss Shyrle very much. Folks
received a swell note from #308.

AUGUST 18, 1945

Played 18 holes of golf with Lou Gingold. Received
second birthday gift from Shyrle. First was an Old Spice
combination set. Second was the recording album of
the Nutcracker's Suite. I love Shyrle more dearly each
day. Received a swell birthday card from #308 signed,
Paul, Molly and Nolan. Very warm indeed. Tomorrow
my 28th birthday. She is to call. Gerry and I attended
"The Great John L", her pre-birthday treat to me. I
find Gerry very enjoyable company. Each day finds
her more ladylike. I am so proud of my little ladies.
Mom, Shyrle and Gerry. Elliot called to wish me a
happy birthday.   What a swell guy (all the way from
Charleston SC). Ken and Hermanie and Gerry and I
went to Bills to celebrate my pre-birthday. Ken is
working on the midnight shift. Their son, Frederick is
quite a lad. Miss Shyrle very much. Every evening
before retiring I look over the photograph of her and
thank "The Old Man."

AUGUST 19, 1945

Merriam called at 10:00AM to extend her best. Also
talked with Dicky. Shyrle called at 11:30AM. How
very wonderful it was to hear her voice. Spoke with
Mrs. Peskind, Mr. Peskind and Nolan. What very fine
and thoughtful people. What a wonderful birthday
they have made for me. It's the first time I've felt
excited and enthusiastic since my first crack at the
Nazi's. Mother wished me happy birthday at exactly
1:15PM...my exact birth time. Attended a fraternity
ritual for Donald Levy at Norry Olander's home. Eliz.
Smith, Mo, his folks and yours truly went to Sac for a
swim. Returned 7:30AM. Although the folks wanted
to fuss I thought it not necessary. Visited a few
minutes with the Guttenbergs. Made an appointment

to play golf with Bob Terk tomorrow. AM. Retired 10:30PM.

AUGUST 20, 1945

Received a special from Shyrle. The folks received a large box of candy from her also. My own darling. She is very thoughtful. I hope she comes east real soon. Played 9 holes of golf with Bob Terk. Fair. Very clear, hot day.

AUGUST 21, 1945

Bob Terk and I (Bob's car) went to Echo Lake. Met Dolores (Dolly) Gangberg. An old sweetheart of Bob's and a sisterly friend of yours truly. Had trouble with the brakes. Finally had them repaired at a Parson's garage in Glenn Falls. Dolly is the nurse at Echo Lake camp. She looks well and somewhat on the plump side. As sweet as ever. Broke her engagement with her fiance. Enjoyed a swim in the lake. Proprietor of camp (Moe) very odd. (psycho-case) Dined at the Half-Way House. Returned Amsterdam 10:00PM.

AUGUST 22, 1945

My darling's letters are most encouraging. She expects to be here next week. I love her so much. Purchased "All of a Sudden My Heart Sings" from "Anchor's Aweigh". Helping mother about the house and fixing the yard. Chatted with Marjorie Stansfield. Feels like Gerry. Wants to prove her worth in life.

AUGUST 23, 1945

Still cleaning house. Could hardly wait until the mailman came. God how terribly disappointing it would have been if he didn't have a letter from Shyrle. Pa wrote my darling. Attended fraternity ritual. Attended "Affairs of Susan." Enjoyable. Clear, warm day. Cool, clear evening.

AUGUST 24, 1945

Received letter from Mrs. Jones, personnel officer, Boston division, Sears Roebuck Co. To be interviewed in the near future. Shyrle to arrive this coming Wednesday. Her folks will be unable to come as they are moving soon. Very fond of all the Peskinds.

AUGUST 25, 1945

Gerry released from her job with Sears in Schenectady. She is planning on going to Boston. Nothing special doing. Been helping mother a lot. Gerry is coming along fine. Pa has slight cold. I go out or rather he takes me out to dinner quite often.

AUGUST 26, 1945

Regular run of the day. Very anxious to hold my darling Shyrle in my arms. Ken, Hermanie, Gerry and yours truly spent the evening at Bills on Market St. Enjoyed a few beers.

The True Diaries of Irving J. Schaffer

AUGUST 27, 1945

Very excited about Shyrle's coming. Reading "Immortal Life". Good. Been reading some Shelley poetry.

AUGUST 28, 1945

Gerry and I met Shyrle at the Schenectady station. Arrived on the Knickerbocker (9:04AM) 40 minutes late. Shyrle looks wonderful. Took train to Amsterdam. Dad met us at the station. Everyone very pleased with everyone else. Shyrle brought some delicious peanut pastry her mother made. Very delicious. Yours truly very, very happy. Merriam's 30th birthday.

AUGUST 29, 1945

Everything percolating wonderfully well. Shyrle and I like walking. Folks very fond of Shyrle. Plans for a February marriage. My only thought is whether I am prepared financially. I'd rather wait a while longer, but whatever makes Shyrle happy, I'll do.

AUGUST 30, 1945

Spoke to Shyrle about ring. Feels very bad about her finger. Seems to have some mental drawback about it. Shyrle fits in the family perfectly.

AUGUST 31, 1945

Shyrle and I and Elliott dined at Merriam's home. Elliott came home yesterday. Very delicious meal. Visited Max Feldman in Gloversville before returning by bus to Amsterdam. Shyrle was very fascinated watching bread being made.

SEPTEMBER 1, 1945

Merriam, Jack, Shyrle and I went to Albany. Shopped around a bit and ate at Howard Johnsons. Slept most the way home. Wonderful wife I am going to have. Raining hard.

SEPTEMBER 2, 1945

Ken, Hermanie, Shyrle and I went up to Bishops (formerly Caseys) at Conklinville. Few drinks. Returned 12:30AM. Shyrle always looks stunning and neat.

SEPTEMBER 3, 1945

Labor Day

Merriam and Jack took the folks and Gerry out on a picnic to Lake George. Shyrle and I spent the evening home as well as the day. Ate at Isabels. We both washed clothes. Gerry, Pa, Shyrle and I played bridge. Retired 12:30AM.

SEPTEMBER 4, 1945

Shyrle had her hair washed. Looks lovely. Pa took Gerry, Shyrle and I to lunch at Brooks. Fair day. Bernard Olendro in the States. Purchased shirt at Morton's. As a rule I've been retiring around 1:00AM. Will feel good when I start work. Received another mustering out paycheck.

The True Diaries of Irving J. Schaffer

SEPTEMBER 5, 1945

Took Shyrle to Max Frankels to be fitted for her engagement ring. There is something very decent and innocent and admirable about Shyrle. She is constantly trying to improve herself. Attended "You Came Along". Too sentimental. Very hot day. Been doing a lot of shopping for mother. Announcement of our engagement in tonight's paper. Finding mother and family very happy about the whole affair. Marjorie Stansfield, Shyrle, Gerry and I played bridge. Shyrle is not feeling too well. System conjested. Very comfortable, clear evening. Retired 2:00AM.

SEPTEMBER 6, 1945

Feeling tired. Shyrle not feeling too well. Have decided that unless she feels better I will take matters in my own hands. Very warm AM. Merriam sent cashier's check completely closing out my account in Gloversville. Somewhat fed up about household work. Shyrle and I and Bob Terk played golf - first nine holes. Perfectly clear day. Shyrle feels much better. Barney Olender (1st Lt, medics) came home.

SEPTEMBER 7, 1945

Barney took Shyrle and I to Albany to pick up Toby (Don's wife). Met Mr. And Mrs. Solomon and son Marcus. Presented Shyrle with her ring. Very happy. Her manner is wonderful. All the family went to Temple. Came in 15 minutes late. All went to Doyle's for ice cream. My first visit to Doyle's in ten years. Very hot and stifling. Retired 2:30AM.

SEPTEMBER 8, 1945

Awoke 9:00AM. Feeling tired, but good. Attended
morning service at Temple. Many congratulations on
our engagement. Rabbi spoke about the forgetting of
the finer things in life - religion. Merriam and family
came down for dinner. Took a ride to Schenectady.
Dicky slept in my bed. Shyrle is wonderful company.
Retired 1:00AM. Elliott returned.

SEPTEMBER 9, 1945

Seems like old times. All the boys were at the house
today; Red Wagner and Jean Chapman stayed for
dinner. Very delicious meal. Seven couples. Went to
Osterbouts, just outside of Albany in the Hilderberts.
Very enjoyable evening. Very grateful for Shyrle when
I look around at the others. Returned to Amsterdam
3:45AM. Shyrle hasn't been feeling well.

SEPTEMBER 10, 1945

Feeling very tired. Must get more rest. Shyrle and I
shopped a bit. The weather is very unseasonable.
Very muggy and close. Elliott will arrive in Charleston
today. Shyrle, Gerry and I were invited to a steak
roast at Stone's. Wonderful dinner. Played bridge.
Mother had a good rest. Returned home 11:30PM.
Mother and Dad came over about 8:00PM.

SEPTEMBER 11, 1945

Awoke 9:05AM. Shyrle and I played golf at 10:00AM.
Returned home after 3 holes due to rain. Shyrle and I
cut the back hedges. Cleared up - beautiful day.
Shyrle, Goody, Janet, Morry, Red, Alie, yours truly

went to Gloversville. Returned 11:30PM. Shyrle and I
are becoming very close.

SEPTEMBER 12, 1945

Awoke 9:00AM. Clear, warm day. Shyrle overslept
and missed appointment with hairdresser. Changed to
11:00AM. Haircut and shopped for mother. Barney,
Shyrle and I drove to Saratoga for a bit of sightseeing.
Visited the "Gaddo". Huge estate. Returned
Amsterdam 5:30PM. Dorothy Sericce, Eleanor
Passera, Barney over for dinner. Mother and Gerry
prepared an excellent meal. Talked until 11:20PM.
Made plans for a WGY broadcast attendance. Clear,
warm day. Retired midnight.

SEPTEMBER 13, 1945

Seems so wonderful having Shyrle around. In another
week she will be leaving for college. After our marriage
in February, Shyrle will lack six credits for a degree
which will be achieved by home study. Her manner
and happiness are rare. Shyrle, Gerry, Barney and I
played golf at the municipal course. Clear, cool day.
Shyrle, Gerry and I went to Merriam's. Picnic at
Caroga Lake. Returned home on 9:20bus. Shyrle
loves the out of doors especially lake and mountainous
country. Both very tired. Pa at Eagles tonight. I love
Shyrle more and more. Retired 11:30PM.

SEPTEMBER 14, 1945

Finally got up at 11:00AM. Raining. Shyrle, Gerry,
Barney and I attended "Junior Miss." Oley treated.
We also attended television broadcast at WGRLB
(Schenectady). Saw broadcast in studio then watched

it on television set. Went dancing at the Town Tavern in Schenectady. Raining. Feeling blue and below par. Sorta spoiled everyone's evening. Retired 12:00AM.

SEPTEMBER 15, 1945

Shyrle awoke me at 9:25AM. Feeling OK. I love her more early each day. Mother feeling very nervous and irritable. Constantly claims of a pain at the base of neck in back. Shyrle and I went downtown shopping with Dad. Victory parade at 3:00PM. Most terrific parade Amsterdam ever had. Barney, Toby, Shyrle and I went to Jack's in Albany for dinner. Very enjoyable. Went to Harold and Ester Hoffman's home. Enjoyed a cocktail party where Morry, Terk, Red and dates met us. Danced at Herberts. Shyrle looks more wonderful each day. After the excitement of the evening died down, my mind became very disturbed about mother. Arrived home 3:30AM. Gerry still awake. Mother and Dad had a spat. Made me very upset. Couldn't sleep until after 5:00AM. Shyrle is very understanding.

SEPTEMBER 16, 1945

Arose 8:00AM. Had a chat with Dad in my room. Disturbed about last night's spat with Mother. Mother feeling a bit on the bad side but I am working with her and everything is OK. All went to Temple services (Day of Atonement). Mr. Hager sang Ko Nidre. Shyrle is very tired. Shyrle and I walked home with Mr. Grossman. A.D. Lurie had a second stroke in Saratoga. Fasting.

The True Diaries of Irving J. Schaffer

SEPTEMBER 17, 1945

Shyrle came in my room at 11:00AM. Folks went to Temple. Shyrle, Gerry and I visited at Mrs. Sochin where we met all the crowd. Shyrle is liked all over. Returned home at 5:00PM and prepared dinner for evening. Broke fast at 6:00PM. Yours truly a bit peeved at the manners of those about me. Shyrle and I walked downtown and back. Coffee at Kansas. The weather suddenly turned cold and our furnace and kitchen stove are percolating. Retired 1:00AM.

SEPTEMBER 18, 1945

Awoke 9:00AM. Eyes very tired and burn. Shyrle and Gerry went to hairdressers. Stores closed for 1/2 hour this AM during A.D. Lurie's funeral. Very cloudy and cold. (unseasonal). Shyrle folks to arrive tomorrow. Shyrle and I very happy.

SEPTEMBER 19, 1945

Joe Gray took Shyrle and I to Schenectady. Mr and Mrs. Peskind arrived on 9:04 (20 minutes late). Both look well and I remember them well. Dad and Gerry met us at station (1:21) Peskinds stopping at McGraths on Guy Park Avenue. Upstairs room. Takes Mrs. Carpenter's overflow. Mother prepared a swell dinner. Sat around and schmoozed all evening. Shyrle still having trouble with system.

SEPTEMBER 20, 1945

Mr and Mrs Peskind, Shyrle and yours truly had breakfast at Kansas. Dad and Mr. Peskind went to Gloversville. Shyrle, Mrs. P and I shopped about

Amsterdam. Dinner at #19. Everyone retired early as we are planning to go to NY tomorrow.

SEPTEMBER 21, 1945

Mr & Mrs P, Shyrle and I left on 8:00AM. Comfortable trip. Arrived Grand Central 12:45 (45 minutes late). Went direct to Andover's and Shyrle picked out her coat (full length brown sheared beaver - very beautiful). Shyrle wears clothes well. Dined at Lindy's The folks shopped in Saks 5th Ave, I Miller. Not too greatly impressed with the city. NY jammed. Enjoy being with my in-laws to be. Returned on 6:30PM. Changed at Albany. Arrived Amsterdam 11:30PM.

SEPTEMBER 22, 1945

Merriam called. Drove her to Schenectady. Looking for maternity dress. Mrs P, Shyrle, Dicky, Gerry and I shopped in Nissbaums. Shyrle and Mrs. P picked out pattern for her sterling silver at Clark and MacDonald. Dined at Gerry's in Scotia. Merriam unable to obtain dress. Mrs. P treated us to ice cream on return trip. Returned #19 5:15PM. We all were treated to dinner by Pop Peskind at Isabells. Very enjoyable. All attended Temple. After Temple, Mr and Mrs Stone, Hermanie, Ken, Barney and Marsha Sterns (Alexander) stopped over. Shyrle to leave on 4:24PM tomorrow. I'll miss her very, very much. All at #19 are very fond of #911 and visa versa. Everything is just wonderful. Retired 2:00AM.

SEPTEMBER 23, 1945

Awoke 9:30AM. Dull, cold AM. Commenced furnace fire. Hate to see Shyrle leave. Mother prepared one of

200

her always delicious meals. We all saw Shyrle off at 4:24PM. How very much I'll miss her. Mother Peskind, Dad, Gerry and I played bridge. Father Peskind took a nap in Gerry's bed. Mother made a buffet luncheon. Mother and father Peskind and yours truly walked for several hours. Father Peskind spoke of future plans and our (Shyrle and my) happiness. What a swell couple. I did not show my feelings as I know Shyrle would like it better that way. I love her dearly.

SEPTEMBER 24, 1945

Met Mother and Father Peskind at 10:00AM for breakfast. Ate at the cafeteria. Marsha (Sterns) Alexander drove us to Schenectady as she and Gerry are dining at Ruth (Sochen) family's home. Had dinner in Pelops. Shopped around a bit. Bid Mother and Father Peskind adieu at 5:53PM at the Schenectady station. Sent my darling a telegram. Received a telegram from my dearest. I miss her very much. It's going to be lonesome. I am anxiously awaiting the mail. All at #19 miss the Peskinds. Every moment of Shyrle's stay was wonderful. It shall seem like an eternity until February. Wrote Shyrle, as I shall do every night.

SEPTEMBER 25, 1945

Awoke 6:10AM. Alarm clock banging away. Ken took me to Schenectady. Interviewed by Mr. Gerling (inspection). To work in Bldg #17 as punch press inspector. (.96) Glass G. Took physical. To commence work Thursday. Would prefer the retail line. Will write and ask Shyrle's advice. Very sweltry day. Very worried about Shyrle. No letter today.

Gerry leaving for Boston tomorrow. I am sure she will make the grade. I will miss her very much. How I long to be with Shyrle. Dad attending store banquet. Retired 11:00PM.

SEPTEMBER 26, 1945

Awoke 8:15AM. Mother, Dad, Gerry and I bid Gerry goodbye at station. We all (me especially) will miss her very much. She looks great. Spoke to Mr. Terk (Luries) about managing one of the men's dept in one of Lurie's stores. (possibility) May work Saturdays in Mortons. Warm, muggy AM. No letter from Shyrle. I hope she is well. Very worried. Sometimes I feel depressed because I don't think I can give Shyrle the things I'd like to. She is so very wonderful and understanding. I love her deeply. Attended fraternity meeting at Synagogue. Appointed temporary Chairman of parent's night. Ice cream at Hills for first time in weeks. Retired 10:30PM.

SEPTEMBER 27, 1945

Awoke 5:45AM. Very sleepless night. Thought lots about my darling. Miss her very much. Gene Zeiser driving yours truly to work. Mr. Allen, foreman, working in Bldg #19 (punch press.) Inspecting unit of cooling system for post-war motors. John Baker (Ballston Spa) who I am relieving, is breaking me in. Very nice fellow and worldly but not too intelligent. Easy job and pleasant surroundings. Mr. Terk called Dad about getting in touch with yours truly. Fair day. Miss Gerry very much. Discharged Fred Ballard (dishonesty). Wants to employ yours truly at $30.00 per week. Agreed to $35.00. Will let him know within a few days. Visited at Mr. Guttenberg's home.

Inquired about Saturdays. He spoke about expansion.
Will ask Ray, then let me know. Fortunately I
understand Mr. G. Although I said nothing wrong I
talked a little more than necessary at Mr. G's about
my business. Retired 11:30PM.

SEPTEMBER 28, 1945

Alarm awoke me at 6:00AM. Mother prepares my
lunch at night. I insist Mother remain in bed in the
morning as it is a simple matter for me to prepare my
breakfast. Mornings are chilly. Today very warm.
Like my job OK. Not much to it and easy to learn.
Wearing safety glasses. Yours truly is torn between
several decisions. Whether to continue on in my
present work or to work for Lurie's or approach Mr.
Guttenberg. I really am desirous in getting back to
business. I trust my decision will meet with the
approval of my darling Shyrle. I wrote Shyrle an eight-
page letter tonight. Red Wagner came over for a while.
Neglected to notify Veteran's Administration at Castle
Point of my reporting for examination tomorrow. Will
write for another appointment. Feeling OK but miss
Shyrle and Gerry. Retired 10:00PM.

SEPTEMBER 29, 1945

Out of the sack at 10:00AM. Chest and back pains.
Mother baked oatmeal cookies for Shyrle. I also
mailed package to Gerry. Getting quite cold. Raining.
Very aggravated about things in general about the
house. I seem to feel it right across my left chest when
I am aggravated. I haven't given it much thought but I
should write Aunt Evelyn. Spoke with Mr. Guttenberg
about Mr. Terk's proposition. Truthfully I believe I will
be better off working for Lurie's than I would for Mr.

Guttenberg. Dad and I talked for quite awhile this night. He is really set on business. Turned clocks back an hour. Retired 12:45AM.

SEPTEMBER 30, 1945

Awoke 9:00AM. Cold, clear AM. Built a furnace fire. Feeling good. Thinking an awful lot about my financial situation. I must provide and provide well for Shyrle. Received a special delivery from my darling. Reciprocated with a telegram. Went walking with Alie Smith. Very cold for September. House is quiet and comfortable. Attended homecoming party for Jewish War Veterans. Stayed 1/2 hour. Herb Sterns gave me a tip about US Treasury (IRS). Retired 11:00PM.

OCTOBER 1, 1945

Awoke 6:00AM. Very pleasant dream about my darling Shyrle. Job coming along OK. Raining. Joe (old timer) took me thru bldg #16 and #18 to show me huge motors and purpose of our job in #19. Mr. Allen (my foreman) invited me to go to Plattsburg with him the week after next to visit his farm. Mr. Terk not in tonight. Doctor Selbert to outfit me with glasses. Gerry called tonight from Boston. To start work tomorrow. Received several letters from Shyrle. I love her more each day. Read in bed.

OCTOBER 2, 1945

Awoke usual time. Raining hard. Job OK, but factory work is not for yours truly. I miss Shyrle more than ever. It seems to increase as the days pass. I wish I were married to my darling now. Met Mr. Terk at the store (Lurie's). Accepted his proposition ($35). Quite a

cut in salary but it's what I want to do. My heart
becomes very heavy when Ma and Pa quarrel. Miss
Gerry. Feel like calling Shyrle tonight. Miss her so
very much. Retired 10:45PM.

OCTOBER 3, 1945

Very cold, clear AM. Very poor night for yours truly.
Restless sleep. Told Mr. Allen (foreman) about my
leaving the GE's employ for work in Amsterdam. Very
decent about the whole thing. Did not jeopardize my
position with the GE. No letter from Shyrle today.
Very much aggravated with domestic conditions at
#19. Furnace cleaned by Mr. Elmer Welch. Walked to
library. Returned "The Emperor's Physician." Took
out "Move Your Merchandise," Goode and
"Salesmanship for the New Era," Mears. Retired
10:00PM

OCTOBER 4, 1945

Cold, frosty AM. Visited GE store in Bldg #56.
Received special and regular letter from Shyrle. I don't
want to reside in Amsterdam anymore than Shyrle
does. However we must be patient. Red, Olie and
yours truly went walking this evening. Gerry is doing
OK.

OCTOBER 5, 1945

Usual clear, cold, sunny morning. Miasmas from
Mohawk causes road to be foggy. Bid adieu to the
General Electric Company. No more stagnate jobs for
this lad. However my associates were nice. Paid
income tax in advance per law. Broke my service with
GE. Walked downtown for first time on Friday

evening. Love walking. Received many congratulations on engagement. I miss my darling more every day. Met Ray Kretzer in Chamberlins. Retired 10:00PM. Reading "Salesmanship for the New Era," Charles Mears.

OCTOBER 6, 1945

Awoke 7:30AM. Read a few hours in bed. Picked up my new glasses at Doctor Selberts. Beautiful fall day. Wrote my darling. Received letter from Nolan and Susan. Visited the Wagners. Registered for fall elections at Thayers. Slight drizzle. Retired 10:30PM.

OCTOBER 7, 1945

Awoke 8:00AM. Read a while. Listened to recordings. I miss Shyrle so very much that I am becoming irritable with myself. Everything seems to grate on my nerves. Dull day. Barney and I started for movies. Ended up at Joe Olender's home. It's such a waste of time kibitzing. Wrote two letters to Shyrle today. Warm day. Retired 10:30PM.

OCTOBER 8, 1945

Woke 7:20AM. Very restless night. Clear, warm AM. Entered store at 8:15AM. Good luck wished to me by mother and Mrs. Wagner. Like my work very much. Enjoy selling. Mr. Cohen, my immediate superior, very pleasant. Store banquet tonight, but yours truly will be on hand for my darling's phone call. I sure love her. Shyrle's call came through at 8:14PM. The time was so short. There were so many things we wanted to talk about. God bless her. Retired 9:45PM.

OCTOBER 9, 1945

Awoke 6:45AM. Always up before alarm. Job OK.
Stock in terrible condition. Mr. Cohen (Terk's brother-
in-law) not too adept in business. Neglectful about his
stock, person, etc. Although he is a pretty nice guy.
Store closes promptly at 5:30PM. Enjoy my work very
much. I want to start putting some of my ideas in
effect. Must be patient. I want to be able to give Shyrle
the things she is used to. Invited to Mo Hyman's
home. Joe Hyman was recently discharged from the
Army. Quite nervous. Mo served good Scotch.
Discussed possibilities of a war with Russia. Retired
12:00AM.

OCTOBER 10, 1945

Awoke 6:40AM. My watch stopped. Usually get my
own breakfast. Walk to work. At store about 8:00AM.
Today is double stamp day. Fairly busy. I plug my
sales. Love my work. Sam Johnson stopped in.
Called Merriam tonight. All goes well. Attended
fraternity meeting. Rabbi Kurtz spoke. Fair. Retired
10:30PM.

OCTOBER 11, 1945

Clear, cool AM. Fairly busy. Yours truly very much
upset over condition of men's dept. Wow, what a sad
set-up. Previous managers must have been stinko.
Enjoy selling. Can't seem to begin to enjoy myself.
Very moody, critical, etc. I keep everything to myself.

OCTOBER 12, 1945

Today is Columbus Day. Fairly busy. I don't' know what's wrong with me. I seem to worry a lot and I believe it's because I can't get my feet planted like I want to. If Shyrle weren't used to being so sheltered and accustomed to fine things, etc, perhaps that might cause me to worry. I so want her to be happy, cause I love her very much. My job is OK, but I can't really do it justice because I have so much on my mind. I pray to God that one day all shall be well.

OCTOBER 13, 1945

I am sleeping fair. Chilly AM. Wish that Shyrle and I were married. I know Shyrle will make me happy. It's going to be wonderful to come home to a nice quiet home and a sweet understanding and lovable wife. Received a letter from Grandpa Geeser. No mail from Shyrle. Retired 11:30PM.

OCTOBER 14, 1945

Rain, dreary day. Merriam and family came down. No special from Shyrle. Contemplating leaving Luries. Not progressive enough. Miss Shyrle very much. Regular run of the mill day.

OCTOBER 15, 1945

Received 3 letters and one special from Shyrle. Miss her very much. Wish we were married. Regular day.

OCTOBER 16, 1945

Not wearing my glasses anymore. Just need rest.
Received from The Boston Electronics Company
"Warsaw Concerto". Don't know who sent it. Very
good recording. Took my usual evening walk. Very
lonely. Not reading in bed anymore. Commencing
calisthenics.

OCTOBER 17, 1945

Advertised Cooper's underwear. Very foolish in my
imagination. Must remove myself from Luries.
Attended fraternity meeting. Temporarily to handle
pledgees. Clear, warm, evening. Shyrle's letters are
quite constant and inspiring.

OCTOBER 18, 1945

Left shirts at Paul's for laundering. Trimmed windows
today. Attended banquet of Brotherhood at Temple.
Tim Healey, radio commentator, speaker. Spoke on
the Jewish problem. Open forum. Pleasant evening.

OCTOBER 19, 1945

I have definitely decided that I shall leave Amsterdam,
probably for Boston. In addition I don't believe it's
advisable for Shyrle and I to live here. However I enjoy
my surroundings at Luries. I must move up. Very
tired. Retired 11:00PM. Call Gerry.

OCTOBER 20, 1945

Generally upset. Very uncomfortable night's sleep. I
constantly think about our future. The only worry will

be our finances. To go to New Castle this Wednesday for examination at the Veteran's hospital for pension purposes. Received a special delivery from my darling at 8:00PM.

OCTOBER 21, 1945

Beautiful fall day. Wrote letters to Markson Bros and Sears Roebuck Company. Received telegram from my darling (via telephone). Went walking with Olie Smith in afternoon. Called Gerry again. Max Feldman, Smitty and I went to see Abbott and Costello. Maxie's mother is feeling good. Had a few beers at Bills. Retired midnight.

OCTOBER 22, 1945

Spoke to Mr. Terk about a interview with another company. Very nice about the whole matter. To go to Boston next week. Attended store banquet at Hotel Amsterdam. Was called upon to speak. Praised dept. Enjoyable dinner. I am finding myself more and more everyday. Mr. Cohen and I and some of our associates (females) spent some time in the Bar and Grill after. Walked home. Felt sorta woozy. Retired 12:45AM.

OCTOBER 23, 1945

Awoke feeling tired. Fairly active day. Mr. Terk spoke to me about Mr. Lewis. Lurie wanting to be become an assistant in the read-to-wear dept. $5.00 increase. Told him I must first go to Boston. Said OK.

OCTOBER 24, 1945

Entrained for Castle Point at 8:00AM. Hour wait in Albany. Palisi brothers bus took me from Beacon to Castle Point Hospital. Waited few minutes. Examined by Captain Lewis Belloff and Colonel Hofnagel. X-rayed, etc. Loosing fluid in my lower joints, also shoulder. Dictaphone recording. Returned 6:07 to Amsterdam. Meet Mr. Russlander, insurance agent (Albany) going and coming. Arrived Amsterdam 8:55.

OCTOBER 25, 1945

Gerry called at noon in response to an advertisement for a store manager in Boston. She is so sincere. Mother Peskind sent me a gift (sport shirt) from Alabama. Shyrle sent me several albums and individual records. I love her dearly. Dreary day.

OCTOBER 26, 1945

Rainy AM. Reply from Mr. Jones. I want to make move to Boston. Only finances worry me.

OCTOBER 27, 1945

Fairly busy day in the store. Nothing special for the day.

OCTOBER 28, 1945

Called Uncle Is in Boston to tell him I am coming. Called Mr. Terk to inform him of my not being in for a few days. Inasmuch as he has Louis Wagner there, he doesn't have to worry about ample help. Kissed mother and Dad goodbye. Caught the 1:12PM out of

Amsterdam. Rode to Albany with Ralph Chapman (naval officer JG). Caught 3:53 out of Albany. Arrived Boston 10:15PM (1 hour late). Train quite crowded. Gerry, Sue and Uncle Is met me at station. Bought them a soda while waiting for baggage to be checked in. Everyone looks fine. Sleeping in den, studio couch. Bed has to be made every day. Talked with Uncle until 2:00AM.

OCTOBER 29, 1945

Awoke to talking in kitchen. Gerry and Uncle Is preparing breakfast for themselves. Uncle Is leaves at 8:10AM. Gerry at 8:30AM. Sue gets up at 8:00 and leaves at 9:05. Sue works for Aunt Lil. Met Gerry at Rogers jewelry store on Washington St where she is asst credit manager to Mr. Hickey. Introduced to Mr. Abrahamson, store manager and Lorraine, Gerry's asst. Store owned by Markson Bros of Boston. Originally started in Maine. Mr. Gully, the man in charge of the men's field is out of town and will be until next Monday. Spoke with Mr. McCrae, in charge of credit jewelry for Markson Bros at #210 South St. Referred me to Mr. Kay at 100 Summer St. Mr. Kay unable to place me at present time. Wise "Jew Boy."

OCTOBER 30, 1945

Uncle Is and I had dinner at Ada Bullocks on Tremont St. Fair meal. Made appointment for me with Mr. Wright of Jordan, Marsh & Co. men's dept at 2:00PM. Mr. Wright buys from Uncle Is at Malcolm Kenneth Co, 136 Harrison Ave for Jordan, Marsh Co. Very decent gentleman. Referred me to Mr. Chase who is one of the executives in charge of the Jordan, Marsh Co junior executive courses. Because the course had started Sept 1st, must wait until '46. However they will hire me at $25.00 per. What a slap in the face. I went into the employment offices of White's and Filenes. Their starting salaries are insulting. Experience is almost immaterial. They pick men from within for executive positions. Generally Sue gets home about 4:30 to 5:00PM and starts supper. Uncle Is about 5:45 and Gerry about 6:30PM. Everyone pitches in with Susie being the mainstay because she knows how to cook, but good. We all help with the dishes, cleaning, etc. All total the time is almost 8:30 before the house is in order.

OCTOBER 31, 1945

Today is Halloween. So what. Boston is a very busy city. In reverse of what most people think, I am of the opinion this city is not too difficult to find your way around. Made the rounds of all the stores seeking employment. Filenes, Whites, etc. The starting salary is almost insulting. Making mention of this again. Registered at Peter's Employment agency. Mr. Packard, gentleman in charge of employing salesmen, sent me to Lerner's regarding a display man. When securing a job through these agencies, you sign a contract for one week's wages up to $2900 per year, 3% up to $3900 etc.   It is very discouraging sometimes. It seems as though a decent job is unobtainable yet I feel like I shall strike something. It will be best if Shyrle and I can start life anew away from our families. As a rule, when I return home I commence making supper. My financial condition is critical. In fact our honeymoon trip etc is to be considered carefully. I'd give Shyrle everything were I so fixed. At any rate our love is beyond everything.

NOVEMBER 1, 1945

Interviewed by Mr. Chase, asst personnel manager of
Jordan Marsh & Co. Spoke of a possibility of my being
considered for the 1946 executive training course. In
the meantime, I could work in the store at $25 per
plus 1/2 of 1% commission. How very ridiculous.
Registered at the American Employment Exchange on
Federal St. Mr. Murphy in charge of sales employment
referred me to a Monday appointment with him.
Everyone here is feeling for me although I don't feel
terribly bad. Uncle called Mr. Friedlander of
Kennedy's in regard to an appointment. I am to call
him tomorrow AM. Grandpa Belloff used to sell
clothing to Kennedy's. Mr. Friedlander owns all the
boy's depts in the 10 Kennedy stores. I feel very
discouraged sometimes but I don't let it be known nor
do I try to show it. Despite it all, living with Uncle Is is
peaceful and I am happy.

NOVEMBER 2, 1945

Made the rounds and nothing doing. I try to write to
Shyrle every day. Uncle Is and I had dinner together.
Regular run of the mill day. I would like some social
activity such as a movie, play, etc. but due to the fact I
am here to find a job and doing so mostly on Uncle's
finances, I feel guilty even thinking about such unless
we all go. My nerves are quite tense as I want to land
something and make Shyrle a very comfortable living.

NOVEMBER 3, 1945

Made an appointment with Mr. Friedlander of
Kennedy's for 1:30PM. Very favorably impressed. To
report back next Friday. A swell man as well as his

assistant Mr. Golden. Mr. Gelin, personnel manager very pleasant. Uncle purchased everything himself for the house. Sue feeling better.

NOVEMBER 4, 1945

We all pitched in and cleaned the house. Aunt Lil and Evelyn and a friend of theirs from Syracuse (1st Lt) came over. Uncle stirred some swell drinks. Snowed all day. Retired 11:00PM.

NOVEMBER 5, 1945

Mr. Packard of the American Employment Exchange requested my seeing Mr. Watson regarding display at Sears, Roebuck and Co on Mass Ave in Cambridge. Mr. Watson seemed very interested and had me fill out an application for employment. The feeling of discouragement is within me, but I shall not give in to it.

NOVEMBER 6, 1945

Today is Election Day. May Mr Hand be the new Mayor. Aunt Bea called and made an appointment for me to call Cy, Mr. Hellman. I am to call him Thursday for a definite appointment. Made the rounds again of all the employment agencies. Uncle's apartment is located at 166 Fuller St., Brookline, Mass. It is on the top floor. The owners are strictly Yiddish. For a home without a mother, it functions wonderfully. Aunt Ann died in April of a brain tumor. Sick for 6 weeks. A few years before a breast was amputated for cancer.

NOVEMBER 7, 1945

Well, Curley won the Boston election for Mayor. I made the rounds of employment agencies, but with little avail. Yes it is discouraging. I do not want to return to Amsterdam for Shyrle and I will be happier elsewhere. It's most important to me - her happiness. Her letters come daily and really pep me up. Complaining only has a tendency to embitter others as well as yourself. I'll try my best and be as honest as I know. Bunny Belloff (Shane) and her husband Don came over for the evening. Bunny was an army nurse and Don is an aviation radio technician in the Coast Guard, who is to be discharged tomorrow. Bunny expects her baby about March. Very fine couple. Uncle served some swell mixed drinks. Retired 12:30AM.

NOVEMBER 8, 1945

Awoke 7:45AM. Uncle Is and Gerry eating breakfast. Made breakfast for Sue and I. Sue starts work at Aunt Lil's at 9:30AM. Works Wed. and Saturday evenings in Coleman's on Tremont St. Inasmuch as Sue hasn't been feeling well, we must watch her accordingly. Had dinner with Uncle. (Lamb potpie). Delicious. Have to almost fight with him to pay the check. Uncle is good company. Called Mr. Cy Hellman in regard to an appointment. Mr. Hellman is a very close friend of Aunt Bea. He is an accountant and has interests in several businesses. As to what he can do for me, I don't know. Perhaps advise. Very warm, clear day. Spent most of the day at #116. Susie and I prepared supper. Baked beans, bananas with whipped cream. Gerry's date, Al Rosenberg, came over about 8:40. Seems to be very nice. Somewhat lackadaisical. Sue went over to Muriel Werners. Uncle Is and I took our usual nightly walk and stopped in for Sue. Met the family. Very nice. Retired 12:00AM.

NOVEMBER 9, 1945

Awoke 7:45AM. Made appointment with Mr. S. J. Helman of SJ Helman & Co, 50 Federal St at 10:00AM. Aunt Bea arranged it. Very pleasant person and very young looking. Gave me a very fine recommendation to Mr. Mark Gully of Markson Bros. Intends to follow up such for me. Seemed to think I should try to sell Rockwool insulation. Had dinner with Uncle. Blonde came over and spoke to us again. Saw Mr. Friedlander at 1:30. Made my own appointment. Nothing special, but I suggested my being temporarily added to the holiday sales force. Suggestion readily accepted. This is to be my trial period. If I prove my worth, I shall be kept on. Starting salary is $40.00. Mr. Wright of Jordan Marsh Co called Uncle Is about my interview with Mr. Chase. After this he requested my coming in to see him which I did at 3:00PM. He introduced me to Mr. Mulligan, Mdse manager of men's clothing and furnishings. Mr. Mulligan is to make appointment for me with general mdse manager of the Co. In all probability they will place me in the men's furnishings field at about $50.00 per while attending the executives training course. I think Kennedy's is my best bet as Jewish personnel are scarce in Jordan Marsh Co. Shyrle will be so very happy. Sue, Gerry and Uncle want to celebrate tomorrow night (Saturday). My darling writes every day. Her letters are my very life's blood. Very warm day. Sent a night letter to Shyrle. I am very happy in this home. Very peaceful. Every night I read from Victor Hugo's "Les Miserables." Retired 10:30PM.

Red Skies at Night

NOVEMBER 10, 1945

Looks like rain. Shall try to see Mr. Mark Gully this AM. I miss Shyrle very much. When I look about I realize how very lucky I am. To return to Amsterdam for a few days before starting work. Elliott no doubt will be in Amsterdam as he was discharged the first part of the week. Presented my letter from Mr. Hellman to Mr. Mark Gully at his office on Washington St. After a very brief interview he made an appointment with me for Monday. May work in the Continental. They (Markson Bros) are going to remodel the entire building and install a jewelry line of which Mr. Gully spoke in reference to me. Shopped with Uncle Is at Coolidge Corners. Helped him shop and wax kitchen floor and adjoining floor. Uncle Is, Sue, Gerry and I had lunch downtown and attended "Rhapsody in Blue" at the Fenway. After Uncle treated us to a sundae at Brighams, Gerry not feeling too well. Raining. Retired 11:30. Very lonesome for Shyrle.

NOVEMBER 11, 1945

Awoke 8:00AM. Again 9:40. Raining. Seem to be suffering more internally. Left side continually gurgles and some pain across the left chest and back. I shall always try to keep happy and make everyone else that way. Gerry and I cleaned house. Uncle finished painting Susie's room. Gerry and I visited Bernice (Werner) at her apt at Alton Court. Also met Ruth, Maurey's wife. Received special from Shyrle. I won't be happy or contented until Shyrle is my wife. Served dinner in the dining room (steak). Retired 11:00PM.

NOVEMBER 12, 1945

Today is officially Armistice Day. Raining. Stores do not open until 1:00PM. Unable to get to Mr. Gully's office as the crowd has already assembled for the Armistice Day parade to see Ike Eisenhower. I caught a glimpse of him as he went by on Washington St. Stores open from 1 to 6. Slight drizzle.

NOVEMBER 13, 1945

At Mr Gully's office at 11:00AM. Mr. Press and he were working on plans for the Continental. Spoke with Mr. Larry Rankin at 210 South St. Later spoke with Bobbie Markson. Bobbie Markson is vice president of Markson Bros. Yoland D Markson is President. Not too favorably impressed with company. Seems like a high pressure outfit. On general principles, I do not like their methods. Called Mr. Gully and told him I am taking a train upstate this PM and would see him on Monday. Missed 3:20PM to Albany by 2 minutes. Took 4:50PM. Met Max Cohen at change in Albany. Max is coming back from a buying trip to NY. Arrived home about 11:40PM. Mother and Dad just retiring. Elliott expected home tomorrow. Raining.

NOVEMBER 14, 1945

Very busy day, but very little accomplished. Closed checking account. Purchased suit in Sochins. Completed balance due me at Mortons. Congratulated Joe Hand on becoming Mayor. Visited Mr. Hill and the Gaskins. Drizzling. Expecting Elliott home. Very nervous.

NOVEMBER 15, 1945

Said goodbye to friends etc. Rushed around like mad all day. Packed and finished my business. Visited Mr. Terk. We went to see Bob and hospital. Having penicillin treatment for stomach disturbance. Visited Marihew and Van Burens - very nervous and upset. Received two letters from Shyrle at #19. Also pictures. Like the sober one best. Retired 11:00PM.

NOVEMBER 16, 1945

Alarm awoke me at 6:45AM. Did not get to sleep until 3:00AM. Very much upset. Mostly due to lack of finances and decision in taking a job. I want Shyrle to be so very happy. Don't know what kind of a honeymoon I can afford. Boarded 8:00AM. Changed at Albany for 10:00 to Boston. Arrived south station 3:40PM. Very hot and stuffy trip. Cold and snow flurries. Brought my grips to Uncle's offices. Made appointment with Mr. Gully and also Mr. Golden in the absence of Mr. Friedlander. So very happy to be back in Boston. Sue had braces put on her bottom teeth. So good to be with Gerry and all. Retired 11:00PM.

NOVEMBER 17, 1945

Uncle called me at 8:00AM. Visited Mr. Gully at his office. Do not like his manner or ways. Requested $65 per. $50 tops. To return at noon. Visited Mr. Golden in the absence of Mr. Friedlander. Agreed to come to work for $40 per. Prefer Kennedy's because they are a real honest concern. I shall make the sacrifice and Shyrle will be happy because I have done the right thing, the honest thing. Spoke with Mr. Wright and Mr. Mulligan of Jordan Marsh & co. Both were very glad to know that I am going to work for Kennedy's. Left them with a very good impression and free to call upon them for advice at any time. Mr. Gully of Markson Bros rather indignant and indifferent about my not going to work for them. It was hard to explain my situation without coming right out and telling them I don't have much respect for the organization and the system. Yes I'll plug and make the grade. Mild day. Starting work Monday. Helped Uncle lug the vegetables and stuff from Coolidge Corners. Such a swell guy. He is a mother and a father to Sue. Raining this evening. Uncle and I took our usual walk. He is very happy about the possibility of Malcolm Kenneth going in for military clothes during civilian times as they did during the war. May be a break for him. I feel so much happier and better in Boston. Retired 11:30PM.

NOVEMBER 18, 1945

Awoke at 10:30AM. Light rain. Should have written Shyrle yesterday as now she will not receive any mail until Tuesday. Worked most of day cleaning house. Had to vacuum house twice because forgot to change band on cleaner. Everyone doing their share. Received a special from my angel. Lamb chop for dinner. We all attended "State Fair" at Coolidge Corners. Had a soda after. Somewhat peeved about a remark. I keep everything within me. Retired 10:30PM.

NOVEMBER 19, 1945

Arrived at Kennedy's at 10:00AM. Mr. Golden introduced me to Mr. Phil Reisman, assistant to Mr. Beauchman, manager of Boston store directly under

Mr. Golden and Mr. Friedlander. Yours truly to roam
about and get acquainted with stock, etc. Met Patrick
Haggerty who was hired under same set up as I.
Formerly with Filene's basement. Met. Mr. Hewitt, Mr.
Ed Kaufman, Al Ross, Paul Ambrosa, and quite a few
of the sales force. Very pleasant atmosphere. Dept
located on 4th floor of bldg, corner Summer and
Hawley St. I split up my sales amongst the salesmen.
One must be very cautious for petty jealousies and
position. I am trying my best in every manner.
Subway jammed. Stores open until 8:30 on Mondays -
$.75 for lunch. Ate at the Hood. Supper with Mr.
Grouvell. Nice gent of about 65 years at bar and
cafeteria on Summer St. Retired 10:30PM.

NOVEMBER 20, 1945

Awoke 7:15AM. At work at 9:00AM. Raining and
chilly. Fairly busy. Enjoy selling. Catching on fast.
Trunk arrived today. Gerry to leave for Amsterdam
tomorrow via car with Bunny Belloff and husband. I
am afraid I shall have to start cutting down on my
correspondence to Shyrle. Time is very scarce. I do
hope she will understand. The atmosphere at
Kennedy's is very homey and pleasant. Generally I
remain a short while after 5:30. Coming and going I
stand while riding the subway. Shyrle is ever so
thoughtful in her correspondence. The days seems so
short. Washing my laundry, making my bed everyday.
Helping prepare supper as well as washing the dishes
consumes much time. Then again you must live
somewhat for the other fellow also. Retired 11:00PM.

The True Diaries of Irving J. Schaffer

NOVEMBER 21, 1945

Arose 7:45 which is about 15 minutes too late. Fairly active day at the store. Really beginning to learn. Being very cautious and diplomatic. At least I think so. Opening checking account with the Chauncey St Exchange of the Shawmut National Bank. There always seems to be activity in the boy's dept. The men's dept is practically out of suits. Uncle Is, Sue and I met Ruth Ann and Dick at the Back Bay station on the 10:00PM from New York. First time I saw either one since 1940. Kibitzed for a while. Sleeping with Uncle. Retired 1:00AM.

NOVEMBER 22, 1945

Awoke 7:30AM. Slept fairly well. Just love having Ruth and Dicky. Sent Shyrle a special - air. Aunt Lil gave a cocktail party before we all went to the Statler for dining. Met cousin Stephanie (8). Very enjoyable meal and floor show. Featured Eddy Peabody (5.25 per). Weather is fair. Enjoying myself immensely with Uncle and all. Met Eve Blockner. Friend of Aunt Lil's that lives at the Hotel Statler. How I wish Shyrle was with me. Spoke of Jerome. After dinner we all went up to Eve's room for drinks. Aunt Lil has bad cold. Retired midnight.

NOVEMBER 23, 1945

Picked up my suit from Coolidge Corner post office from Sockins. Mr. Friedlander came back and it certainly is a pleasure just to know the man is around. Very busy (10,000). I find very little trouble selling because I enjoy it. Very much want to forge ahead but must be patient. Shyrle's letters are so very understanding. She even suggested her working. I don't want her to. Feel very tired as I did not fall asleep until 3:00AM. Muriel and Sue met Gerry at South Station on the 9:00PM from Albany. Retired late again - 12:00.

NOVEMBER 24, 1945

Very busy day at the store. Mr. Friedlander spoke with me again. Very decent person. Sore throat. Ruth Ann and Dick prepared a swell dinner. Uncle's boss Mr. Cohen, gave him a 16 lb turkey. Retired 11:00PM.

NOVEMBER 25, 1945

Received a special from Shyrle. I love her more everyday. Bad cold settling in me. We all prepared a swell dinner. Aunt Lil and Bea, Stephanie, Eve and I had a swell dinner. I did not go to the train to see Ruth Ann and Dick off as I must write Shyrle. Such a grand wife. Warm clear day.

NOVEMBER 26, 1945

Came in at 9:30 this morning. Arranging stock. Nothing special. Mr. Ed Gelim invited me to attend speaker at Temple tomorrow evening. Heavy, tight cold.

NOVEMBER 27, 1945

Mr. Friedlander asked me to take over supervision of the under-grads furnishings. Girls are a ticklish problem. Meet Mr. Gelim at Temple Ohakem Shalom,

corner Beacon and Kent St. Mrs. Helen Gahagen
Douglass was main speaker. Spoke about Russia and
our cooperating with her. Also about atomic energy.
About 800 attended. All men. Affair run of Neiman
society. Retired midnight.

NOVEMBER 28, 1945

Western Union called in Shyrle's telegram at 8:30AM.
Trying to do my best in my new job. Gerry, Uncle and
I had dinner at Aunt Lil's. Very delicious meal. To
start looking for apt. I wish I had more time to write to
Shyrle. Such a swell person. Retired midnight.

NOVEMBER 29, 1945

Awoke to a very rainy blustery day. Subways jammed.
Business quiet. Mr. Friedlander and Mr. Golden are
about the store occasionally. Must somewhat retard
my ambition. Rained hard all day. No letter from my
darling.

NOVEMBER 30, 1945

Awoke to a heavy snowstorm. About 8" of snow
already on ground. Overshoes sure come in handy.
Arrived work 9:20AM. Feeling good. Cold settled in
chest and head. Doesn't seem to loosen up. No
headache, fever or the like. Ed Gelin, John Mooney
and yours truly took cab home from store. Walked in
from Coolidge Corners. Gerry and I went to Bernice's
(Werner) home (Alton Court) for dinner. Maurey
Epstein (Lt SG) home. Looks good. Ruth (Maurey's
wife) Helen (her sister), James and Carl, (cousins) and
Harriet (Bernice's daughter). Very nice dinner. Well
served and well prepared. Sociable gathering. Still

snowing. Sheppard (Bernice's husband) drove us home. Miserable night. Retired 12:00AM.

DECEMBER 1, 1945

It is now 1:50AM and I am writing in my diary in the kitchen. My conjested chest is a great discomfort. Very difficult breathing. I don't like to disturb anyone, as Gerry isn't well either. I do need rest very badly. It's been so long since I have slept as I used to.

Today it is DECEMBER 12 and many things have happened since I last wrote in this diary. Elliott stayed with us for a few days before starting work in NY. I have started apt hunting. It's plenty tough. I am quite worried about many things. In fact I probably look 10 years older. I like my job but it has plenty of headaches. I am too ambitious and don't stop to think enough. One day I shall be in my own business. Because I have so many things to do, I have cut down a little everywhere; even on Shyrle's correspondence. This hurt me very much. If I don't start sleeping soon I'll be coming to a fast end. My chest is as sore as ever.

My Shyrle is entitled to anything I have. I only hope she does not want to read this diary. However if she sincerely wants to I'll permit her. Many of my inner thoughts are not recorded as when I am low I feel differently than when I feel OK, so I do not record. I do know I like living at Uncle's. Very peaceful and happy. I shall try very hard to make our marriage a success. I know Shyrle will hold up her end. We both have our faults and when I was my angel's age I probably couldn't hold a candle to her.

I am first getting used to Boston. It's huge in population but like a small town. There is plenty of culture to be had. As yet I haven't had time to absorb any. I don't believe I could enjoy anything without Shyrle.

Elliott is starting out in New York and is finding it plenty tough. No news about Jerome. Oh how my heart aches for him. God some night please tell me where he is.

Mother and Dad are very lonesome I know. It's not much of a reward after bringing up five children. After the fine way we were brought up. Such is life.

Here it is <u>DECEMBER</u> 13th. May I find more sleep-filled nights in the future. Retired 11:00PM.

DECEMBER 14, 1945

Slept like a top for the first time in months. Taking it easy at the store. Woke up to about three inches of snow. No letter from Shyrle. Received letter from Veteran's Administration informing me I have arthritis, chronic. I am to receive $11.50 pension per month. Although my general condition isn't bad I wonder if I should write to Shyrle about it. I must talk it over with someone. Uncle and I decided it best to let it wait awhile. Retired 11:00PM.

DECEMBER 15, 1945

Slept quite well. Very busy day. New girl in dept. Rose Marie Haye. Quite efficient. We all ate at Peroni's and after saw "Mildred Pierce." Theater very uncomfortable. Retired 12:30AM.

DECEMBER 16, 1945

Awoke 9:00AM. Slept well. Miss Shyrle very much. Uncle and I repaired gas stove. Called Phil Saltman to tell him how much we enjoyed his program over WEEI.

Well, here it is DEC. 21. Friday evening and I have been so busy that I am still neglecting my diary. However, I am not neglecting writing to Shyrle. My angel left Madison for home on Wednesday morning. The day before a terrible snow storm struck the Chicago area as well as Boston. Received a check from Israel Friedlander for $5.04 after social security and income tax had been deducted. Trying very hard to keep my department in A-1 shape. Like every job, mine also has its ups and downs. Gerry wasn't feeling well for a few days but is OK now. I think I shall send Shyrle roses for Christmas. Sleeping better. Still have a sore chest. Left arm acted up a bit. Very busy in store. Some of our days run into 15,000. Getting about 7 hours rest a night. May go home for New Years.

DECEMBER 22, 1945

Picked up my suit and Uncle's pants from cleaners on Commonwealth Ave near Fuller St. Very busy day at store. How I hate to keep after the girls. But they must do their work and wait on customers. Uncle and I went walking. I miss my angel more and more.

The True Diaries of Irving J. Schaffer

DECEMBER 23, 1945

Awoke about 9:15AM. Cleaned turkey and helped clean house. Wrote Shyrle a special which she should receive for Christmas. My chest is giving me a lot of trouble today. All of a sudden my breathing becomes heavy. It feels like some kind of pressure just at the base of the front of my neck. Like something pressing against my windpipe. I should go to a doctor but I can't afford it. It frightens me sometimes. Sue and Gerry are stuffing the chicken.

DECEMBER 24, 1945

In two months Shyrle and I will be married. I miss her so very much. Quite a busy day. Party at store after 4:30. Just couldn't get in the swing of things without Shyrle. Sent Shyrle a corsage of orchids. I wish I could afford much more. Finished wrapping gifts. Retired 11:00PM. Starting to read Phillips E Oppenheim "The Great Impersonation."

DECEMBER 25, 1945

We began looking for our gifts about 10:00AM. It was such a nice morning. Shyrle's gift was saved until last. What a wonderful girl. She sent Gerry a pair of nylons and for me two white shirts of excellent quality and a beautiful fully lined silk robe. I don't want her to do these things but I just can't take away all her happiness. It almost makes me cry. I put a call in to her at 12:00. 3 1/2 to 4 hour delay. I miss her so very much. We all went over to Aunt Bea's. Aunt Lil and Eve also there. We killed a bottle of domestic Burgundy. Tried Shyrle's call again. On way out of studio, heard heating system acting up. Some smoke.

Shut off system because of Stephanie being in bed.
Mary (Lil's maid) came over to take care of Stephanie.
Finally got Shyrle's call through at 12:20AM. My it
was wonderful talking to her. She tried to call me
Christmas Eve. To be married at Park Plaza. I feel
very lonesome. I slept so sound after talking to Shyrle.

DECEMBER 26, 1945

Exchanges and refunds are plenty. Taking down
decorations, etc. Received 3 letters from Shyrle
including a special. Sue left for New York on 12:00PM
to visit Ruth Ann and Dick. Gerry worked until
7:30PM. Uncle prepared supper. Eating turkey until it
comes out of our ears. Dicky's birthday.

DECEMBER 27, 1945

Looked over rooms at 164 Beacon. No kitchen
privilege or private baths. Rent range from $30 to $80.
Warm day.

DECEMBER 28, 1945

Elliott's birthday. Nothing special happening.

DECEMBER 29, 1945

Gerry and I boarded 4:53 to Albany. Left at 5:30.
Jammed. Snowing in Boston. Gerry treated me to
dinner on train. Pulled in Schenectady at 2:30AM
Sunday. Gerry found a dollar in snow outside of
Schenectady station. Hired taxi to Amsterdam. Cost
$6.00, $1 tip Gerry found. After we greeted Mom and
Dad, we hit the sack at 4:00AM.

DECEMBER 30, 1945

Called most of the boys and visited many of the neighbors. Elliott arrived at 1:00PM with his friend Ray Bolger. On the radio, he goes under the name of Bob Schall. Swell guy. Merriam, Jack and Dicky came down. Everyone looks well. Merriam is expecting her youngster the first of February. Called Shyrle. My how wonderful it was to hear her voice. Thank God our marriage isn't too far off. I love her so much.

DECEMBER 31, 1945

This is the last day of the old year. Sent 9 night letters to arrive New Year's Day. Ray, Elliott and I stopped in for a few minutes at Goody's New Year's Eve party at his apt. Met Jackie Cornman who is visiting Seymour Meisel. She attends the University of Illinois and is a sorority sister of Phyllis Peskind, Shyrle's cousin. Returned home in time for midnight and we all celebrated. I retired early. The rest sat up and kibitzed until 4:00AM. I am so lonesome for Shyrle.

JANUARY 1, 1946

Here it is the first day of the New Year. Gerry and I departed on 1:18 out of Amsterdam. 3:53 out of Albany. Train jammed. Gave my seat to a lady. Arrived South Station (Bay) 10:30, 1 1/2 hours late. Taxi home. Uncle came in at 11:30. Sue remaining in NY to see doctor about plastic surgery on nose. Very expensive trip for me. Max Frankel to have wedding band made up for Shyrle. Glad to be back in Boston.

JANUARY 2, 1946

Feels great to be back on the job. Business is slow.
Mr. Friedlander and Mr. Golden left for New York
buying trip. Shyrle's letters come through daily. A
day seems incomplete without at least a note from her.
As the days go on I find myself becoming more silent.
It's a trait I've always wanted to acquire. Been
smoking cigars quite regularly. If Shyrle wishes me to
stop, I shall.

JANUARY 3, 1945

El Gelin invited me to a Brotherhood meeting and
dinner. George Alpert and Rabbi Irving Miller were the
main speakers. The Jewish problem was the tropic.
Turkey topped the menu. Ed has certainly been swell
to me. We received a 1 pound box of Busy Bee candy
from Shyrle.

JANUARY 4, 1946

Nothing special. Very mild weather.

JANUARY 5, 1946

Mr. Golden and I bought ties from S Snieber & Co.
About 300 dozen for all the stores. Eventually I hope
to assume that responsibility solely. Mr. Wolfgang of
the Milwaukee Boston store visiting us to learn of the
success of our business. Pleasant man.
Merchandiser. Uncle, Gerry, Sue and I attended the
"Dolly Sisters" at Coolidge Corner. Met Ed Gelin and
wife in theater. Retired 1:00PM.

JANUARY 6, 1946

Up at 9:00AM. Bathed, laundry, etc. Shyrle called on the dot of 10:30. It was wonderful hearing her voice. I don't imagine as though I sounded too enthusiastic. Shyrle has a cold. In 7 weeks we will be married. Attended banquet in Hancock Room of the Hotel Statler. Executives from surrounding stores attended. Enjoyable meal. Mr. Friedlander and Mr. Golden spoke of future plans. Although my position is somewhat indefinite, I have a general idea I'll buy the under-grad furnishings for all the stores. Meeting broke up about 3:50PM. Very warm day. Feeling conjested again in chest. I feel an early death but also immense wealth. Jerome has been continually on my mind. I hope he returns.

It is Sunday again. JANUARY 13, 1946. My darling Shyrle has been very kind to me. Her correspondence is continuous and very warm, lovable with deep unwritten passion. I pray with all my heart that I shall not break my heart in being unable to give Shyrle the many things she is used to and she should have. I realize her folks want us to be very happy and money is one of the keys to happiness. I am sure my angel will understand; she always has. I realize we can't live on love even though it is so deeply rooted. Oh if only we can pull through without any help for about six months. I also realize Shyrle's happiness, but I must achieve my goal on my own. I don't know what it is inside me but when I am obligated or indebted, I feel tortured, broken depressed. Perhaps I am this way as so-called favors have been thrown back in my face. I shall never intend, surmise or even entertain reciprocation for any assistance I might give or offer. I shall never stop loving my to-be wife Shryle. I shall always be honest, sincere in business. I shall reach

233

the top one day. I shall be very successful, but shall be claimed by death before I can enjoy my wealth. I realize all this but being as I am, I cannot take any other course. I am being selfish but God knows my heart and soul are full of love, romance and warmth and love for others.

The job is progressing OK. It is not easy competing for advancement especially being the junior member in years and seniority of the executive staff. One has to be secretive in not displaying emotion either good or bad. One has to be very tolerant. Some of the help, especially the girls and women are neurotic. They have to be continually kept after. That's why some of us rise, others remain permanent, others sink.

In about five weeks, Shyrle and I will be one, man and wife. Despite all the problems confronting me, I am confident matters will adjust properly. My mind is somewhat relieved and I am sleeping better. I think I'll be able to make our honeymoon OK, as far as finances are concerned. As yet no apt. All these things worry me, as I want to bring Shyrle to a decent home. She deserves at least that. She is a good scout and would be satisfied with almost anything.

Mr. Friedlander left for Miami Beach for a month. Despite little activity we are doubling our business over 1945. I have been doing some buying with Mr. Golden.

I hope Mother and Dad have ample finances for the wedding. It's a big pull for them, but their being there is as good a wedding gift as I could want and I am sure my darling will understand. I hope I shall live long enough to see my children become adults. I can give them great wisdom, something that neither book or experience can at their age. I hope that whoever reads this diary shall absorb it in all seriousness. I hope Shyrle never reads this as it may destroy part of her happiness and create sort of a pity for me. That I would never want.

My chest remains as sore as ever. My upper body trembles whenever I lean with any pressure. My skin seems to be drying out and wrinkling. Had I the finances, I'd visit some good doctors. It doesn't seem fair to Shyrle yet I can't tell her. I know she is the type that would rather have a seemingly short but very, very happy marriage. If I ever lost her, I'd loose my ambition - I lust for success. My life would be a void.

Today it is very clear and cold. Shyrle's special arrived while I was vacuuming the dining room. I love her dearly.

JANUARY 27, 1946

Here it is two weeks since I last wrote in the diary. I've decided to more or less let certain things ride as I have so much to do that I must neglect something, so this is it. Well, in four more weeks, Shyrle and I will be man and wife. I can't bring myself around to tell Shyrle just how meager our finances are. I need shoes, suits, etc, but I just can't afford them as I need the money for our honeymoon. Shyrle must have all the possible happiness I can give her. I am so very happy about our love. Our happiness shall be everlasting. Bob Stolz was in Boston on business and a visit. Swell guy. Reading "Bitter Glory," Thornber. (Life of Chopin

with George Sand). Gerry and Sue do not get along too
well. Similar personalities. It's not easy to please two
women. Uncle is as great as ever.   Elliott is now
located in Baltimore with Dr School. Merriam is
expecting very soon. Mom and Dad are preparing for
the wedding. No news about Jerome. Shyrle called
and I was very thrilled. The apt situation is worrying
her and I can't say as though I blame her much. I too
am worried. Why trouble her with these things.
Grandma Peskind is quite ill with pneumonia. I am
contacting a spot for our honeymoon destination
somewhere in New England. Thank God my darling is
not the demanding type. She is very considerate and
understanding.

The job is progressing nicely. We have just finished
taking inventory. Everyday I manage to learn
something. Everyday I try to improve myself and
understand my associates. My only drawback is my
health.   God only knows my efforts are sincere, honest
and right. I am extremely careful not to repeat a
mistake. One day I must become very powerful in the
business world. I shall with Shyrle at my side.

The True Diaries of Irving J. Schaffer

(We have included here just a couple of comments from the author that we thought might be helpful to a fuller understanding of the context. We also are pleased to inform you that after a brief period in Boston and approximately 12 years in St. Louis, Irv and Shyrle Schaffer moved to Phoenix, Arizona, USA with their two daughters, Linda and Barbara, where they established a highly successful men's wear store catering to a distinguished clientele. Irv and Shyrle are still happily married.)

Like any big brother, Jerome taught me a lot. I admired him and loved him. Jerome had expected to go to the United States Military Academy at West Point, passed all the exams well, but his vision kept him out. So he joined the Army in February 1934 and, after considerable schooling in radio communications and secret codes, became an accomplished cryptographer. Highly capable, he was assigned to as an instructor at West Point, teaching code and telegraphy. Then as pending war with Japan intensified, he was transferred to the army base in Panama to decode intercepted secret Japanese messages. Japan was telling Washington one story, but decoded messages told quite a different story. With the war in Europe raging, and fear increasing about Japan entering the war, decoding encrypted messages was our only way to try and discover their true plans. Jerome couldn't tell us about his work, but he always wrote home. Then while traveling in Southern Mexico, carrying secret information, twenty-nine year-old Jerome was killed or kidnapped. His last letter was postmarked March 21, 1941.

Fortunately I recuperated from most of my illnesses and injuries from WWII, although it did take 10 to 12 years for this to happen. I give full credit to my wife, Shyrle, for her patience, consideration and understanding what I went through. It was always very difficult and I very, very seldom discussed my years in combat.

NOTE with respect to entries on and around:

NOVEMBER 22, 1944

I really had no idea I was going to be awarded the Distinguished Flying Cross. I knew I would probably get the purple heart, because I had been wounded and I knew I would probably get more clusters to my air medal, but receiving the DFC was something far and above what I expected. However, in looking back, I realize that I did certain things during that one terrible mission that I never even believed I could do, such as releasing a 500-pound bomb in the bomb bay with the bomb bay doors open. After the bombardier had dropped, this one bomb got hung up in the bomb bay. Don't ask how I got the strength to do it, but our tail gunner held my feet and I went down headfirst into the bomb bay looking at the earth 10,000 feet below and somehow or other, God gave me the strength to release that bomb.

The True Diaries of Irving J. Schaffer

As I read this diary, everything seems to be coming back – the faces that I flew with, mess halls, planes, the guys that I knew, the activities, the trips and so forth. Sometimes, it all seems like a dream. One of the toughest parts of my tour of duty was stand down missions. That would be due to another storm coming up over the area, or another bomber took out the target. The anticipation, the anxiety even though it was not expressed, it was in our system. It did eat at us and did cause us to do certain things that we normally wouldn't do. Although I never flew with young Rubenstein, he was a good gunner, a good airman, a very patriotic American and it's a case where he became so internally and emotionally loaded that he couldn't take it anymore. He wouldn't go in and talk to the doctor, though, or any of us, and one night he committed suicide at age 19.

APPENDIX A

Citation with respect to Distinguished Flying Cross, USAAF awardedby GO 224 Hq 12 AF 5 Nov 44.

Reads, in part, that Irving J. Schaffer did: on October 20, 1944, ... For extraordinary achievement ... removed wounded comrade from the tail of the plane and administered first aid. ... repaired the radio ... manually lowered the flaps ... without further injury to his crew. His outstanding proficiency in combat and steadfast devotion to duty reflect great credit upon himself and the Armed Forces of the United States.

Citation with respect to the AIR MEDAL of USAAF awarded by GO 229 Hq 12 AF 8 Nov 44

Reads:
For meritorious achievement while participating in aerial flight as radio gunner of a B-25 type aircraft during an attack upon a road bridge at Pavia, Italy on 4 September 1944. Staff Sergeant Schaffer's proficiency in combat reflects great credit upon himself and the Military Service of the United States.

FIVE ADDITIONAL "Clusters" were awarded to add to this award from November 11, through March 28, 1945 for other notable contributions.

CPSIA information can be obtained at www.ICGtesting.com
Printed in the USA
BVOW062144290212

284153BV00002B/7/A

9 781411 642775